MW00425210

I Was Gone Long Before I Left

I Was Gone Long Before I Left

What Living in the Monastery
for Twenty-Five Years Taught Me about Life

Peter C. Wilcox

RESOURCE *Publications* · Eugene, Oregon

I WAS GONE LONG BEFORE I LEFT
What Living in the Monastery for Twenty-Five Years Taught Me about Life

Resource Publications
An Imprint of Wipf and Stock Publishers
199 W. 8th Ave., Suite 3
Eugene, OR 97401

www.wipfandstock.com

PAPERBACK ISBN: 978-1-7252-8033-5
HARDCOVER ISBN: 978-1-7252-8032-8
EBOOK ISBN: 978-1-7252-8035-9

Manufactured in the U.S.A.   08/11/20

To my Capuchin Franciscan brothers who were very inspirational to me over the years. Also, to my wife, Margaret, for her love and support in so many ways for over thirty-six years of marriage, and for her encouragement and helpfulness in writing this book.

Contents

Introduction

JOURNAL ENTRY, MAY 30, 1981, Annapolis, MD. I left the monastery today. No drama. No fanfare. After 20 years, no one said goodbye. It was an agonizing time for me and took me years to make this painful decision. Somehow, leaving the seminary or monastery was always done this way. Leave quietly, so no one sees you. This always seemed so strange to me, even cruel. After living, praying, and serving with the same people for years, a person just quietly walked away, always at night, while everyone was asleep.

All of that happened 39 years ago. When I left, I felt like a broken man. My spirit was broken, my ideals had been shattered. And even though I knew I had to make this change, I still felt guilty and ashamed. I continued to berate myself. Sometimes, I heard this voice inside of me saying, "you're a failure, you're weak, you couldn't do it, you had to give in." And maybe that was true. Maybe I was weak. Maybe I was a failure. In some ways, it certainly felt like that. But after years of struggling to live my vows as best I could in the monastery, I just knew that I had to make a change. After years of trying my best to live this way of life, I realized that for my own mental and physical health, I had to leave.

When I left, I was afraid. I had so many questions and so few answers. Including my years in the high school seminary, I had lived this religious life style for 25 years. I had given this way of life "my best shot," so to speak, but felt I just couldn't do it anymore if I wanted to avoid a mental breakdown. It was only after years of spiritual direction and intensive therapy, that I came to this conclusion. I could certainly identify with the prayer of spiritual writer and Cistercian monk Thomas Merton when he prayed,

> My Lord God, I have no idea where I am going. I do not see the road ahead of me. I cannot know for certain where it will end.

Nor do I really know myself, and the fact that I think that I am
following your will does not mean that I am actually doing so.
But I believe this: I believe that the desire to please you does,
in fact, please you. I hope I have that desire in everything I do.
I hope I never do anything apart from that desire. And I know
that if I do this you will lead me by the right road though I may
know nothing about it at the time. Therefore, I will trust you
always for though I may seem to be lost, and in the shadow of
death, I will not be afraid because I know you will never leave
me to face my troubles alone. Amen[1]

When I left the monastery on that day so many years ago, there were
only two things that I knew for sure. One, I had a place to live and two, I
had a job. Outside of these two things, I could certainly pray with Merton
that "I had no idea of where I was going and I did not see the road ahead
of me," but I tried to trust that the Lord would lead me by the right road
even though I didn't know where this road would take me.

Fortunately, one of these right roads emerged when a couple who
were friends of mine, offered me a room in their basement. It was very
sparse, but adequate. Another "right road" emerged when I was able to
find a job through a friend as the personnel director for a large construction company. However, approximately three years later, this construction company began to downsize and I was "let go." Basically, I was fired.
Interestingly enough, this happened on Good Friday in April, 1987. So,
now the question became what was I going to do?

In the monastery, counseling and spiritual direction had always
been one of my main ministries. So, after thinking and praying about this
for several weeks, I decided to investigate the criteria that was necessary
to become a psychotherapist. After discovering that I had already completed all the course work and internship requirements, I learned that
all I needed to do was to pass the state licensing exam which I quickly
accomplished. On reflection, I realized that this was another "right road"
that the Lord was leading me down. This was the beginning of my career
in counseling that I very much enjoyed for over twenty-four years.

Ernest Hemingway once wrote that "the world breaks everyone
and afterward many are strong in the broken places."[2] Since most of my
world up to that point had been my life in the monastery, this was the
world that broke me down. But with my many years as a psychotherapist,

1. Merton, *Thoughts in Solitude*, 81.

2. Quoted in Hemingway, *A Farewell to Arms*. See also www.goodreads.com/
quotes/ernesthemingway.

I truly believe that I became strong in my broken places. Moreover, since I struggled for years to make my decision to leave the monastery, and because the emotions of guilt, shame, and depression were so much a part of my dilemma, I have tried to help others who were also struggling with these issues.

Everybody is a story. Every person has a story. My story begins with that journal entry written so many years ago in 1981. It seems like a simple journal entry but what it took for me to reach this decision was extremely difficult. In my case, it was the culmination of many years of mental anguish, confusion, and depression. This book is about my journey through these years and how I was finally able to come to my decision. For many of us, the ability to make real life, concrete decisions about some aspect of our lives can be extremely painful. In over twenty years as a psychotherapist and spiritual director, I have so often found this to be true. And now, as I reflect back on these years, I hope that my story will be healing and helpful to others who are struggling to make the right decision in their lives.

For over thirty-eight years, I have been unable to write about the experiences of my life in the monastery because I felt ashamed. For years, I thought about leaving the monastery but couldn't make this decision because of the feelings of guilt and shame. Psychologically and emotionally, I felt paralyzed. Finally, after all these years, I have decided to tell my story.

This book has been written from a place deep inside me. It has been germinating inside of me for the last thirty-eight years. It comes out of the well of my own journey and life experiences. It's always difficult and risky to try to put our lives into words. I found that to be especially true with this book. It has brought back many painful memories. It asked much of me. It called for a painful honesty and vulnerability that I found daunting. It asked me to go deep into myself, to share my story, to invite you into what had been a very difficult time in my life.

In St. Teresa of Avila's classical spiritual book *Interior Castle,* she describes a difficult period of time in her own spiritual journey. She said "when I think of myself I feel like a bird with a broken wing."[3] This was the way I felt for a long time.

In this book, I have tried to grapple with the important questions of life, with my journey and the mystery of the human soul as I have tried to grow spiritually, emotionally, and psychologically. I have tried to open up a path that is grounded in the Scriptures, in centuries of Christian

---

3. Teresa of Avila, *Interior Castle.* www.notable-quotes.com/teresa_of_avila.

spiritual writing, and developmental psychology. I have also tried to offer down to earth truths from my own life, as well as profound truths from the great tradition of Christian spirituality. Weaving the parts of my story together has been like making a tapestry. It's like trying to put all of the pieces of a puzzle together without knowing the final picture.

I Was Gone Long Before I Left is my story about living in a Catholic monastery for twenty years as a member of a religious community. For fourteen of those years, I was also a priest. It explores the reasons why I went to the monastery, why I stayed, why I eventually left, and what I have learned. Maybe more importantly, I have tried to understand the painful process I went through to make the decision to leave.

From the beginning, I want to make it clear that in writing this book, I have "no axes to grind." I am not bitter. I seek no revenge. I don't want to punish anyone. Moreover, I am not anti-Catholic Church and have no need to disparage religious life. I simply want to share my story—my journey, hoping that it will be helpful to others.

Over the years, I have come to believe that all of us try to make the best decisions we can with the information we have at our disposal at any given time. For a variety of reasons, sometimes it takes a long time for everything to come together in our lives that enables us to make those decisions which can dramatically influence the direction of our lives. This is the way it was for me.

As a psychotherapist and spiritual director for over twenty-four years, I have tried to help people make all kinds of decisions about their lives. Many times, these have been extremely painful decisions that have been very difficult for them and others. It is my hope that this book will validate their decision making process and give encouragement to others as they struggle to make decisions in their own lives. Finally, it is my hope that my effort to write this book will bring continued healing to those wounded parts of my own life.

Anne Morrow Lindberg, in her book *War Within and Without,* said that "one writes not to be read but to breathe . . . one writes to think, to pray, to analyze. One writes to clear one's mind, to dissipate one's fears, to face one's doubts, to look at one's mistakes—in order to retrieve them. One writes to capture and crystallize one's joy, but also to disperse one's gloom. Like prayer—you go to it in sorrow more than joy, for help, a road back to grace."[4] It is in this spirit that I invite you to join me on my journey.

4. Lindberg, *War Within and Without.* www.goodreads.com-work-quotes-106051-war-within-and-without.

Part One

Why I Went to the Monastery

1

My Journey Begins

"The Longest Journey is the Journey Inward"

(DAG HAMMARSKJOLD)

IT WAS OCTOBER, 1979 and the autumn leaves were changing to shades of bright reds, orange, and yellow. I went into the woods to find my favorite bench which overlooked the Severn River. It was a beautiful spot which always seemed to invite me to prayer. It was probably my favorite place during my days when I lived at St. Conrad Friary (Monastery) near Annapolis, Maryland.[1] It was actually the second time I had been assigned there. The first time, in the mid 1970s, I was the assistant novice master teaching the novices about our Capuchin Franciscan way of life. This time I was trying to finish writing my doctoral dissertation on Cardinal John Henry Newman at Catholic University.

These were difficult days for me. For the last several years, there was an intense aching in my soul. I seemed to be lost in a baffling crisis of spirit. For some months, I was aware of a growing darkness within me, as if something in my depths was crying out. A whole chorus of voices. Orphaned voices. They seemed to speak for all the unloved parts of me

---

1. In the Catholic Church, the Franciscans are one of the Mendicant Orders. Men belonging to this Order, are friars (brothers) and they live in friaries (monasteries). Technically speaking, monks live in monasteries. However, for my purposes in this book, they can be interchangeable.

and came with a tremendous force. At times, they seemed to explode the boundaries of my existence. Years later, I know now that they were the clamor of a new self struggling to be born.

A. The Autumn of My Discontent

It was a frightening time for me. I knew I couldn't go on this way. Years of depression, headaches every day, stomach ulcers, and digestive problems were telling me that something had to be done. In one sense, I was standing on the shifting ground of midlife. I was thirty-seven now and had come upon that time in life when one is called to an inner transformation, to perhaps a crossing over from one identity to another. When the winds of change swirl through our lives, especially at mid-life, they often call us to undertake a new passage of the spiritual journey. But that requires us to confront the lost and counterfeit places within us and to release our deeper innermost self—our *true* self. They call us to come home to ourselves, to become who we really are.

However, that autumn of my discontent, should not have surprised me. For years, I had been struggling with these issues and questions. Should I stay in religious life or not? Was God inviting me to embrace this darkness and discover a deeper way of being? A deeper relationship with Him? These seemed to be the same kinds of questions I had been struggling with for the last seventeen years.

In a sense, I should have remembered that the life of the spirit is never static. But it can certainly be upsetting. We are born on one level, only to find some new struggle toward wholeness waiting to be born. That is the sacred intent of God—to move us continuously toward growth. During these times of turmoil, we are invited to recover everything that has been lost or orphaned within us and to restore the divine image imprinted on our soul. And rarely do significant shifts come without a sense of our being lost in dark woods, or in what T.S. Eliot called the "vast interstellar spaces."[2]

As I sat on my favorite bench in the woods on that autumn morning, I wondered how I could escape the emotional, psychological and spiritual pain I was in. The familiar circles of my life left me with a suffocating feeling. My religious structures were stifling. Things that used to matter were

---

2. Eliot, *"East Coker,"* 126.

no longer important. Things that had never mattered became paramount. My life had curled up into the frightening mark of a question.

Nevertheless, in spite of all this, I always continued to go about my responsibilities. I would work on writing my dissertation through the morning and early afternoon, pray through the day with my brothers, sometimes see people for spiritual direction, and generally participate in our community life. I have always been very accomplished at fulfilling my duties, even during a crisis. Outwardly, I appeared just fine. Inside, I was a mess.

In one sense, I wanted things to go back to the comfortable way they were before. I wanted to "snap out of it" so to speak, and had ordered myself to do just that on numerous occasions. But it was sort of like looking at an incoming wave and telling it to recede. Simply demanding it, didn't make it happen.

For a moment, I thought about my external, everyday self—the self I presented to the world. I contemplated the masks I had worn, the "inner selves" or dominant patterns embedded in my personality that had influenced my way of living in the world.

Referring to the multiplicity of our inner selves that inhabit each one of us, Elizabeth O'Connor wrote, "it was during a time of painful conflict that I first began to experience myself as more than one. It was as though I sat in the midst of many selves."[3]

I reflected on my many selves. The Pleaser, Performer, and Perfectionist—my trinity of P's. I was learning how closely these old roles were connected to another powerful role that I played out: the Good Little Boy. He was that part of me that possessed little self-validation or autonomy. He was that part of me that tended to define life by others and their expectations. As a man, I sometimes felt that I had been scripted to be all things to all people. But when I tried, I usually ended up forfeiting my deepest identity, my own uniqueness as a child of God.

My Good Little Boy endured everything with a smile on his face. He feared coloring outside of the traditional lines, and frequently cut himself off from his real thoughts and feelings. He was well adapted to thinking other people's thoughts and following the path of least resistance.

Now, oddly, I could feel the movements of an unknown person locked away inside of me who wanted life and breath, who wanted to shed what wasn't real and vital and recover my own uniqueness. I felt

3. O'Connor, *Our Many Selves*, 3.

the vibrations of a deeper, authentic self who wanted to live out his own unique vision of being an individual and embrace his own mystery. Who was this self inside of me who cried out to be?

During the previous four months, I had been reading the poetry of T.S. Eliot, who at times seemed like a soulmate to me. In his "Love Song of J. Alfred Prufrock," I found my story, the quiet agony of someone who came upon an unsuspecting darkness buried in midlife and met the overwhelming question: "Do I dare/ Disturb the universe? . . . I have measured out my life with coffee spoons;/ I know the voices dying with a dying fall/ Beneath the music from a farther room."[4] In my life, there seemed to be some kind of music coming from a distant room that I couldn't find. Voices dying to be heard. Did I dare disturb the universe within myself?

Believe me, when I say I wanted to shove all this away and pretend it didn't exist. In fact, I had actually done that for a long time. But I couldn't do that any more. My life had become too painful. At times, I found myself shut in a closet of pain, unable to find the door. In my blackest moments, I actually fantasized about running away to find the vital part of me that I had lost.

B. Embracing the Confusion

As I sat on that bench that autumn day beneath a beautiful, crisp blue sky, I felt like everything inside me was churning, trying to find a way out. And suddenly, at the height of my chaos, I began to entertain the over-whelming question confronting me. Actually, I had been circling it for a long time, but now, at last, I walked right into the center of it. In a sense, it was a dangerous thing to do because those who enter the heart of a sacred question and feel the searing heat it gives off are usually compelled to live on into the answer.

Is it possible, I asked myself, that I am being summoned from some deep and holy place within? Am I being asked to enter a new passage in the spiritual life—the journey from false self to true self? Am I being asked to dismantle old masks and patterns and unfold a deeper, more authentic self—the one God created me to be? Am I being invited to dis-turb my inner universe in quest of the undiscovered person who clamors from within?

4. Eliot, "The Love Song of J. Alfred Prufrock," 4–5.

Unfortunately, there has been little emphasis on this summons within Christian circles. And, when it comes, we don't understand that we are being thrust into personal transformation. Most of us tend to write it off as just another predicament or plight—perhaps the result of burnout or our dissatisfaction with life.

I believe, however, that in such a summons we are actually being presented with a spiritual developmental task. We are being asked to unfold a deeper self—what we might call the life of Christ within us.

As I reflected on my struggle that afternoon, I remembered the discoveries I had made in the writings of the famous Swiss psychiatrist Carl Jung. I had been studying his works over the past several years, trying to understand his approach to how we grow psychologically as we age. When I told a friend that I was doing this, he reminded me that I was looking for truth in rather unorthodox places. However, I told him that this was like what Abraham Heschel said in his book *I Asked for Wonder*, "God is hiding in the world. Our task is to let the divine emerge from our deeds."[5]

Moreover, for the past six years, I had been teaching theology in the Washington Theological Union. My area of concentration was teaching courses in Christian spirituality. During the years when I was working on my doctoral degree in theology from Catholic University, I had studied the classic Western spiritual writers like St. Teresa of Avila, St. John of the Cross, Julian of Norwich, Meister Eckhart, and especially the contemporary Cistercian monk and spiritual writer Thomas Merton. In fact, I had been teaching a course on Merton, entitled The Theology and Spirituality of Thomas Merton. Since Merton had recently died in 1968, there always seemed to be a lot of interest in him and his understanding of how we grow spiritually. In trying to comprehend Merton's understanding of the contemplative journey, I discovered that Merton believed that the spiritual life always involved entering the depths of oneself. Later, when I began to study Jung, I was amazed at how much of his work in depth psychology paralleled the spirituality of Thomas Merton that I had come to know, and how they enriched one another.

Jung believed that "every midlife crisis is a spiritual crisis, that invites us to die to the old self, the fruit of the first half of life and liberate the new man or woman within us." I recalled Jung's words in *Stages of Life*:

> Wholly unprepared, they embark upon the second half of life.
> Or are there perhaps colleges for forty-year-olds which prepare

5. Heschel, *I Asked for Wonder,* 124.

them for their coming life and its demands as the ordinary colleges introduce our young people to a knowledge of the world and of life? No, there are none. Thoroughly unprepared we take the step into the afternoon of life; worse still, we take this step with the false presupposition that our truths and ideas will serve as hitherto. But we cannot live the afternoon of life according to the program of life's morning—for what was great in the morning will be little at evening, and what in the morning was true will at evening have become a lie.[6]

Jung divided life into two major phases. The first phase, or "morning," is reserved for relating and orienting to the outer world by developing the ego. The second half, or "afternoon," is for adapting to the inner world by developing our true self. The midlife transition between these two, Jung likened to a difficult birth. This was certainly what I had been experiencing.

This transition is always very difficult, Jung believed, because it involves a real breakdown of our old spiritual and psychic structures—the old masks and personas that have served us well in the past but that no longer fit. The overarching roles that created the theme song for my life—Perfectionist, Performer, Pleaser, Good Little Boy, began to lose their music. It's agonizing to come to that place in life where you know all the words but none of the music.

In our youth, we set up inner myths and stories to live by, but around the midlife juncture these patterns begin to crumble. It feels like an inner collapsing of everything inside of us. This is why it is so painful and confusing. As John Shea writes, "when order crumbles, mystery rises."[7]

One of my favorite passages in Scripture comes from the Old Testament Book of Ecclesiastes. "To everything there is a season, and a time to every purpose under heaven: a time to be born, and a time to die, a time to plant, and a time to pluck up that which is planted" (Eccles. 3:1–2).

Most of us need reassurance that it's okay to let the old masks die, and to "pluck up" what was planted long ago. And as I was struggling with whether to embrace this experience or run away from it, a friend said to me "if you think God always leads you only beside still waters, think again. God will also lead you beside turbulent waters. If you have the courage to enter, you will think you are drowning. But actually, you are being churned into something new. It's okay, Pete, dive in." All I had

---

6. Jung, *Stages of Life*, 783.

7. Shea, *Stories of God*.

to do was trust the process. So, I told myself that if I could stay with this process and not run away from it, I would discover that a sacred voice at the heart of me would cry out, shaking my old foundation. It would draw me into a turbulence that would force me to confront the false roles, identities, and illusions that had become a part of my life.

I leaned back on that little bench that chilly autumn day in October and tried very hard to say yes to what was struggling inside of me. It seemed to me that my quest was to find the part of me that I had lost. Jung said that we all have a "shadow." It's the rejected, inferior person inside that we have always ignored and fought becoming. For me, my shadow seemed to represent an essential part of me that was buried in darkness. It was that part of me hidden beneath the masks and fabrications. It was that part of me struggling to find the light.

I suppose in some way I kept hoping that some wise, loving person would come to my rescue and lead me out of my darkness. In fact, by this time, I had already been sharing my struggle with my spiritual director and seeing a psychiatrist to help me through this difficult time. I talked with both of them about my "dark night of the soul," but I hadn't yet been able to find my own vision of transformation. How would I be able to do this? What was being asked of me?

2

Learning to Live with My Questions

"We are closer to God when we are asking questions
than when we have the answers"

(ABRAHAM JOSHUA HESCHEL)

ON THAT AUTUMN DAY back in 1979, I remember thinking that I was now moving into my "second half of life," my "afternoon of life," as Jung liked to call it. And I also recall thinking about the writings of one of my favorite writers, Rainer Maria Rilke, who always encouraged people to live with their questions until they discovered their answers for themselves. In fact in 1902, a young poet by the name of Franz Xavier Kappus wrote his first letter to Rilke. In it, he asked Rilke to read and critique his poetry. Rilke refused to do that but began a conversation with the young man. Kappus later published the letters he received from Rilke as *Letters to a Young Poet*. In this book, Rilke advised his young friend

> . . . to be patient toward all that is unsolved in your heart and
> try to love the questions themselves like locked rooms and like
> books that are written in a very foreign tongue. Do not seek the
> answers, which cannot be given you because you would not be
> able to live them. And the point is, to live everything. *Live* the
> questions now. Perhaps you will then gradually, without notic-
> ing it, live along some distant day into the answer.[1]

1. Rilke, *Letters to a Young Poet*, 34–35.

Live the questions now so that at some point you will live your way into the answers. There is an art to living your questions. You peel them. You listen to them. You struggle with them. You let them spawn new questions. You hold the unknowing inside. You linger with them instead of rushing into half-baked answers. The Jesuit writer Anthony de Mello put it very well: "some people will never learn anything because they grasp too soon. Wisdom, after all, is not a station you arrive at, but a manner of traveling . . . To know exactly where you are headed may be the best way to go astray. Not all who loiter are lost."[2] As a matter of fact, those who *loiter* in the question long enough will live into the answer. "Search and you will find," Jesus said (Matt. 7:7). I sometimes wonder if this means search long enough and you will find. It is the patient act of dwelling in the darkness of a question that eventually unravels the answer.

Kappus sought out Rilke with one question: is there a great poet waiting to be born in me or should I let that dream go? Kappus was looking for a road map, some critical help, and a direct answer regarding this, his deepest question. He never got that. Instead, he got a conversation about life, love and purpose. Rilke could have answered directly, but he didn't. Instead, he told Kappus to "try to love the questions themselves." Kappus needed to learn that sometimes the answers aren't as important as the way we learn to live among the questions.

I have never been very good at living with my questions about life. I have always been the type of person who searches for answers. However, the question I was struggling with in 1979 was should I stay in religious life and the priesthood or, as Kappus asked Rilke, "should I let this dream go?" In fact, it was a question I had been struggling with for years. In the past, I was always afraid to actually ask this question because it raised such turmoil inside of me. Whenever it tried to break into my consciousness, I would push it down or try to run away from it. Emotionally and psychologically, I couldn't sit with this question. It was too scary, too frightening to me. But this time, because of some things that had recently surfaced in my life, I decided to try and let this question have life.

Most of us know the feeling of longing for answers to our questions that do not come to us. Rilke, a devout believer, would have readily extended his advice to the spiritual level. In prayer, we too seek answers to our deepest questions. What am I doing *in* my life, *with* my life, with my love, my time, my gifts? Particularly, in the dark night seasons of our

2. de Mello, *The Heart of the Enlightened,* 38.

lives, our questions can be many but the answers few. The challenge in those times is to befriend our questions. But for me, how could I befriend a question that upset me so much? How could I entertain a question that had the potential to alter the course of my life?

It is interesting to discover that the Scriptures give us many examples of people asking questions and not getting answers, or at least not getting answers to the questions they asked. For example, the rich young man asked Jesus, "what must I do to gain eternal life?" He seems to have been a pious, devout young man but he left with a new set of questions to think about. How could he learn to love the questions? Perhaps by re-evaluating his sense of personal pride in his perceived holiness. The woman at the well seemed to ask Jesus a diversion question about the place of proper worship. I don't think she really cared, but she didn't like where the conversation with Jesus was going. The answer she received left new questions. How might she learn to love the new questions? Maybe by sharing her experience of Jesus with her fellow Samaritans. The disciples, afraid of drowning in the storm while Jesus slept in the boat, asked "don't you care if we die?" Jesus' response left them with a new question about the depth of their faith if they would be right in Jesus' presence and still be so afraid. How could this new question bless them? Maybe by reminding them that neither life nor death in the company of the Lord is the last word.

In Rilke's first letter, he told Kappus "nobody can advise you and help you, nobody." What might Rilke's adamant negative response have produced in Kappus? I can imagine anger, frustration, or maybe despair. "If you can't help me, who can?" But Rilke's next two sentences are interesting. While refusing to be the solution himself, he does offer a path forward. "There is only one way. Go into yourself."

For myself, as I struggled with my question of whether or not to leave religious life and the priesthood, I sensed that my answer could only be found within myself. Although I had been sharing my question with my spiritual director and psychiatrist who were both trying to help me sort out the issues involved in trying to make a decision, I realized that ultimately the decision was mine. For me, realizing this was scary. Like Rilke suggested, I had to go into myself. But where would it lead?

The reason why the questions we ask in life are so important is because they give direction to our lives. It's the questions we ask that give rise to our answers which in turn influence the many choices we make about how to live our lives. This is why it is crucial to ask the right questions. And it's our choices in life that will determine the kind of person we will become.

In 1968, Thomas Merton wrote his second diary, which he called *Conjectures of a Guilty Bystander*. He said that this book was completely different in its style and content from his first diary, *The Sign of Jonas*, which he wrote in 1953. This second diary was "a personal vision of the world in the 1960s." It was different, he felt, because his questions about life, society, and issues in the world were very different. Over those fifteen years, Merton said: "these notes . . . are an implicit dialogue with other minds, a dialogue in which questions are raised. But do not expect to find answers. I do not have clear answers to current questions. I do have questions, and, as a matter of fact, I think a man is known better by his questions than by his answers."[3]

After being in the monastery for twenty-seven years, Merton had come to realize the importance of asking the right questions for our lives. It is our questions that allow us to grow spiritually, emotionally, and psychologically.

Sometimes, we have to deal with other questions before we can find the right question. That is the way it was for me. Ever since I was a novice in our Order in 1962, I was constantly plagued by questions whether I could live this life. Could I live my vows in a healthy way and not be crippled by them? Could I find happiness in living community life? Over the years, I had lived with some friars who seemed to be unhappy all the time. For a variety of reasons, they were difficult to live with. Had religious life made them this way? Did living the vows end up having this kind of negative impact on their development? I was afraid that this might happen to me.

Later on, some of my other questions focused on several physical ailments I was constantly experiencing. What was causing these daily headaches that were so difficult to treat? Why was my stomach always bothering me? At other times, my questions would center around the depression I was struggling with. Not only why was I depressed but what could I do about it? I struggled with these types of questions for years looking for answers before I allowed the *right* question to seep into my consciousness—should I stay in religious life and the priesthood or not? What was the "afternoon of my life" saying to me?

3. Merton, *Conjectures*, 1.

3

Entering the Monastery

"Our Beliefs Become Our Prisons"

(RACHEL REMEN)

BACK IN THE 1950s, it was a great honor to have a vocation to become a priest. The word vocation itself meant a "calling" and we were constantly encouraged in my catholic high school to pray about whether we felt we were being called to become a priest. And if we felt we were being called by God, it was important to respond to that calling by nurturing this vocation. You didn't want to deny this calling or simply not act on it. Therefore, the best way to affirm and nurture this call was to go to the seminary. So, this is what I did in September, 1957.

Back in the 1950s, going to a catholic school meant going to Mass and other church functions for a variety of reasons. About mid-way through my sophomore year, I began to think more seriously about going to the seminary and to pray more earnestly about this idea. In addition, I began to read more. Three books were especially formative in my decision-making process. 1) *The Seven Story Mountain* by Thomas Merton. He was an extremely important spiritual writer in the mid-twentieth century and his autobiography detailed the way Merton went through a major conversion in the 1940s and then entered the Cistercian Order which was very strict at the time. This book greatly inspired me. 2) *Damien, the Leper* was also an influential book in helping me make a decision.

Damien was a missionary priest from Holland who went to the island of Molokai in the state of Hawaii to minister to and take care of the lepers in 1864. In those days, leprosy was a dreaded disease for which there was no cure. Molokai was the island to which many of the lepers were banished. Damien went there to take care of the lepers, knowing full well that he himself would probably contract and die from this disease. After ministering to them in a totally unselfish way for twelve years, he did contract leprosy and died from it on Molokai in 1889. This book inspired me because at the time, I also thought I wanted to be a missionary priest like Damien. 3) A third book that greatly inspired me and influenced my decision was *The Life of Padre Pio*. He was a Capuchin Franciscan priest living in Italy from 1887–1968, who had received the Stigmata of Jesus. These were the wounds of Jesus given to him because of his holiness. His hands and feet bore the holes where the nails went through the hands and feet of Jesus. His wounds, like the wounds of Christ, bled regularly. The Stigmata was not given to very many people and his life and holiness became an inspiration to me. He was also a wonderful confessor who spent long hours comforting people in the Sacrament of Reconciliation and he also possessed the gift of being able to make very accurate predictions about the lives of people.

Besides these three very influential books, there was a fourth thing that was a powerful influence on me. This was a family vacation trip we made to the Shrine of St. Anne de Beaupre in Montreal, Canada in 1956. We had gone to Canada on vacation during the summer following my freshman year of high school. I can still vividly remember visiting this beautiful church with large stone pillars on the inside. And what really impressed me was the presence of hundreds of crutches, canes, and wheelchairs that were attached to these pillars. These had all been left there as a testament to miracles that had been granted to people over the years. To myself, a young fourteen year old, this was truly amazing and inspiring.

Another factor that played a role in my decision to go to the seminary was the belief that everyone in the Catholic Church had about priests. We were always taught that there was no greater vocation on earth. Priests were admired by everyone. Accompanying this belief was the corresponding belief that if you went to the seminary to become a priest, you would also be admired. I'm not sure how much this idea influenced my decision to go to the seminary, but I know that it was present. Now that I am older, and hopefully somewhat wiser, I can understand this factor more clearly. However, as a fifteen year old boy, I thought my reasons were mostly altruistic.

For me, it was a huge decision to go to the seminary. In my own mind as a teenager, I was giving up a lot of things. After all, I was president of our class in the tenth grade. I was very popular in school, good in sports, had a great time at parties and our school dances, and was just beginning to enjoy dating. To go to the seminary meant giving up all of these things.

Everyone knows that youth is a time of idealism. In a naive sort of way, another reason I wanted to go to the seminary and become a priest was because this would help me to become a saint. Most of the men and women that I was familiar with and had been reading about and had become saints were either priests or members of a religious community. I thought if they could become a saint, maybe I could too.

Coupled with this desire to become a saint was my desire to go to heaven and avoid going to hell. Remember, it was the Catholic Church of the 1950s. This idea about the fear of going to hell also played a significant role in my decision to go to the seminary. For some reason, my fear of going to hell was becoming more pronounced within me, so I thought that if I was able to become a priest, I would have the best chance of avoiding serious sin which would help me go to heaven and avoid going to hell. At this time, there were many sermons about this topic which struck the fear of God in me. Also, some of the preaching at our parish missions seemed to greatly emphasize this idea. I especially remember going to one of our parish missions where the priest was preaching about venial and mortal sin and what happened to you if you died with an unforgiven mortal sin on your soul. To a young teenager, this was very scary.

Although I was thinking more about going to the seminary, I had no idea which one to go to. The only thing I knew at the time was that I wanted to be a missionary priest rather than a diocesan priest. During the winter of my sophomore year, I remembered that I had a friend when we lived in Pittsburgh who had gone to a seminary that was run by the Capuchin Franciscan religious order. So, I thought I would write to him about what his experience at the seminary had been like. He was very positive about his life there. The name of this seminary was St. Fidelis and it was located about thirty miles north of Pittsburgh. After exchanging several letters, he invited me to come for a visit. So, during my Easter vacation of that year, my parents and I drove to Butler, Pennsylvania to take a look at St. Fidelis High School and College Seminary. Of course, we were shown around by my friend and listened to him describe life in the seminary. Although it sounded rather strict and had a lot of rules to follow, I remember thinking that I was very impressed with what this seminary had to offer. Moreover, it also fulfilled the one requirement that I seemed to want, i.e. that of being a seminary run by a religious order that had some of their priests working in the missions. It was not a diocesan seminary which prepared priests to work in the parishes of a particular diocese.

After my visit to St. Fidelis, and discussing my thoughts with my parents, I decided that this was the seminary I would like to attend. Then, after completing the application, the only thing remaining to do was to have the vocation director of the Capuchin Province, which was headquartered in Pittsburgh, come to our house for a home visit. That occurred during the summer. The purpose of this kind of visit was to introduce himself and the Capuchin Order to me and my family and for us to meet him. It gave all of us a chance to ask any questions we might have as he tried to explain what life was like in the seminary. After showing him my high school grades, he assured me that I would be accepted into my junior year of high school at St. Fidelis with no problems. Later on this became a huge problem for me. This was important at the time because most boys either went to the seminary in the ninth grade to begin their high school years or waited until they finished high school at home and then went to the seminary to begin college. There were not many boys in my situation, i.e. entering half way through high school.

After this home visit by the vocation director, I had to wait for several weeks for an answer to my application. My acceptance letter came one day in the middle of the summer. Now, I had a few weeks to get ready and pack things that I would be taking with me. In a few weeks, this new adventure would begin.

A. The Catholic Church in the 1950s

I entered St. Fidelis High School Seminary in September 1957. I was fifteen years old. This decision was entirely my own. I had no pressure from anyone. Although my parents never discussed with me the pros and cons of my decision, they were supportive and encouraged me to pursue this desire if that was what I wanted. Interestingly enough, I later discovered that my mother didn't think I would last very long. She thought I would be back home fairly quickly!

Today, most psychologists agree that the way most people make important decisions in their lives is a very complex process. I have also found this to be true in my career as a psychotherapist. For over twenty-four years, I have accompanied people who have struggled to make all kinds of decisions. Sometimes, these decisions are life changing and involve a great deal of anguish and soul searching. No matter whether the issue involves a relationship, a career, or a financial decision, it is never an easy process.

In order to understand the interlocking reasons as to why I went to the seminary in 1957, it is important to understand what was happening in the Catholic Church in the 1950s. Until the last fifty years, the Roman Catholic Church was characterized by a number of clear, distinct emphases. You were considered a practicing catholic if you went regularly to church, prayed privately, tried to live the commandments, were not publicly at odds with the church's teaching on marriage and sexuality, were contributing to the support of the church, and were not in some public way causing scandal. This, however, was seen as the minimum. Doing these things merely made you a catholic, but did not necessarily define you as a healthy one.

What helped to define you as "healthy" was participation within certain spiritual practices, especially certain devotional and ascetical ones. Therefore, you were not just a catholic because you went to church and respected the church's laws on sex and marriage. You were also one because you did a number of other things: you were a catholic because you did not eat meat on Fridays, fasted during Lent, gave money to the poor, prayed the rosary, supported foreign missions, and participated in various other devotional practices. To be a catholic also meant attending benediction, praying the stations of the cross, saying litanies to the Blessed Virgin Mary, St. Joseph, and the Sacred Heart, going to church on first Fridays, reading the lives of the saints and other devotional books, praying for the souls in purgatory, incorporating certain sacramentals, like holy water, and blessed medals into your life.

Moreover, for the last century, ever since Pope Leo XIII's social encyclical of 1870 entitled *Rerum Novarum*, the need to practice social justice has been growing as an important component within catholic spirituality. This, or its absence, also helped to define you as a catholic. However, except for a few exceptions, this imperative never was able to lodge itself as centrally within the heart of Roman Catholic spirituality as did the devotional and sacramental elements just named.

As a young boy, I grew up in this Roman Catholic Church as it existed prior to the changes ushered in by the Second Vatican Council in the 1960s. Generally speaking, all catholics went to church and the church's rhythms pretty much dictated things. The Mass was celebrated in Latin and although most people did not understand this language, we had missals where we could follow along in English. Children who went to a catholic school or public school children who were catholics and attended religious education classes, had to memorize a common catechism in a question and answer format that became familiar to everyone. Rectories, convents, and seminaries teemed with life and, by and large, the church enjoyed considerable respect within the larger culture. For Roman Catholics, in the Western world, this was a certain golden time. There was a universal ethos within the body of Roman Catholicism that we may perhaps never again approximate. Whatever its dysfunctions, and there were some of those too, the Roman Catholic Church of my youth was a powerful incarnation expression of the Body of Christ. And for me, it was the vehicle through which I received the Christian faith. This was the church I was participating in when I decided to apply for acceptance into the seminary in 1957.

B. My Family

Our families are the cradle of our existence and they have a profound influence on our growth and development. It is within our families that our personalities are formed and nurtured.

Huntington, West Virginia was probably the second largest city in the state in 1957. Tucked away between the mountains, the city thrived on the presence of several industries. More importantly, it was a lovely place in which to raise a family and many generations of families seemed to remain there for years. We used to have a saying that there was "a lot of old money" in Huntington.

This is the place where I was born on January 10, 1942. We lived there for the first five years of my life, moved to Pittsburgh, Pennsylvania for several years and then, because of my Dad's job, came back to Huntington in 1955. It was from here that I went to the seminary in 1957.

I have an older sister and one younger brother. My father sold automotive parts and at times had to travel a great deal. My mother was a nurse by profession but was able to be a stay at home Mom when we were growing up. Later on, she went to work as the head nurse of the pediatric unit at St. Mary's, our local hospital. Interestingly enough, this was also where she met my father. Being so young, I don't remember very much about these first years, except for the fact that I had several friends that I used to play with regularly.

When I was five years old, my father's job took us to Pittsburgh. He received a promotion to a sales manager position which also included more traveling. Consequently, we didn't get to see him as much. There were many young families in our neighborhood with a lot of children my age and I had many good friends. These were basically happy years for me.

For my first year of school, I went to St. Bernard's, a Catholic elementary school several miles away. This was the beginning of my catholic education. After this first year of school, the county built a new public elementary school very close to our home and so, all three of us were able to walk to school every day. Although I had many teachers during these years, I have always remembered Mrs. Jones, my third grade teacher. She was a very kind person who seemed to take an interest in me.

When I reflect on these years, there are certain things I vividly remember. Fortunately, many of them were very positive experiences for me. Maybe this is one reason why I can easily recall them.

For some reason, one of the games that I remember playing at school was marbles. It could be played with any number of kids, as long as they had sone marbles. One player would draw a large circle in the sand and every player would place five marbles in the sand wherever they chose. Then, each player took turns trying to knock the marbles out of the circle. Everyone would have their *special* shooting marble in which they would place the marble between their thumb and first finger and try to hit the marbles in the circle completely out of the circle. If you were able to do this, then each player could keep the marbles they managed to knock out of the circle. At that age, it was really a fun game and one that I was very good at. Every day, many of us would bring our bag of marbles with us and play at recess as well as before and after school. I think one of the reasons why I remember this game so well is because I began to realize that I was a very competitive person.

I also loved playing sports—mostly baseball and football at the time and because I was a good athlete, I was able to play for a number of teams.

I particularly remember one Little League baseball game in which I hit a home run to win the game for our team and after the game my mother took me out to an ice cream store for a milkshake! Interesting sometimes, the things we can remember, even if they happened so long ago.

My family was also a big Pittsburgh Steelers football and Pirates baseball fan. Once in a while, we would have tickets to a football game and even though it might be extremely cold and/or snowy and windy, we would brave the elements and go to a game.

My family also had the first TV in the neighborhood which was a new phenomenon back in the 1950s. Consequently, we could always count on our friends to come over to our house and watch The Lone Ranger Show or a Roy Rogers or Gene Autry Show. In those days, having a TV was a big deal and we had a lot of fun using this new piece of equipment. And how many of us can remember several of the first TV programs called The Howdy Doody Show and Kukla, Fran and Ollie? Back in those days, these were certainly some of our favorites and our home became a gathering place for kids in our neighborhood.

The summers were especially fun times for me growing up. Often, three or four of us would get permission to sleep outside in our tent and we always had a great time doing this. Moreover, in the summers of 1953 and 1954, my brother and I along with one of our cousins and several friends went to Camp Lakewood for two weeks. This was a structured event in West Virginia where we went swimming and fishing, played "capture the flag" with the other guys, slept in cabins and did a lot of fun activities at the camp site and out in the woods. Reviewing our pictures of these experiences always bring back happy memories.

Probably my best friends in the neighborhood lived two houses up the street from us. There were three boys in their family and all of us really liked working with our model train sets. We were always comparing and competing with each other as to who had the better trains. Of course, my brother and I thought our Lionel trains were the best and our friends thought their American Flyer trains were even better. In a good way, we were always battling each other as to who had the best overall train set up. Great fun!

After finishing elementary school, I went to Bethel Park Junior High School. That is what we would call middle school today and these years encompassed the sixth, seventh, and eighth grades. Two things stand out to me as I reflect on these years. The first important thing I remember is going on a diet to lose weight! In elementary school, I had always been somewhat "chubby" or overweight. In fact, I used to go around our house asking my mother and sister if they thought I was too fat? So, in the eighth grade, I decided to go on a diet and eat only a sandwich and a piece of fruit for lunch. It must have worked because when I began the ninth grade I felt slimmer! The reason why this is important involves the second thing I can remember about my junior high school years. I was beginning to become very interested in girls. Although I didn't have a real girl friend during these years, I can still remember two girls that I liked. Even now, I can still see their faces and remember their names.

Toward the end of the eighth grade, it became clear that we were going to move again—back to Huntington, West Virginia. My father received another promotion and plans were made to move there during the summer. Several of my friends heard about our impending move. Near our school, there was a beautiful public park. One of my good friends talked me into going to this park one day after school on the pretense of playing baseball. When I got there, a group of around thirty kids and a number of parents were there to surprise me with a "going away party." We had a great time playing games and eating hot dogs and hamburgers. What a great sendoff! I had no idea that I meant so much to these friends. It was one of those experiences in my life that was terribly important to me and one that I have never forgotten.

During that summer after finishing the eighth grade, my family moved back to Huntington, the place where I was born. For several months, we lived in an apartment while the house we were building got finished. I began my high school years as a freshman at St. Joseph Catholic High School. Compared to the public schools in our area, it was a relatively small school. But there was a great spirit among the students and faculty. It was from here that I went to the seminary after my sophomore year.

These two years—the ninth and tenth grades—were also very happy years for me. My transition to this new school was easy because everyone was extremely welcoming. The school was staffed by the Sisters of St. Joseph who were very good educators and who had a good rapport with all of us teenagers. During these years, I was popular, got good grades, and played on the high school baseball team. During the summer after the ninth grade, I went on my first date. I had learned that one of the girls in my class liked me and even though I liked someone else more at the time, I decided to ask this girl if she would like to go to a movie. I was brand new to this whole dating thing, but we had a very nice time and enjoyed ourselves very much. Another thing I enjoyed was going to our school dances. I was considered to be a very good dancer and really enjoyed these occasions. It gave me a chance to dance with the girl that I liked, although I knew she liked an upper classman at the time. I have always remembered these dances as very special times during my high school years.

In the tenth grade, I was elected president of our tenth grade class at the beginning of the school year. This was a surprise and a very nice honor for me. Also, one of my friends was older and already had his driver's license. I can so vividly remember that one day in October he picked up me and four of my classmates and drove us to a beautiful place called Ritter Park. We had gotten an assignment from our biology teacher to collect a variety of leaves and make a booklet out of them. We were studying plants and trees at the time and a public park seemed like a good place to find a lot of different species. It was such a fun day and among our group was the girl that I liked a lot which made the day even more interesting and enjoyable.

1) My Father

Both of my parents were teenagers during the Depression and this had a profound impact on their personalities. My father was fourteen when the Depression began and he came from a very troubled family. I never remember my Dad talking about his family life. The only people I ever knew in his family was his only sister, one aunt and one cousin. My father was born and grew up in Huntington. His parents divorced when he was very young which was extremely traumatic for him. His father remarried but my Dad didn't like his step mother, so he left home as a teenager. He got a job and found a place to live on his own.

My father became a convert to the Catholic religion when he and my mother got married in 1939. They raised the three of us and in those early years, my Dad had a good job as a salesman of automobile parts. He was mostly an extrovert which contributed to his success as a salesman and he enjoyed family gatherings and parties. However, he had difficulties with his emotional life. With his troubled family background, he had difficulty expressing his emotions. He could be aloof emotionally. But if he got upset at my brother and me, he could become angry very quickly and yell at us at times. Expressing his anger appropriately seemed to be his most difficult emotion and this fear that I had of him and his anger, has greatly affected me later on as an adult. He also had a difficult time relaxing or just taking it easy. And because of leaving home as a teenager and the Depression beginning when he was about fourteen, he always felt he had to work hard. But he loved sports and this was how we generally connected. I remember that he liked boxing and when I was young we used to watch a TV program together called the "Friday Night Fights."

As a family, we had some wonderful vacations. One year, all of us, along with my grandmother, drove to Ft. Lauderdale, Florida where we had a really nice time. Also, my Dad liked to hunt and fish, and on several occasions he took me and my brother as well as my uncle and one of my cousins on fishing trips to Canada. I have great memories of these trips. Dad also loved ice cream and I can always remember on many Sunday evenings after he would finish his business reports, he would take us to a local ice cream parlor for ice cream. Every time, he would order a chocolate milk shake.

As the years went by, two things emerged in his personality that made life difficult for him and for our family. First of all, when we lived in Pittsburgh in the 1950s, there were some beginning signs of a problem with alcohol. Later on in his life, this became a major problem. Eventually, this caused tremendous problems in my parents' marriage. The second factor that became a huge problem for him and our family was several bad business decisions he made. After having some kind of business disagreement with his boss in the auto parts company, Dad decided to leave that company and join another similar type of company near Chicago, Illinois. This, of course, required moving to Illinois which was very difficult on my family. Moreover, for some reason Dad did not investigate the finances of this company well enough and although he worked extremely hard and very long hours, he wasn't able to turn this company around. After a couple of years, he decided to take another job with an automobile parts company in Hayward, California which meant another move out west. However, despite his best efforts and long hours, this endeavor also never became very successful. Mostly, because my mother became very unhappy and my father's health began to deteriorate from high blood pressure, my parents decided to leave California and return to Huntington to be closer to my mother's family. These two bad business decisions had a huge negative impact on our family.

During these rather tumultuous years, I was away in the seminary in Butler, Pennsylvania but saw the impact these decisions had on everyone when I would come home for vacation. After moving back to Huntington, my father bought a small pizza carry-out store that was moderately successful. However, after several years, the lady that owned the building where the business was located, sold her land to the state for road improvements and so my Dad also lost his business. After his pizza store business collapsed, he was out of work for a while. Eventually, he managed to get a job with the state and became the supervisor of a toll bridge in Huntington. After working at this position for several years, he told my mother that he wanted to move and retire to Florida. Well, by this time, my mother said she did not want to move away again. After my parents moved back to Huntington from California, my mother got a job as a nurse at the local hospital and didn't want to give that up. Eventually, my father moved to North Carolina which devastated my mother. Several years later, he told her that he wanted a divorce and this hurt her even more. I can remember the few times when I got to leave the monastery and visit my mother, she would be terribly distraught, crying and very depressed. Needless to say, these were extremely difficult visits for me and I just tried to comfort her as best I could.

Over the following years, with my dad living in North Carolina, I wasn't able to have much contact with him because I had no address and no phone number. It felt like he wanted nothing to do with his family. I remember one time that my brother and I drove to the little town in North Carolina where we knew he lived, hoping to find him. I will always remember that we spotted him going in the other direction in his car but by the time we could turn around, we lost him. We checked around with some places that we thought might know him but to no avail.

In the summer of 1980, I was teaching a summer course at St. Bonaventure University in Olean, New York. One morning, I received a phone call from a priest in my community saying that my father had died. It seems as though he had a massive heart attack. I was still in the priesthood then, so I drove to North Carolina several days later and presided at his funeral. This was overwhelmingly difficult for me. As I was trying to share some thoughts about him at the funeral Mass, I broke down completely and couldn't finish my homily. It was the end of a long, painful journey for my father.

During the course of my own therapy, I came to understand more about my relationship to my Dad. Because of his very troubled family life, my father found it difficult to express his emotions. I felt emotionally distant from him, yet needed and wanted his love and attention. My own

difficulties expressing my emotions through the years has been a struggle
for me and I have worked hard on this dimension of my life. Although he
did the best he could, I have often wished that we could have been closer
and shared more of our life together.

2) My Mother

My mother was born in 1917 which meant that she too was also a teenager through the Depression years. Her parents were Italian immigrants
who came to America around the turn of the century. Because her parents had other relatives living and working in Fairmont, West Virginia,
they settled there first. Several years later, they moved to the small coal
mining town of Smithers, along the Kanawha river, where they raised
their family and spent the rest of their lives. In Italy, my grandfather had
trained and developed his skill as a stone mason but couldn't find work
here in that field and so he went to work in the coal mines. This was an
extremely difficult job and in those days the coal mines were not very
safe. Nevertheless, he remained in this job for over thirty years. When we
were visiting my mother's family over the years, I can still see my grandfather walking up the street toward their house covered with coal dust.

Although I knew very little about my father's family, my mother
came from a very tight knit group and we saw them several times a year.
My mother was one of six children and she and her only brother were
the only ones who moved away from the Smithers area. Every year, we
would vacation there for two weeks. I have great memories of those vacations. My cousin, Paul, was about my age and he, my brother, and I had a
great time doing a variety of things—playing all kinds of games, running
around the neighborhood, going to movies, fishing in the local creek,
and going to a lovely park for large, family picnics. Also, my uncle had a
hunting and fishing cabin that we all enjoyed very much. Basically, it was
at this cabin that I learned how to hunt and fish. These memories have
vividly remained with me over the years and they gave me a sense of the
joy that one's extended family can bring to a person.

When my mother was in high school, she was quite fit as she explained to us how she could swim across the Kanawha river! This was
no small feat given that it was a wide river. I think she felt very proud of
herself that she was able to accomplish this. With regard to her career,
she went to nursing school in Huntington, West Virginia and became

a registered nurse in the 1930s. After receiving this nursing degree, she remained in Huntington and worked as a nurse at St. Mary's Hospital. It was here that she met and married my father. She, her brother, and one sister, were the only children in her family that were able to go on to higher education. Although she was a stay at home mom when she was raising us, this nursing degree proved to be very valuable when my parents moved back to Huntington from California. Her nursing degree enabled her to find a good job that helped support our family.

With regard to her personality, my mother was an introvert—quiet and more reserved. Although she enjoyed the company of other people, she always seemed to be quite content in her own home doing a variety of things around the house. She loved flowers and gardening, quilting, classical and especially operatic music, and enjoyed several early TV shows that I would sometimes watch with her, like "I Remember Mama," and "Life is Worth Living," a show featuring Bishop Fulton J. Sheen.

One of the traits that I always greatly admired about my mother was her kindness. I don't ever remembering her saying an unkind word about anyone or ever remember her spreading any kind of gossip.

After my father's business venture fell apart in California in the mid 1970s, my family moved back to Huntington to be closer to family and friends. This began a very difficult period of time for my mother. As my dad's drinking problem increased, my parents' relationship deteriorated. When they returned to Huntington, my mother was able to resume her career as a nurse and became the head nurse on the pediatric floor at St. Mary's Hospital. When my father filed for a divorce, my mother was devastated and she fell into a deep depression which lasted for several years. After this, she decided to move back to her home town of Smithers to be closer to her family. She purchased a mobile home and lived next door to one of her sisters. I can still vividly remember going home during the late 1970s, trying to console her. She was very sad and depressed and could never figure out why my father left her. After living in her mobile home for about two years, my aunt's husband died and then my mother sold her mobile home and moved in with her sister. This enabled them to help each other by sharing expenses and also having some companionship. And although my mother continued to struggle with depression, this move to my aunt's house kept her from being isolated.

This living arrangement seemed to work fairly well for about twelve years. Then, in the summer of 1991, I received a call from her. She was very distraught and said that she and her sister had an argument. After listening and talking to her for several more days and then talking to my wife, Margaret, we agreed that it would be best for her to come and live with us in Maryland. This was mutually helpful because my mom would be able to take care of our daughter, Colleen, who was nine months old at the time, until we came home from work. However, this part of the arrangement had to be put on hold for awhile because when my mother came to live with us, she again was going through a major depression. I had her talk to a colleague of mine who was a psychiatrist, and he thought she needed to be hospitalized. So, after spending several weeks in the hospital, my mother came back to our house where she continued to receive outpatient counseling and work with the psychiatrist who could monitor her medications. She began taking care of our daughter which was very helpful to us. Up until this time, we took Colleen to a sitter's house because both Margaret and I were working full time. Having my mother watch her during the day helped my mother have a renewed sense of purpose and allowed us to know that Colleen was receiving excellent care. This arrangement also allowed my mother and Colleen to form a very special bond which remained throughout the rest of her life.

In the late 1990s, my mother began to show some signs of dementia. At this time, she was still driving, and one evening she went to church and couldn't find her way home. At this point, we knew that this would be the end of her driving. Gradually, as her condition became worse, we took her to a geriatric physician. After administering several tests, he concluded that she had early stage Alzheimer's and put her on some medication to help slow down the progression of the disease.

As with most Alzheimer's patients, mom's condition continued to deteriorate. She continued to live with us and we were only able to keep her with us because of the love and care of my wife. Margaret cared for her as if she were her own mother. I will never be able to thank her enough for everything she did for her every day. She would come home from work, make her dinner, pray the rosary with her which my mother loved, get her ready for bed, and made sure she took her medications. I certainly could not have done it without her.

Gradually, as my mother's condition deteriorated, we realized that she needed twenty-four hour care. Every time we had to go somewhere, my mother would become extremely anxious and beg us not to leave her. Fortunately, we were able to have mom go to a nursing home which was only about four miles from our home. This allowed us to still visit her regularly. I will always remember the big smile she had on her face when we walked into her room. The staff of the nursing home said that she was always cooperative and pleasant to be around. Some people afflicted with this disease become very angry and belligerent. Fortunately, this was not the case with her.

Mom was ninety-one when she died peacefully in her sleep. Margaret, Colleen, and I were extremely fortunate in that my mother always recognized us right up until the very end. We found great comfort in that. The last time we saw her, we encouraged her to let go because the Lord was waiting for her. This seemed to help her find peace.

In terms of my personality, I am obviously a mixture of both of my parents. But I think I am probably more like my mother in some fundamental ways. Like her, I tend to be more of an introvert, enjoy my quiet time, and have struggled with depression through the years. But perhaps the one thing that I did not learn from either parent was the ability to express my emotions. Both my father and mother did not know how to talk and share their feelings very well. Consequently, I never really learned how to do this either and, as we will see, this inability has left me wounded in different ways.

C. My Years at St. Fidelis High School Seminary

Back in the 1950s, there were basically two types of high school seminaries. One kind was established for boys who wanted to become diocesan priests. These young men were usually ordained for a particular diocese and they would be assigned by their bishops to staff local parishes throughout their diocese. If a young man went to a diocesan seminary, he could expect to spend four years in high school, then four years of college, majoring in philosophy, and the final four years studying theology. From the freshman year of high school until ordination, usually took twelve years.

If a young man chose to go to a seminary to become a priest as a member of a religious order, he would go to the seminary as a high school freshman, then go to college for his first two years and then take a year off from college and go to the novitiate of the religious order. All religious orders had a novitiate year. Basically, this was a very strict year devoted to prayer and learning about the spirituality of the founder of the religious order. It was essentially a year of discernment. For the novice, it was an opportunity to see if the person could be happy and thrive as a member of their particular community. For the religious community, it was an opportunity to observe, assess, and ultimately make a judgment about the suitability of each novice to live this way of life. After being a novice for a year and taking the religious vows of poverty, chastity, and obedience for a certain number of years—usually three—the young man would go back and finish his last two years of college and then move on to study theology for the next four years before he could be ordained a priest. Moreover, if you were a member of a religious order, your assignments would come from your religious superior rather than a bishop. Because of the year of discernment as a novice, it usually took one more year to be ordained compared to diocesan priests.

And so, over sixty three years ago, I entered St. Fidelis High School Seminary to begin my long journey to the priesthood. I can still vividly remember that day back in 1957, and my feelings of excitement and anticipation, along with some fear of the unknown.

My very first day was extremely traumatic for me. I remember it to this day, like it was yesterday. After my parents drove me to the Capuchin seminary outside of Butler, Pennsylvania, and helped me unpack, we said our tearful goodbyes, and I returned to the alcove to which I had been assigned. Alcoves were small enclosed areas, large enough for a bed and a small metal closet where you kept your clothes. After finishing my unpacking, I walked over to a sign on the door and looked for the classroom that I had been assigned to. I was shocked to find my name on the list for ninth graders! Panic set in. What was I to do? When the vocation director visited my home during the summer, he had promised me that I would be going directly into my junior year of high school. Now, I find my name of the list of freshmen. After the initial shock, I calmed down somewhat and decided to go and try to find the principal. At this point, I had no idea who the principal was or even where his office was located. Having met what looked like an older boy in the hallway, I asked him how I could find the principal's office. Then, following his directions in this very large building, I found his office, and knocked on the door. Fr. P. came to the door and I introduced myself. He was an elderly priest who gently smiled at me. I was terrified inside as I tried to explain my situation. Being fifteen and not knowing anyone in a completely strange place, I told him that the vocation director had promised me that I would be going into the eleventh grade. However, I found my name on the freshmen list. I also told him that if I had known that I would not be going into the eleventh grade, I know for sure that I would not have gone to the seminary that year. I would have at least waited until I finished high school at home and then gone to St. Fidelis as a college freshman. In any case, the principal listened to me as I tried to explain my situation and then he said that he was concerned that I would be behind in Latin and that I had not studied the German language. I later found out that German was required during the first two years of high school because the Capuchins of the Pittsburgh Province had originally come from Germany and for this reason, it was now a requirement in high school. In addition, I told him that I had taken two years of Latin in my high school at home. Finally, he told me to try the tenth grade rather than the ninth grade and we would see how it goes.

Needless to say, I was devastated! What more could I do? Having to repeat the tenth grade made me so angry and upset and yet there didn't seem to be anything I could do about it. My parents were already on their way back home to West Virginia. Remember, there were no cell phones back in 1957! So, I couldn't call them and there was no other way I could get in touch with them. I felt like I wanted to run away from this place. And so, this was the painful beginning of my seminary experience.

Following this difficult and painful beginning, I seemed to fit into seminary life fairly well. I struggled to resign myself to repeating the tenth grade and waited to see how things went. Fortunately, I was pretty much accepted by my new classmates. Being the "new kid on the block," I became involved in my studies and, being good in sports, allowed me to participate in a lot of activities. The days were busy and it seemed like there was hardly a free moment. We were either in class, in a study hall, or in the chapel. In general, the routine of the day was very structured and although life in the seminary was strict, it did not seem oppressive to me. We were up early. The bell rang loud throughout the dormitories at 5:30 am and we had twenty-minutes to get to the chapel for our morning prayers and daily Mass. We were in the chapel for prayers several times a day. This was followed by breakfast and then classes until noon. After lunch, we had class again from 1:00 pm to 3:00 pm and then free time until the bell sounded at 4:30 pm to bring us back inside, get cleaned up, and ready for study hall from 5:00 pm to 5:45 pm. From here, we went back to the chapel for prayers before dinner at 6:00 pm. Following dinner, we were free until 7:30 pm when the bell sounded again calling us for a study hall until 8:30 pm. Finally, after this last study hall of the day, we returned to chapel one last time for our night prayers and then off to bed. This was pretty much our schedule for the weekdays. The weekends were more relaxing and less structured, mostly because we had no classes, although there continued to be lengthly study halls.

As it turned out, I was behind my classmates in Latin and German, and so, another student and I were tutored in these subjects for about six months to help us catch up. Although this certainly did not compensate for having to repeat my sophomore year, it was necessary for me if I was going to be able to stay at St. Fidelis.

Besides needing to maintain good grades, everyone also needed to have good marks in conduct. There was a behavior card that every seminarian received each month describing certain behaviors with the numbers 1, 2, or 3 listed beside each each one. You were expected to get all one's on this card beside each category. Number two meant that you had been caught misbehaving in some way and number three meant you were liable for expulsion. You would certainly be asked to leave the seminary if you received several three's. For example, one of the very important behaviors that we were expected to follow was called the "Great Silence." This was a rule that said there would be no talking after night prayers, around 9:30 pm until breakfast the following day. So, if someone got caught talking or fooling around in any way, that person was likely to receive a "2" or "3" on their behavior card. If you didn't improve the next month, you might be eligible for expulsion. There were many other rules that we were expected to obey but observing the "Great Silence" was a major one.

For the most part, these early years of seminary life were positive experiences for me. Despite having to repeat my sophomore year, I seemed to adapt to seminary life without a great deal of difficulty. Although my studies were challenging, I was able to maintain at least a "B" average. And, although my behavior card was not perfect, I managed to obey the rules without a lot of strain.

One very positive thing happened to me when I was a senior in high school. I was chosen to be a sacristan. It was probably the most covenanted position in the seminary. A sacristan was the person who was designated to help prepare the priests for Mass, set up the altars, and handle the sacred vessels that were used for Mass. At this time in the church, only a few people were permitted to handle the sacred vessels. One person was chosen from the senior high school class, and one from both the freshmen and sophomore college classes. It was quite an honor for me to be chosen and I enjoyed this work very much.

1) Understanding "Seminary Culture"

I discovered very quickly what we, as seminarians, called the "seminary culture." This meant that everything was done to promote and guard your vocation. Everything was done to foster what the priests at the seminary thought was best for the formation of the seminarians, leading ultimately to the priesthood. This meant several things. First of all, it meant that obedience ruled. As a seminarian, you were expected to obey the rules. You were not encouraged to question authority in any way or to think for yourself. A good seminarian simply followed the rules as best he could. However, there were some rules of seminary life that were difficult to understand. For example, the seminary building was one large structure with three floors but the rules divided it up into sections, depending on what year you were in. So, if you were a freshman in high school, you occupied one section of the building and had to use a certain set of stairs to move from one section to another. Then, as you were there longer, you could occupy another section of the building and again use another set of designated stairs to get to the upper floors. Similarly, students in each year had there own designated recreational space in the building. This meant that if you had any free time and just wanted to "hangout" with your friends, you had to do this in the appropriate area according to the year you were in.

I suppose, in a sense, these kinds of rules existed to give the students a sense of progressing to a higher level of seminary life as one moved through the years. Although there didn't seem to be any important reasons for these kind of rules, everyone certainly knew about them and abided by them. Following the rule was the name of the game.

In a similar way, the dormitory areas were also divided up according to the year you were in. For example, if you were just beginning as a freshman in high school, you slept in an open air dormitory with bunk beds. Then, for your sophomore and junior years, you graduated to a private alcove separated by metal sections and a curtain. At least these arrangements gave each person a certain amount of privacy. After this, if you were a senior in high school or in the first or second year of college, you were eligible for a private room. These private rooms, of course, were coveted by everyone because you had your own space in which to study and sleep.

A second aspect of seminary culture emphasized what was called "custody of the eyes." Because the priesthood required a celibate life style, as a seminarian you were always expected and encouraged to remember this admonition. This meant that you should not look at girls or women in a way that might cause you temptation or possibly jeopardize your vocation. You were supposed to always protect your vocation and not allow any temptations to become a problem. This was always difficult for me even in the minor seminary because on one Sunday a month, there would be a visiting day. What this meant was that during four hours on a Sunday afternoon, the families of the seminarians were encouraged to come and visit their sons. Well, since my family was living in West Virginia at the time, it was at least a six hour drive, so my family rarely came on these visiting day Sundays. However, several of my friends always invited me to visit with their families, and so I had the opportunity to meet a lot of people and among them were some very pretty girls. How was I expected to practice "custody of the eyes" in these situations? Honestly, I don't think I ever figured this one out. In fact, I must admit that I enjoyed seeing them!

Maybe more importantly, this admonition to practice "custody of the eyes," also meant that when you were home on vacation at Christmas, Easter, or the summer, there should obviously be no dating. Doing this could put your vocation in danger, or worse, become an occasion of sin. Naturally, there was a very strong emphasis on this, especially while we were home for the summer months.

A third facet of this "seminary culture" was unspoken silence. You didn't talk about things openly, especially if you were having problems. For example, if you were thinking about leaving the seminary, you never spoke to a friend about this. That might cause your friend to have the same problem and maybe think about leaving too. If you had any problems at all, you were expected to only talk with your spiritual director—one of the priests—-about this sort of thing. It never ceased to amaze me that some days you would wake up, go to morning prayers and Mass, then go down to breakfast and discover an empty seat at one of the tables. Someone had left the seminary during the night. This always seemed so strange to me because it could have been a good friend who left, but no one probably ever knew he was having trouble and thinking about leaving. Moreover, you never got to say goodbye. Inevitably, whenever someone left, it was mostly done in secret, at night. Most guys left during the summer months. Each September, you would return to St. Fidelis and find out that several classmates didn't return. But once in a while, a boy would leave during the school year but it was always a secret. In all my five years in the minor seminary, I never saw one person leave during the day. It felt like the person leaving had some sort of contagious disease and if you got too close you would catch it and leave too. Silence was the name of the game. Your vocation had to be protected at all times! This type of secrecy began in the minor seminary but, as I will share later, grew worse in the monastery.

A fourth dimension of our "seminary culture," involved our seminary spirituality. From early on, we were always taught to "offer it up." It was a way of "spiritualizing" everything that happened to you in life. This way of dealing with life was ingrained in us from the beginning of our seminary days. If we had any difficulties or problems in life, we were encouraged to "offer it up" to Jesus, to align our difficulties or suffering with those of Jesus on the cross. The thinking here was that if we were able to do this, we would then be able to grow in our spiritual life. While this way of living our lives made good theological sense at the time, it was not always healthy emotionally or psychologically. If we could always "spiritualize" everything that happened to us, it might give us a way of denying or burying important emotional or psychological issues rather than dealing with them at the time. Living this way was something that I learned to do very well in the minor seminary, but I know now that it came back to haunt me later on. In order to be emotionally and psychologically healthy and grow spiritually, it is imperative that we learn to handle issues as they arise in our lives and not bury or deny them by sweeping them "under the rug."

D. Entering St. Conrad Monastery

On a balmy Texas afternoon in September 1962, President John F. Kennedy took to the podium at Rice University and laid out his administration's ambitious space program. In a tone laden with confidence, he said "we choose to go to the moon in this decade and do the other things, not because they are easy, but because they are hard; because that good will serve to organize and measure the best of our energies and skills, because that challenge is one that we are willing to accept."[1]

Approximately two months before Kennedy uttered these words, I entered the Capuchin novitiate on July 15, 1962. His words certainly applied to me as I thought about this decision. I knew it would not be easy,

1. www.jfklibrary.org_historic speeches.

but hard. I knew my goal would serve to organize and measure the best of my energies and skills. I understood that this challenge was one that I was willing to accept.

However, before I entered in July, I had to formally apply to be accepted as a novice in the Capuchin Franciscan Order in the spring of my sophomore year in college. Our province's headquarters was in Pittsburgh, Pennsylvania. Having done well in my five years at St. Fidelis, this was mostly a formality at this point. Nevertheless, in May, 1962, I received my acceptance letter from the Provincial.

After completing several more weeks of school and passing my final exams, I completed my sophomore year of college. That gave me about six weeks to prepare for going to the novitiate at St. Conrad Friary near Annapolis, Maryland. We had to be there on July 15, which was the day my formal novitiate year began. I visited my family and friends to say goodbye because by entering the monastery in 1962, I didn't know when I might see them again. In those days, there were no formal vacation days and only on rare occasions would we be allowed to go home. These rare occasions were usually for a serious illness or death in the family. I remember that my sister got married in June, 1963, and even though I only had about six more weeks to go in the novitiate, I was not allowed to attend. That was painful for me since I wanted to be there to support my sister and family on this joyous occasion. But I knew this was the rule when I entered the novitiate.

When you were in the minor seminary, there was a certain mystique about the novitiate. Stories about the novitiate year abounded and you were never quite sure what was true or what it was really like. Everyone knew that it was an extremely strict year and one that would test your resolve to see if you could endure it and thrive in this type of lifestyle. One of the things that made me apprehensive about going to the novitiate was the fact that the year before I entered, I knew there were two young men in the year ahead of me that had found the year to be overwhelming. Knowing what happened to them actually frightened me. One had been a good friend of mine in the high school seminary. During the course of his novitiate year, Fred became extremely depressed—so much so that he had to leave the novitiate because of his depression. Furthermore, he needed to be hospitalized and so he was admitted to the psych ward of a hospital back in Pittsburgh where he underwent electro-shock therapy and intense counseling for months. Finally, he was able to leave the hospital and began the long road to recovery. Eventually, he went back to school and got a degree in social work and worked for years helping people as a manager in the Salvation Army. But the novitiate year had certainly been traumatic for Fred and one in which he told me years later, had been devastating to him as a person. He said in some ways, it seemed as though he never truly recovered from his experiences that year.

That same year, 1961, Sam was also a novice in the Capuchin novitiate. He too became severely depressed, even suicidal. Sam managed to leave the novitiate on his own and he wrote about his efforts to cope with life after his return home to his family in Pittsburgh. Sam described his "suicidal gloom," as he called it, brought on by what he thought was a serious problem of scrupulosity. Later on, he understood that he suffered from a serious case of obsessive compulsive disorder which kept him tied up in knots.

When Sam left the Capuchin novitiate in February, 1962, after six years of training in the high school seminary, he said he felt like a "disgraced failure." He described himself as a goody-goody, overheated Catholic boy who possessed an undeveloped conscience of a first communicant frozen in the body of a virginal twenty-year old. He was engulfed with shame and felt that he was both damned and crazy. Added to this was the fact that he was returning home to his dangerous family where his father was a raging alcoholic. And, with his seven younger siblings, there was really no room for him at home. He said that he had to sleep in the hall outside the bathroom on a metal bed whose iron posts had to be hacksawed until they fit under the slant of the attic stairs.

In a curious sort of way, Sam felt that it was his scrupulosity that was his constant nemesis and companion which also in the end, saved his life. Why? Because he couldn't figure out a way of committing suicide without it being what he thought was a mortal sin. It all came together one day for Sam as he trudged through the muddy clay and dead weeds toward the banks of the swollen Allegheny river in Pittsburgh. Sam said there was no one around as he wondered if he could devise a drowning that would not be a mortal sin. A leap from one of the many nearby bridges would be deliberate and therefore culpable, damning him forever. That option was out. But walking the concrete steps of the riverbank, the lower ones flooded by churning water and ice, Sam wondered how he might twist an ankle or misjudge a step. If he would stumble, he would strike his head and slip into the inviting, rising water. Like his father, Sam was unable to swim and was terrified of water. He imagined that he would flail in the ice, panic, try to survive, uttering a perfect Act of Contrition as he was swept away. Drowning in the cold Allegheny river, he thought he would at last finally be delivered from his own personal darkness and wake before the face of God.

But then he thought that if he hoped he would fall in and, hysterical, go under, wouldn't he already be culpable, committing a sin of the mind? If he succeeded, wouldn't he still end up in hell? He said that he walked closer to the water's edge, backed off and continued to stroll along the banks of the Allegheny. By then, his scrupulous conscience kept raising new rationales, questions, counterarguments and scenarios—endless loops of rumination that had dominated his life for years. This was the tormented logic of his religious, compulsive thinking, but also a nonstop questioning that kept him alive.

In his bottomless hunger for certainty, he would not end his life in this way. He never turned his ankle, his foot never slipped, and the river continued to flow without the freight of his young body. Finally, as the late winter afternoon sky darkened, Sam trudged back up the hill to the Greyhound bus terminal and took the bus home. In the end, he felt that all he had produced was more grist for the ceaseless grinding of the millstones of his conscience, another serious sin to cough up in agony the next time he went to confession.

Several days later, Sam found himself going to confession, seeking absolution once again for what he thought was a serious sin. At its height several months earlier as a Capuchin novice, Sam would force himself to go to confession several times a day. Every thought and feeling was a sin. Sam thought that seeking forgiveness in the sacrament of penance would ease the pain of his tormented mind.

Several weeks later, Sam received a call from a priest friend of his who had found him a live-in job at a convent in the Pittsburgh area. This turned out to be a life saving event for him. Sam began working and living there with four other men who gradually became his first friends after leaving the Capuchin novitiate. But more importantly, Sam just felt safe there. Safe from his novitiate experience where his scrupulous conscience dominated his every waking moment. And, safe too from his dad and his alcoholic behavior.

Over the next several years, Sam got help for his scrupulosity. He came to understand that what he truly struggled with was obsessive compulsive disorder. And this new understanding gradually allowed him to become free from what had plagued him for so many years. Eventually,

Sam went back to college to complete a degree in English and became a very successful college professor.

Because I knew what these two guys had gone through in the novitiate, I was worried that something like this might happen to me. Along with this fear, was the fact that we had heard "through the grapevine" that we were probably going to be getting a new novice master. The current novice master was a priest who had served in this capacity for over twenty-five years. Now, his health was beginning to fail and he was transferred to another monastery where he could receive better health care. So, there was a lot of anticipation about what this new person would bring to the job. There were numerous stories about how strict and demanding this current novice master was and now our class would be the first one to "break in" and inaugurate this new one. I actually knew this priest who had recently been appointed as our new novice master. He had been the person who came to visit our home when I was thinking about going to the seminary five years earlier.

My class was the largest ever in the history of the province to enter the novitiate. There were twenty-two of us. These were still the days when there were many people entering the priesthood and religious life. So, we had a new novice master and the largest class ever. Sounded like it would be an interesting year.

Every religious order had a novitiate that each person participated in at some point during the early years of their formation. It was like "training." As I mentioned earlier, it was an intense year of religious formation in which the novices would receive instruction on the spirituality of their order, prayer, and the particular rules of their congregation. It was meant to be a difficult year, to discern whether a candidate was suited for this particular way of life. It certainly tested the resolve and perseverance of each novice and gave the Order a chance to observe the novices on a daily basis so that ultimately a judgment could be made about a novice's suitability to become a member of this particular community.

The Order that I joined was the Capuchin Franciscan Order. The Capuchins were a reform branch of the Franciscans back in 1525. There are three major branches of the Franciscans and the Capuchins are known to be the most strict. Moreover, if you joined the Capuchins, you could either become a priest or a brother. Both are members of the community, but each had their own functions. If you became a priest, you would participate in the ministry that all priests participated in, i.e. celebrating Mass and administering the other sacraments, preaching, and working in a variety of ministries like working in a parish, going to the missions or some other ministry that your particular province would be involved in. If you became a brother, your ministry, back in the 1960s, would mostly be work in the community, like cooking, taking care of the gardens, making sandals or greeting people at the monastery door. Today, there are also many other opportunities for brothers to become involved in a variety of outside ministries. In any case, we would all be brothers to each other living together in community life.

Although I didn't realize it at the time when I entered religious life in 1962, I soon discovered that I had embarked on this journey at a particularly inauspicious time. Members of religious orders were involved in a painful period of change and were trying to decide what exactly it meant to be a priest or brother in a religious community in modern society. The Catholic Church itself was also seeking transformation in the postwar world. During my first few months in the novitiate, the Second Vatican Council convened in Rome in 1962. It had been summoned by St. Pope John XXIII to fling open the windows of the church and let the fresh air of modernity and the Holy Spirit sweep through the musty corridors of the Vatican.

One of the areas tackled by the council fathers was religious life, which urgently needed reform. Many of the religious orders had gotten stuck in a traditional rut. Customs that had made perfect sense in the nineteenth and early years of the twentieth century, now seemed arbitrary and unnatural. Practices that had no intrinsic spiritual value became cultural relics of the Victorian age. But somehow these practices had acquired a certain sacred significance and change was regarded as betrayal. The council urged religious orders to go back to the original spirit of their founders, who had been men and women of insight and imagination, innovators, pioneers, and visionaries, not guardians of the status quo. Nuns and monks should also let the bracing spirit of change invade their cloisters. They should discard the rubble that had accumulated over the years and craft a new lifestyle that was more in tune with the times.

But this proved to be a monumentally complex task. Members of religious orders had to decide what was essential in their rule, and then translate this into present day reality. However, this was no easy task because they themselves had been shaped by the old regime at a profound level, and many found that they could not think in any other way. They could modernize their clothes but they could not change the habits of their minds and hearts, because these had been formed by a training that had been carefully designed in a different world and was meant to last a lifetime. For some, this was a time of great anguish. They saw a cherished way of life disappearing, yet nothing of equal value had emerged to take its place.

It was into this religious milieu that I began my novitiate year on July 15, 1962. I felt a great deal of excitement and anticipation as a I entered the doors of St. Conrad Friary. It was the beginning of a new adventure that I had been preparing for since going to the minor seminary five years ago. I was looking forward to wearing my brown Capuchin habit and sandals and officially becoming a member of the Capuchin Order of Friars Minor. But before I received the habit, all of us had to participate in an eight day silent retreat. I looked upon this as an opportunity to be alone with God and really prepare myself for the year ahead. After finishing our retreat, investiture day arrived and all twenty-two of us received the Capuchin habit.

Our novitiate complex, St. Conrad Friary, sat on top of a beautiful hill overlooking the Severn River, near Annapolis, Maryland. Although it sat on about twelve acres of land, most of it was extremely hilly and not useful because most of the land sloped down steeply toward the river. The house itself was a lovely former mansion that the Capuchins purchased in the 1950s with the plan to add on to it so that it could function as a monastery. A chapel, dormitory, and dining area were added after the initial purchase.

I quickly got into the flow of the day. Our daily schedule revolved around prayer, meditation, classes studying Franciscan spirituality, the Capuchin rule of life as well as our Capuchin Constitutions, which were the practices that interpreted our Rule of Life for daily living. We arose at 5:30 am, went to chapel at 6:00 am for a half hour of personal meditation, prayed part of the Divine Office for the day, which is now called the Liturgy of the Hours, and then celebrated Mass at 7:00 am. At 8:00 am we all went to breakfast, then to class until 11:45 am at which time we went back to the chapel again for the noonday prayer of the Divine Office. This was followed by lunch at 12:00 pm. After lunch, we had about forty-five minutes of recreation until we went to do our manual labor jobs from 1:30 pm–3:00 pm. These jobs could be almost anything to keep the monastery and surrounding outdoor areas neat and clean. During the nice weather months, this often meant working on the lawns, shrubs and bushes outside. Sometimes, it meant working in the gardens or repairing broken equipment or painting. We would also spend time cleaning the monastery, waxing the floors, or doing laundry. Since we were always trying to be self-sufficient as much as we could, there was always plenty of work to be done. After finishing our jobs, we had free or recreational time from 3:00 pm–4:30 pm, where we could choose to participate in a variety of sports, or go swimming in the Severn River on warm days, or just relax on our own. Then from 4:30 pm–5:30 pm, we were expected to be in our rooms reading or studying. At 5:30 pm we went to the chapel again for our second half hour period of meditation, followed by our late afternoon praying of the Divine Office. This was followed by dinner at 6:15 pm and then we had some free time from 7:00 pm–7:30 pm. After this, we were back in our rooms until 8:30 pm for reading and studying. We then went back to the chapel for our night prayers, including the last part of the Divine Office for the day. Following this, we were expected to be in bed by 9:30 pm. The weekends were a bit more relaxing with more free time for playing sports or just relaxing. It certainly was a full schedule and kept us very busy.

As you can imagine, one of the major reasons for entering a novitiate year, was to give the novices a prolonged opportunity to learn how to pray. So much of our daily routine was structured around the importance and practice of prayer. We celebrated Mass daily, prayed the Divine Office (in Latin!) four times a day and had two thirty minute periods of time for private meditation. The silence of our days were designed to enable us to listen to God. "Be still and know that I am God" (Ps. 46:10) was what we were trying to learn how to do.

Every morning at 6:00 am, we went to our chapel for a half hour of meditation, according to the method that St. Ignatius of Loyola had designed for his Jesuits in the *Spiritual Exercises*. This method of praying was a highly structured discipline which was used by many religious orders back in the 1960s because there was a set method of learning how to meditate. At least this was the intent. As a preliminary step, we prepared the topic for meditation the previous night. Each novice had the same meditation book that gave us a beginning scripture passage and several questions for our reflection. Ignatius' method of meditation was based on a three part program: see, judge, and act. First, we all stood in silence for a few minutes, reciting to ourselves a prayer that reminded us that we were in the presence of God. Then, we took out our meditation book and began with "see." This meant that we had to use our imaginations to picture the gospel scene which we had read the previous night. We were supposed to try and place ourselves in this particular gospel passage in some concrete way by imagining that we are in the crowd following Jesus or that perhaps Jesus is speaking directly to us. Ignatius thought that it was very important that all of a person's faculties be engaged, so that the whole person was brought into this experience. This "composition of place," as it was called, was also meant to ward off distractions. If you were busy picturing the road from Jerusalem to Jericho or imagining that you were one of the brothers in the story of the Prodigal Son, your imagination was less likely to stray to worldly topics. At least, that was the theory.

Next came "judge," when the intellect was brought into play. This was the point when you were supposed to reflect on the main idea of the gospel passage, to think about what Jesus might be trying to say to you. Finally, you proceeded to "act," which, for Ignatius, was the true moment of prayer. Then, as a result of your deliberations, you made an act of the will, applying the lessons you had learned to the day that lay ahead. There had to be a specific resolution. It was not good enough to somehow vaguely vow to live a better life from that day forward. You had to settle for something concrete: to try harder to be more patient with a fellow novice, or to make a special effort not to think uncharitable thoughts about one of the novices who irritated you beyond endurance. Prayer, Ignatius thought, was an act of the will. It had nothing to do with pious thoughts or feelings; these were simply a preparation for the moment of decision. Ignatian spirituality was never an end in itself, but was always directed toward some kind of action. He wanted his Jesuits to be effective in the world, and their daily meditation ensured that their activities would proceed from God.

But we were Franciscans—not Jesuits. As we continued to try and learn how to meditate according to St. Ignatius, I kept wondering how we could learn how to pray/meditate according to St. Francis of Assisi. Francis was much more of a free spirit and didn't want to be encumbered by a lot of rules, even with regard to prayer. He wanted his followers to develop a personal relationship with Jesus and then one's prayer life would flow from this. But, because we were just novices, beginners as it were, we were lumped together with so many other religious orders in following the rules for prayer from St. Ignatius. Later on, as I learned more about Franciscan spirituality, I discovered my own method of prayer/meditation which I have utilized to this day.

1) Spiraling Downward

After the initial excitement of receiving the habit wore off, I tried to settle into the rhythm of the day as best I could. However, as these early days and weeks went by, I began to notice my feelings changing which was both confusing and unsettling for me. Since I am more of an introvert by nature, I tended to keep things bottled up inside myself rather than being able to talk to others about them. I began to feel a vague sense of dread that was upsetting to me but I kept thinking this was more of a temporary feeling after the "newness" of novitiate life wore off. What made me feel this way was unclear to me at the time and so, I kept going and tried to be the best novice I could be. After all, we had been told that the novitiate year was going to be difficult and I simply presumed that this feeling of dread was part of the deal, so to speak, and that eventually these feelings would pass.

The Christmas season brought some relief to me. There were a lot of things to do to keep all of us busy preparing to celebrate the birth of Jesus. Besides cleaning and waxing the floor of the chapel on our hands and knees, we had to practice several four part hymns for midnight Mass which took a lot of time and attention. This, plus the spirit of the season, lifted my spirits somewhat. Also, we were studying the life of St. Francis and I learned that this feast was very special for him and so I was trying to incorporate his ideas about Christmas into my own prayer life. Because St. Francis was a man who wanted to experience things with all of his senses, he decided one Christmas to depict the birth of Jesus with live animals and real people. This "first creche" was created at Greccio in 1223. Our tradition of having a Christmas creche in our homes and churches continues this practice begun all those years ago. This emphasis of St. Francis on the humanity of Jesus, helped me discover a new way of understanding the Incarnation and I tried to incorporate this into my own prayer life. This new reality enabled me to celebrate my first Christmas in the monastery in a deeper way.

Winters in the Annapolis area can be severe and the winter of 1962 was particularly harsh. Very cold days with a significant amount of snow made the months of January and February particularly difficult for me. I could feel my spirit sinking. I began to feel very confined. After all, I had been in this monastery, with these same people for almost seven months now. I had not left these monastery grounds since arriving in July, not even to go to the doctor. Imagine literally staying in one place and with the same people and never leaving for such a long period of time. I also began to feel very restless, feeling like I would just like to go somewhere, anywhere, if only for a ride in a car. This feeling of confinement was so difficult for me and brought back the feeling of dread once again.

Coupled with this feeling of confinement was the feeling of isolation. We were literally isolated from the outside world in what seemed to me an unhealthy way. Except for two Catholic newspapers and a couple of Catholic magazines, we had no contact with anything or anyone outside the monastery grounds. There were no TV's and no secular newspapers. We had no visitors. We were only allowed to write one letter home a month and I can remember keeping a daily diary during each month in order to include things in my monthly letter. However, after a couple of months, I discovered that I didn't really need to do this because there was so little variation in our day to day schedule. There really wasn't very much that was new to incorporate in my letters home.

During my entire novitiate year, I only left the monastery grounds twice. The first time our entire class walked about two miles to visit a Jesuit retreat house called Manresa. It felt so good to simply be able to go somewhere, to be able to leave the confines of the novitiate and enjoy seeing different things. It gave me a feeling of something new and fresh—a feeling that I had not experienced in a long time. The only other time I left St. Conrad's during the entire year was an afternoon trip that all of us made to visit the cathedral church in Baltimore which was about fifteen miles away. We were studying the local church situation in class and the novice master thought it would be helpful to see the main church, the Baltimore Basilica, in the archdiocese of Baltimore. A bus ride never felt so good!

2) The "Age Factor"

As the days and weeks of winter continued, the daily routine began to bother me more and more. Living so closely with my brother novices began to be extremely difficult and took a toll on me emotionally. Much of this anxiety was caused by what I call the "age factor." In monastic life, everything was done according to the age of each person. What that meant was not only did all twenty-two of us do everything together 24/7, but more particularly, every novice did many other things with the same person on each side of them. So, everyone prayed together four times a day and ate our meals together with the same person next to you three times day. This "age factor" was really difficult for me. I could never get a break from these brother novices, not even to sit by myself or next to other novices to pray. Because of this, after a while, I began to experience some idiosyncrasies in the novices next to me that I had not noticed before. For example, the Divine Office which we prayed together four times a day was all in Latin. For some reason, the way in which the novices around me pronounced the words we were praying grated on me and became increasingly annoying. However, because of this "age factor," I couldn't move to another place in the chapel. I had to stay where I was in the age group. For me, knowing that I had to do this four times every day became very difficult. Even though it was difficult for me, I tried talking to them about this issue but somehow things never changed very much. Moreover, at our meals, we also had to sit next to these same people three times a day, every day, for the entire year. So, if you had a disagreement or argument with one of the novices next to you, you still had to remain in your place. You were supposed to "offer it up to Jesus." This "age factor" permeated every aspect of our lives.

3) My Severn River Experience

Spring is beautiful in the Annapolis area. As the cold, early dark evenings of winter gave way to spring, there was new life everywhere. First, the daffodils peeked out of the ground. Then the buds began to flower on the dogwood trees and the beautiful azalea plants began to bloom. There was a fresh hint of newness everywhere. Most of our work was outside now which I cherished, and for a time it picked up my spirits. However, I noticed within myself a definite turn inwards. Being mostly an introvert by nature, I became even more quiet and introspective. This was not healthy for me because it led me by late spring to become depressed. More importantly, I began to think about leaving. These thoughts became more troublesome for me because two other novices had recently left. And, it happened in exactly the same way that a seminarian would leave when I was in the high school seminary. Everything was done in secret—at night. No one seemed to know that these two novices were even thinking about leaving. One morning, we just woke up and they were gone. We never even got to say goodbye to these young men that we had known and lived with for six years. It was like the Capuchin Order was afraid to let us know they were leaving for fear it would encourage more of us to leave. This way of dealing with life—and religious life—seemed so unhealthy to me.

With only two more months to go before we made our first vows, this thought about leaving began to dominate my thoughts. Did I want to stay in this religious order in which the life style had become so difficult? Should I stay? Can I be happy in this way of life? During these days, there was a definite part of me that wanted to leave, but somehow I felt that I should stay and that I would be displeasing to God if I left. This thought pattern quickly morphed into feelings of guilt which plagued me for years.

As the days became hotter and as we headed into the summer months, I realized that I only had a few weeks before we would be making our first vows. During this time, I remained very confused and full of doubts. Then one day in early June, the most singular event occurred which is my strongest memory of my entire novitiate year.

When the weather was warm enough, and we had some free time, we were permitted to go down to the boat dock on the Severn River to swim. There were also several large inner tubes which we were free to float around in and relax on the river. One day in early June, I decided to take one of these inner tubes out in the river and just lay in it and relax for awhile. After I had floated around for several minutes, I looked up and saw the Severn River bridge in front of me. Cars were crossing the bridge in both directions. Then I thought to myself 'how I wish I could be in one of those cars and leave this place.' I kept floating in the inner tube for a while longer thinking about this idea. It wouldn't leave me. Eventually, it was time to head back to the monastery for a period of reading and studying. So, I made my way back to shore, placed the inner tube in the boathouse and walked back up the steep steps to my room.

For some reason, this experience has vividly remained with me for over fifty–seven years. I can remember it like it happened yesterday. As I have grown older and reflected on my novitiate year, this time of floating on the Severn River and wanting to be in one of those cars is one of my most vivid memories. I wish that I would have had the courage to act on this thought. For reasons that are much clearer to me now, I didn't. However, hind sight is often better and can help us see more clearly. This is the way it has been for me over the years. I think in some way, I have beat myself up thinking about this experience and this time in my life. I guess it's about time for me to forgive myself for thinking this way and not acting on it.

We were scheduled to make our first vows of poverty, chastity, and obedience on July 15, 1963, about five weeks away. Again, this was an extremely confusing and painful time for me. Part of me wanted to take my vows trusting that when I left the novitiate, these thoughts about leaving would fade away because my environment would be different. Another part of me wanted to follow these thoughts and feelings, leave the monastery, and try another path in life. Little did I know at the time that these thoughts about wanting to leave would haunt me for years. But, I kept telling myself that we all try to do the best we can with the information we have at the time.

In the Capuchin Franciscan Order, a novice would take his vows at the end of the novitiate year. These first vows of poverty, chastity, and obedience were made for a three year period. Following these three years, these same three vows would be promised for life. As the time of my first vows approached, I remained very conflicted. I wanted to talk with someone about my doubts but the only other priests living at St. Conrad's were the ones on what we called the mission band. Usually, these four or five priests were involved in the preaching ministry and they would travel throughout the United States conducting retreats and mission days in parishes. The only other person that was available to talk with was the novice master himself but I was reluctant to talk to him because I didn't want him to think less of me and know that I was having all these doubts. In addition, he was the one person who would be making the final judgment about the suitability of each novice to make his vows. Interestingly enough, our novice master never once during the entire year addressed the issue of what we, as novices should do if we were having any difficulties. Moreover, I had never heard any of my brother novices say that they had ever spoken to him about any problems they were having. To me, it seemed to be another example of the fear of talking about problems. Again, looking back, I really should have swallowed my pride and talked with him to get his perspective on what I should do. It's easy for me to understand now what I should have done. But as a confused twenty-year old, who didn't want to let anyone down, this was very difficult for me to do.

Reflecting back on this period of time, I want to make it clear that there was never any pressure, from any source other than myself, to stay. We were free to stay or leave whenever we wanted to. I believe my family would have supported me with whatever decision I made. The pressure to stay was all on me internally. Unknowingly, I put this kind of pressure on myself. I didn't want to appear weak. With my desire to be perfect, to please others, and not disappoint anyone who thought highly of me both inside and outside the Order, I had myself tied up into knots.

As the day of my first profession of vows drew closer, I remained unsure of what I should do. For me, it was a time of excitement, anticipation, and fear. To end the year, we had to make another silent eight day retreat just like we had done to begin the year. I was hoping and praying for some clarity during this time of quiet prayer. Unfortunately, this never came. The same internal conflicts remained. So, at the end of my retreat, I decided to make my first profession, hoping that in the next phase of my formation, I would have a better chance to sort things out and then make an informed decision. But in some ways, it also felt like I was "kicking the can down the road."

Profession day is a very important occasion in a religious order. Leading up to it, all of us were busy cleaning the entire monastery in anticipation for the arrival of our families, relatives, friends, and many other Capuchins who came to celebrate this occasion. After visiting with my family the previous evening, I went to bed realizing I was in this conflicted state but hoping that later on I would be able to find an answer. Each novice took his vows of poverty, chastity, and obedience within the context of the Mass. When my turn came to approach the altar, I walked to where our provincial was seated, placed my folded hands in his and said my vows. It was a lovely celebration. After a light lunch, all of us departed with our families.

After our profession day, we were allowed to go home for a week. Imagine, this was only the third time during the entire year that I had left the grounds of the novitiate. As we got in our car for the six hour drive home to Huntington, West Virginia, I had this marvelous feeling of freedom. It was the first time I was in, or drove a car, in over a year. It felt so good to be leaving this place that had been so difficult for me. As we drove along the highway, I just sat back and relaxed, admiring the beautiful landscape of the West Virginia mountains. Interesting, how we can forget or at least take for granted the beauty of God's creation. For me, having been deprived of this beauty for an entire year, it was a beautiful sight.

Our memories can be either precious or painful. As I remember my novitiate year so long ago, I can still place myself there in the monastery or outside on the grounds doing a variety of things. But the dominant feelings I remember are confinement, isolation, internal turmoil, and depression. Some memories never seem to go away.

4) A Bird With a Broken Wing

Wolfgang Amadeus Mozart is one of the greatest composers the world has ever known. But it wasn't always so clear that he would have left such an impactful legacy. Mozart was a child prodigy in his own right. His father, Leopold, himself a talented musician and composer, noticed this when Mozart was four. He had an uncanny ability to sit still and he loved to practice. When he turned five, Mozart could compose his own pieces.

As Mozart grew older, he would follow his father to perform in front of royalty across Europe. He would win applause no matter which capital he set foot in, and he generated a nice income for his family. It was a comfortable life, and Mozart was a success by any standard.

However, as Mozart grew into his teenage years, he felt confused. Playing for a royal audience meant that he could never stray from the more conventional pieces. There was also another question that made him uneasy—was it music that he enjoyed, or was it fame and attention?

An answer would appear when he was twenty-one. After the death of his mother, Mozart finally understood why he had spent all this time pleasing the nobility, a task which he considered beneath his position. It wasn't fame or riches that he craved; it was his father's love and attention that he had desired all this time. And so, realizing that his father was holding him back from composing—the one thing he loved—Mozart never returned to Salzburg, where he was born and raised. Only then did his most famous compositions start pouring out of him.

Mozart's search for his mission is probably familiar to many of us. It certainly was for me. We hear of people having mid-life crises and struggling with their identity. A career or way of life that sounded promising in our twenties becomes soul-draining some ten years later. It happens often.

Robert Greene calls this the false path. He explains in *Mastery*: "A false path in life is generally something we are attracted to for the wrong reasons—money, fame, attention, approval, and so on . . . Because the field we chose does not correspond with our deepest inclinations, we rarely find the fulfillment that we crave. Our work suffers for this, and the attention and approval we may have gotten in the beginning starts to fade—a painful process."[2]

At that point, Greene explains, our only recourse is to actively rebel against the forces that have pushed us away from our true path. Like how Mozart had to leave his father, painful steps are required at this point. This left me wondering how we are drawn to this false path in the first place. If we could figure that out, we would save ourselves a lot of pain.

When I had left home and gone to the seminary at fifteen and then entered religious life, I had been certain that if I only tried hard enough, I would be successful and that I would see the world transfigured by the presence of God. Then, I thought, like the Bible promised, I would soar like an eagle.

But at the conclusion of my novitiate year, I not only felt I would not soar like an eagle, but I felt more like a bird with a broken wing. I knew that the novitiate was going to be a difficult year but I had no idea it would be this hard. T.S. Eliot wrote "human kind cannot bear very much reality."[3] If my life was going to be like my novitiate year, there was no way I was going to be able to bear this kind of reality for a life time.

Needless to say, my year in the novitiate was not what I expected. I entered in 1962, an ardent, idealistic, unrealistic and immature twenty-year old young man, and finished it feeling broken and damaged. This was nobody's fault, even though I assumed that the failure was entirely my own doing.

In Matthew's Gospel, Jesus tells his disciples that only a few find the narrow gate that leads to life. By the end of my novitiate year, I had come to the conclusion that only a very small number of people could live up to the demands of a life that required the entire subjugation of the ego and a self-abandonment that—I realized sadly—might be beyond me. I knew priests and brothers in our Capuchin Order who beautifully enshrined this ideal, but I was coming to realize that perhaps I might not be one of them. This was difficult for me to say to myself but maybe it was true.

The novitiate year for me was like a conditioning process rather than a discernment process. For the entire year, we were completely isolated from the outside world. This meant that the novitiate became our whole world. No other world existed for us and so the whims and moods of our novice master acquired monumental importance. For example, smoking

2. Greene, *Mastery*, 37.

3. www. goodreads.com/quotest.s.eliot.

took on a huge sense of importance. There were only two times during the day that smoking was permitted. One was immediately after lunch for about half an hour and the second time was immediately after dinner for approximately one hour. The only problem was, we never knew whether the novice master was going to give us cigarettes or not. It just depended on his mood for the day. The cigarettes were kept in a box that he kept at all times. So, on those days when he allowed us to smoke, he would bring the box over to our recreation room and give them to us. Those of us who smoked, camped out at the door every recreation period hoping he would permit us to smoke. Of course, if he gave them to us, we were very happy campers. But if he didn't, we were all depressed! This was an example of how small our world had become. To allow ourselves to be controlled by smoking was truly sad, as I reflect back on it. This was just one example of how we became entirely dependent upon our novice master's every move.

This type of conditioning and isolation was central to the rituals of initiation practiced in the ancient world and in many indigenous societies today. On reaching puberty, boys are taken away from their mothers, separated from their tribe, and subjected to a series of frightening ordeals that changed them irrevocably. It is like a process of death and resurrection. Those who were initiated, die to their childhood and rise again to an entirely different life as mature human beings. They are often told that they are about to suffer a horrible death. They are forced to lie in a cave or a tomb. Sometimes, they are buried alive and experience intense physical pain. Often, the boys would be circumcised or tattooed as well as undergoing terrifying rituals. The idea is that in these extreme circumstances, the young men discover inner resources that will enable them to serve their people as fully functioning adults. The purpose of these rights of passage is to transform dependent children into responsible, self-reliant men who are ready to risk their lives as hunters and warriors, and, if necessary, to die in order to protect their people.

Essentially, our training in the novitiate was like this kind of initiation. We too had been separated from the world, deprived of normal affection and interaction with others, and subjected to trials that were designed to test our resolve. We too were to be warriors of sorts—soldiers of God, who practiced the military obedience devised by St. Ignatius of Loyola, the founder of the Jesuits. Our training was designed to make us wholly self-reliant, so that we no longer needed human love and affection or approval. We too were told that we were to die to our old selves and to our worldly, secular way of looking at life. Of course, we were not buried alive in a tomb or anything like that, but the constant isolation and confinement felt like a tomb to me. As St. Ignatius's Rule put it, we were to become utterly pliable to the will of God as expressed through our superiors. Dead to ourselves and to any worldly existence, we would live a fuller, enhanced existence, as Jesus had promised in a text that was often quoted to us: "unless the grain of wheat falls into the ground and dies, it will remain nothing but a grain of wheat. But if it dies, it will bear much fruit" (John 12:24).

Now, it seemed to me that I had indeed died, but I was certainly not bringing forth much fruit. I felt as though I had entered a twilight zone between life and death, and instead of being transfigured, as I had hoped, I had gotten the worst of all worlds. Instead of being full of courage, fearless, active, and protective of others, like the initiate of a tribal rite of passage, I was simply afraid. I had wanted to be transformed and enriched; instead I felt diminished. Instead of becoming strong, I was simply hard. The coldness and frequent unkindness that was sometimes a part of community life was difficult to cope with. This made me question my ability to cope with the idea of living in close quarters with others. Our training was designed to make us transcend ourselves, and go beyond the egoism and selfishness that hold us back from God. But now I felt stuck inside myself, unable either to escape or to reach out to others.

This way of reacting to my year in the novitiate was my own way of coping with these experiences. My novice master had certainly not intended this to happen to me. He had not meant to push me into this way of thinking. In the end, I blamed myself. I felt that I had not responded properly to my training. I had been too weak to go all the way, to let myself truly die. I had kept on longing for love and affection, but was too weak to endure these robust austerities. Maybe I had attempted something that was beyond my capacities. This was on me. This is what I had to sort out.

Part Two

Why I Stayed in the Monastery

4

Living a Life of Quiet Desperation

"It may be that when we no longer know what to do
we have come to our real work, and that when we no longer
know which way to go we have come to our real journey."

(WENDELL BERRY)

AFTER THE CONCLUSION OF my novitiate year, it felt really good to be home for a week's vacation. Although I didn't do very much, it still felt like such a relief for me. I no longer had the daily pressure of living the schedule of religious life. Just having the freedom to do what I felt like doing was healing for me. Going to Mass, visiting with my family, several relatives, and a few friends made up my days and the week flew by very quickly.

After this week at home, I returned to St. Fidelis College to finish my junior and senior years. The college was located next to the high school seminary near Butler, Pennsylvania, about thirty miles north of Pittsburgh. However, since we were now members of the Capuchin Order, we lived in St. Mary's Monastery which was part of the complex but separate from the seminary. It was July, 1963. Although Vatican Council II had just begun, the decree on religious life had not yet been promulgated. Because of this, there still were no major changes in monastic life. This meant that monastic formation programs continued to be very traditional and nothing new had been implemented. Consequently, I didn't expect much to change with regard to our formation over the next two years.

As we drove to St. Mary's Monastery, I had mixed emotions. On the one hand I was hopeful and filled with anticipation as I began to live in this new monastery. I thought that perhaps this new monastic experience would give me a fresh start. Maybe I could recover some of the positive experiences of my earlier seminary days. But, on the other hand, I was very worried because I knew that monastic life would continue to be filled with confinement and isolation, and would stress the importance of the "age factor." These three factors in daily living in our monastic life had been so difficult for me to cope with in the novitiate. I worried that these would be repeated in living monastic life at St. Mary's. However, I wanted to be open and hopeful about the possibilities as I began this new phase of my life.

During our drive back to St. Mary's, I remembered the words of Wendell Berry. These words seemed to be speaking to me personally. At the conclusion of the novitiate year, some religious become more sure of their vocational choice. They feel more at home with the vocation they have chosen. Not me. For me, it was just the opposite. Like Berry said, "when we no longer know what to do, we have come to our real work and when we no longer know which way to go, we have come to our real journey."[1] Going back to St. Mary's Monastery to finish my junior and senior years of college, I knew this was going to be my task. Deep within me, besides studying philosophy, I knew what my real work was going to be, and because I still didn't know whether to stay in religious life or not, I knew that I had to enter into my real journey.

These last two years of college would focus on the study of philosophy. After I arrived at the monastery, and reported in to the superior, I found my room, unpacked, and went to meet my brothers who were also arriving during the afternoon. Since this was our junior and senior years of college, the seniors were already there since they had just finished their junior year. However, since they were only one year ahead of my class all the way through the minor seminary, I already knew them pretty well. It was good to see everyone again. After visiting with the other guys for awhile, I went back to my room to find the daily schedule which had been placed on a "welcome" folder on my desk. Glancing at it quickly, it looked very similar to our religious life routines in the novitiate.

The following schedule would be our daily routine:

---

1. www.goodreads.com_author_quotes_8567.WendellBerry.

5:30 am	rise
6:00—6:30 am	first meditation
6:30—6:45 am	pray the Divine Office
6:45—7:30 am	Mass
7:30—8:15 am	breakfast
8:30—11:30 am	class
11:30—11:45 am	pray the Divine Office
11:45—12:30 am	lunch
12:30—1:30 pm	community recreation
1:30—3:00 pm	community work period
3:00—4:00 pm	free time/sports
4:00—5:00 pm	study in rooms
5:00—5:30 pm	second meditation
5:30—6:00 pm	pray the Divine Office
6:00—6:45 pm	dinner
6:45—7:30 pm	community recreation
7:30—9:00 pm	study in rooms
9:00—9:30 pm	pray the Divine Office
9:30 pm	bed

As you can see, it was a very structured, regimented day, very similar to our novitiate schedule. However, on the weekends, since we didn't have class, more time was allowed for study and recreation.

For these next two years, everyone had to major in the study of philosophy. There were no academic choices. Courses in metaphysics, epistemology, cosmology and logic were very challenging to say the least. For me, the subject matter of these courses was not very interesting but at the time, all seminarians had to major in philosophy. These courses were all the more challenging because some of our text books were in Latin! So, in order to learn the material, everyone had to first translate from the Latin to English and then comprehend the information.

This made these two years of philosophy extremely challenging intellectually. But in order to become a priest, everyone had to master these subjects, as well as Scripture courses in both the Old and New Testaments, along with church history. However, in these courses, the textbooks were in English, so at least there was no translating involved. These were the more enjoyable courses for me. Although they were challenging, I managed to do well in them.

In 1957, when I began thinking about going to the seminary, one of the ideas that appealed to me was joining a religious order where living in a community with other men was a major part of one's lifestyle. At the time, I didn't think I wanted to become a diocesan priest because the lifestyle seemed too lonely to me. However, from my early days in the novitiate, I quickly discovered that living in a community with the same guys 24/7 was extremely challenging, to say the least.

When I began my last two years of college in July 1963, I was hopeful that my experience of living in community would be more positive than what I had experienced in the novitiate. My hope was that the beginning of Vatican II would also encourage a renewal of religious life that would bring some fresh ideas to community living which urgently needed reform. Hopefully, some of the arcane rules of religious life would be changed or at least modified. What had been handed down as healthy spiritual practices since the Middle Ages might be understood as good for a certain period of time but were no longer valid for living a healthy spirituality. For example, one of the practices that we learned about and practiced in the novitiate was called "the discipline." What this meant was that every Monday, Wednesday, and Friday before we went to bed, each novice stood at the entrance to his room, pulled up his habit, took a metal chain, and whipped ourselves across our buttocks while our novice master recited a penitential psalm. This went on for about three minutes. This was done in order to remind ourselves of two things. First, it was supposed to remind us of the Passion of Christ when he was whipped and scourged for us. And secondly, it was supposed to remind us of our weak human natures and that the sins of the flesh must be avoided. I'm not sure that these three whippings a week ever accomplished that but it sure did hurt! Fortunately, this practice has now been eliminated.

Many religious orders at this time were stuck in a very traditional rut. Customs that made perfect sense in the sixteenth century when the Capuchins were founded, now seemed arbitrary and unnatural. Practices that had no intrinsic spiritual value but were cultural relics of the Victorian age had acquired a sacred significance, and changing them was regarded as betrayal by some members of the community.

One of the guidelines for renewing religious life was to return to the ideals of the founders of our religious orders. I was hopeful that as Franciscans that would mean returning to the ideals and way of life of our founder, St. Francis of Assisi. One of the things that inspired me initially about joining the Capuchin Franciscan Order was the free spirit of St. Francis. He wanted his brothers to be free—to be unencumbered by a lot of rules and regulations so that they would be free to preach the gospel wherever they were. However, over the centuries as things became more institutionalized, the Franciscans, along with most religious orders, became more driven by the same arcane rules and regulations as everyone else. Essentially, no matter what the special charism of a religious order's founder might have been, most religious communities basically lived the same daily routine of religious life.

A. An Ache in My Soul

Even though St. Mary's Monastery was different than St. Conrad's, many of the same difficulties that I experienced in the novitiate followed me to St. Mary's. Some of my struggles again centered around the "age factor" in religious life. This meant again that you did everything by one's age. So, I prayed four times a day next to the same two guys, I ate every meal next to them, and our rooms were next to each other. Any time we did anything as a group, we were *always* next to each other. Irritating idiosyncrasies took on monumental proportions. Perhaps even more difficult for me was the isolation and confinement of living in the monastery. St. Mary's Monastery was situated in the country, approximately eight miles from the nearest town. During my two years there, just like in the novitiate, I hardly ever left the monastery grounds. Moreover, we were allowed family visits once a year and never got a break from our daily monastic routine even during the summers. In addition, there was no such thing as a summer vacation. And so, as the days and weeks wore on, I could feel myself wanting some kind of contact with the outside world. I think this could have been so helpful to me. But that kind of freedom would not come for several more years. As a result, I could also feel myself slipping into depression once again. Just coping with everything on a daily basis—and—knowing that it was not going to change any time soon, sent me into an emotional tailspin during these two years. For me, it was one thing to go through some aspect of monastic life that was difficult and a struggle but when I realized that this was not going to change any time soon, I became more depressed and reclusive.

Another dimension of religious life that greatly troubled me was the emotional frigidity of our lives. This was one of the areas of religious life that most desperately needed reform. Friendship was frowned upon, and the atmosphere in the monastery was cold and sometimes unkind. Increasingly, it seemed to me to have moved an immeasurably long distance from the spirit of the gospels. For some reason, there seemed to be a terrible fear among my superiors of what was called having a *particular friendship*. This kind of indoctrination about friendship began in the high school seminary and it was drilled into us all through the years of our formation. No one ever explicitly explained why but most of us suspected that it was connected to the whole idea of homosexuality. There was a great fear of guys who might be gay and so the way it was dealt with was to make us all afraid of particular friendships. This had been drummed into us at such an early age when we were teenagers in the high school seminary, that I found it all very confusing.

It seemed to me that all this negativity around the issue of friendship harmed me more than I realized at the time. Because of these fears, I began to feel that my capacity for affection had either atrophied or been so badly damaged that it could not function normally. I felt frozen and could understand what people meant when they said that their heart had turned to stone. I could almost feel this new hardness within, like a cold, heavy weight. I had become a person who was afraid of love and who seemed incapable of reaching out to others. Whether I liked it or not, I was now a garden enclosed, a well sealed up. It would take me several more years to understand what all this meant and find a way to let go of some of this fear.

Sometimes, the help we need at a certain time in our lives comes from some unexpected and unusual places. This is what happened to me. There were four positive things that happened to me during these last two years of college which enabled me to cope with my difficult situation at the time and influenced my decision to stay in the monastery. Probably the most important one was learning how to play the guitar. Every evening, after cleaning up the dishes following dinner, we had about an hour of recreational time before going to our rooms to study. One evening, about a month after our class arrived at St. Mary's Monastery, one of the Capuchin priests who taught in the high school seminary showed up in our recreation room with his guitar. It was August 1963 and folk music was just becoming popular. These were the days of Peter, Paul, and Mary, the Kingston Trio and Joan Baez. This priest played and sang for us songs like, Five Hundred Miles, If I Had a Hammer, and This Land is Your Land. I really liked this music and one of my friends and I began practicing the guitar and learning some of these songs. It was interesting because there was one guitar in the community room and we had to share the time that each of us was able to use it. Without realizing it at the time, this was important to me because it gave me something to look forward to each day. Learning how to play the guitar and practicing these songs allowed me to focus my interest and energy into something I truly enjoyed. Later on, when we moved to our house of theology to continue our theological studies, four of us formed a folk group which became an important ministry for us. We got to be fairly well known in the Washington, DC area and often were asked to play for a variety of groups in some of the local churches and organizations.

The second thing that helped me during these two years was going to the library to read and study psychology. After completing my junior year of college studying philosophy, a new Capuchin priest who had just finished his PhD in psychology was assigned to St. Fidelis High School Seminary as director of students. When we began our senior year, he offered a new course entitled Introduction to Psychology which I enjoyed very much. Because I had been struggling with depression since going to the novitiate, I became very interested in psychology, especially studying human development. Not only did I like this course, but I would often go to the library on my own to read as much as I could on the writings of Carl Jung, Albert Adler, and especially Carl Rogers. I was essentially trying to understand myself and the impact of my family life on my development so that I could try to find some ways of coping with my depression issues. Little did I realize at the time, but this became very important to me eighteen years later when I left religious life. Eventually, I would return to graduate school to obtain another degree and become a psychotherapist. My twenty-four year career in counseling was something I thoroughly enjoyed. Sometimes, we don't know the importance of something we do at one time in our lives which becomes a significant part of our lives later on.

The third positive thing that I engaged in was playing sports, Whenever we had some free time, both the juniors and seniors would play all kinds of sports depending on the time of the year. In addition, during the previous year, when I was in the novitiate, St. Fidelis High School and College built a new gymnasium which allowed us to play basketball during the long winter months. Playing sports allowed me to burn up excessive energy, get the endorphins moving and in general helped me to feel good about myself. Fortunately, I had always been a good athlete and engaging in these activities helped to build my self-esteem.

Finally, an unsuspected dimension of our daily routine became encouraging for me. Usually, we had some kind of physical work to do four or five times a week. After we had come to St. Mary's Monastery to begin our junior year of college in July, I was asked by my superior to be the custodian of our outdoor swimming pool. I was happy to be assigned to this kind of work because it was outdoors and something I could do on my own. I could be by myself outside the monastery walls for an hour and a half and not have to interact with anyone. It just felt freeing to me and was like an emotional relief. Moreover, it wasn't really a difficult job at all. Mostly, it involved testing and balancing the pH of the water in the pool by using the proper amount of chemicals as well as cleaning it daily and removing any kind of debris. But this little job was important to me because again, it gave me something to look forward to each day. Sometimes, doing something simple, can have important implications for our lives.

Early on, after my arrival in July, I asked one of the priests to be my spiritual director. After he agreed to my request, I began to see him on a regular basis. Since I was continuing to struggle with depression, I knew I had to talk about this issue with someone and try to figure out why I was continuing to struggle with this and, maybe more importantly, what to do about it. But I also knew that I still hadn't resolved the most fundamental issue for me which was to either stay in or leave religious life. Although it was helpful to talk about these issues, the spiritual direction I received did not enable me to reach any significant conclusions. I think that he knew that although he could help me to possibly sort out some things, it would ultimately have to be my decision to stay or leave.

When I was in the monastery in 1963, it was easy to feel disconnected from what was going on in our society and in the world. Although we had a bit more knowledge of what was happening through our limited access to newspapers, magazines, and watching the news on television than we had in the novitiate, I also felt that we were never encouraged to become too interested in these worldly things. After all, at the time, we were supposed to be giving up worldly things and ideas. It was thought that these could become major distractions from growing in our spiritual life. Nevertheless, I can still vividly remember where I was and what I was doing when we got the news that John F. Kennedy had been assassinated. As with most of America, we were shocked by this news and got permission to watch television throughout the day and evening to follow the story.

Our Capuchin Franciscan community at St. Mary's Monastery was very different than the one we had in the novitiate. For one thing, St. Mary's was much larger. Including our junior and senior classes of about thirty student friars, there were probably fifty of us altogether. Many of these men were involved in other ministries. The majority of them taught in the high school seminary, while others were serving in parishes or hospitals in the area. Although we lived in different sections of the building, we still prayed and ate our meals together. In addition, we would often have a significant amount of contact with some of them as we all went about living our daily routines. Many of the older religious seemed happy and content. They were always pleasant to be around and seemed to take an active interest in how we younger friars were doing. They enjoyed talking with us and they seemed to like the ministries they were involved in. Several of them were truly edifying. The way they lived their daily religious lives was inspirational to me. I knew that if I stayed in religious life, I wanted to become like them. On the other hand, there were other friars who seemed to be very unhappy. It was clear to many of us that some of them had major problems. This realization created a great deal of fear inside of me. Some of these friars were terribly withdrawn and hardly ever spoke to anyone; some seemed to be depressed; others were "grouchy" and always complaining about something; one was an active alcoholic. Since I was already uncertain about my vocation, I was afraid that if I stayed in religious life, I could end up like them.

B. Tied into Knots

Although my daily routine was a struggle for me, a greater difficulty emerged during my senior year in college. For some reasons that are still not clear to me, I developed a severe case of scrupulosity. In some ways, it was difficult to know where this came from. But the one thing I did know was that this was a very difficult time for me. I now understood in a more personal way what Sam had struggled with in the novitiate.

Essentially, a scrupulous person sees sin everywhere. They are constantly thinking about their actions to see if they have committed a sin. For me, I would continually ruminate about my thoughts and behaviors to see if I had committed a sin. And, if I thought I had done something wrong, I would then worry about whether it was a serious sin or not. Of course, going to confession all of the time was always a part of the process. It felt like I was trapped inside my brain without the ability to stop these thoughts, like I was "tied up in knots" inside myself.

I certainly shared this struggle with my spiritual director and he tried to assure me that often these thoughts were not sins at all but rather came from an overly active conscience. I certainly had that! I can still hear him saying to me, "you know Pete, only good people become scrupulous. People with no conscience or an undeveloped conscience never worry about these things." While I could understand how this was true, it didn't concretely help me very much at the time.

Sigmund Freud would obviously say that a scrupulous person has a super ego that is out of control. This would be that part of us that incorrectly sees wrong doing everywhere and punishes ourself for being less than perfect. In addition, for me it involved my relationship with God and affected my prayer life. It made me feel that God was a punitive God watching my every move and waiting to punish me if I even thought of doing anything wrong.

In a sense, entering religious life can set up a person to become scrupulous. This is because the primary reason for entering religious life is to strive for holiness. Didn't Jesus say, "be perfect as your heavenly Father is perfect" (Matt. 5:48)? Scrupulous people tend to take this to the extreme.

I don't really know exactly how I overcame this problem. But what I remember doing in talking about this with my spiritual director was three things. First, and most importantly, I began to think about my relationship to God and to understand that God is not a policeman watching my every move and waiting to punish me. He is a God who loves me even though I do sin at times and he has mercy on me. The second thing I did was to read the Gospels and put myself in the place of so many individuals who met Jesus and to imagine him responding to me in the same way that he responded to others, with mercy and kindness. Thirdly, although I tried my best not to think about sin all the time, whenever I did, I tried to realize whether or not I truly *intended* to do something. Gradually, over the course of about a year, I managed, with God's grace, to free myself from the grip of this insidious problem.

Sometimes, what we experience and struggle with in life can end up being a blessing to others. This was true for me with this issue of scrupulosity. Years later, after I had become a psychotherapist, I was able to help people who were struggling with this issue. Psychologically, we would say today that this is a form of obsessive compulsive disorder and I would help my clients work through their scrupulosity issues with a combination of talk therapy, behavior management strategies as well as medication. But back in the 1960s, there were not a lot of medications to help people with this problem. In any case, because I had to struggle with this issue in my own life, I could certainly empathize with these clients and try to help them alleviate their pain.

Needless to say, I was happy when May, 1965 rolled around. I was more than ready to graduate and move on to my next phase of formation, our house of theology in Washington, DC. These two years had continued to be very difficult and challenging to me and I still had not found any way out of my dilemma of whether to stay in or leave religious life. I was hoping again that I would be able to do this while moving on to study theology.

Our graduation from college was a very nice occasion. Although our numbers were extremely small, there was a major sense of accomplishment as we received our diplomas. Family and friends gathered at St. Mary's for the occasion and on this day at least, my struggles of the last two years faded to the background with the reality that I now had finished college. No matter what I ended up doing, I now had my degree.

After a reception for everyone who had come to celebrate our graduation, we all headed home for another week's vacation. I was certainly looking forward to that. As the hills of St. Mary's faded in the distance, I was ready for some rest and relaxation before heading to Washington, DC. A milestone had been reached.

5

Capuchin College
Our House of Theology

"Walking Inside the Ragged Meadow of my Soul"

(E. E. CUMMINGS)

A. The Burden of Myself

SOMEHOW, IT IS THE task of each person to bear the burden of oneself. Some of us carry it easily because we fail to recognize the extent of its existence. Others carry it with difficulty; some fall beneath its pressure and fail to rise again. But we also find ourselves born into a society where as St. Paul says, we are invited "to carry each other's burdens" (Gal. 6:2).

After spending a week's vacation at home having graduated from college, I left for our house of theology in Washington, DC in July, 1965. I was clearly feeling the burden of myself, continually trying to figure out whether I should stay in religious life or not. And up to this point, I found it very difficult to find anyone else to help me carry this burden of myself. I felt like I had to be strong. If I shared my burden with anyone else, I thought I would be considered weak. So, I trudged on by myself. However, I also knew that this would be a pivotal year for me because by the next summer, we were expected to take our final vows of poverty, chastity, and obedience or leave. Our first three year commitment to our vows was coming to a close.

68

Needless to say, my first three years in religious life was not what I expected. I never dreamed it would be this difficult. I entered the novitiate in 1962, as an idealistic and somewhat immature twenty-year old. Now, as I approached my first year of theology in Washington, DC, I continued to feel conflicted. It was difficult to constantly bear the burden of myself.

B. Cultural and Societal Issues in the 1960s

The decade of the 1960s in America was both challenging and tumultuous. So many forces were at work both nationally and internationally that seriously affected American life and culture. The cold war and nuclear disarmament with Russia continued to be an ongoing problem, and the Cuban missile crisis in 1961 was extremely dangerous. The race into space continued to be challenging and although Russia beat us into space with the deployment of Sputnik in 1957, we nevertheless were the first to land a man on the moon in 1969. Last year in 2019, we celebrated the fiftieth anniversary of this amazing accomplishment.

Closer to home here in the United States, it was a decade of civil unrest. In the days following the assassination of JFK in November of 1963, the country fell into a kind of collective stupor. Civil disobedience and protests of all kinds took center stage in our cities. People marched to protest for civil rights following the preaching of Dr. Martin Luther King. Riots on university campuses like Kent State led to the death of innocent people. Those for and against the war in Vietnam kept the country in constant turmoil and upheaval. Then, in March 1968, Martin Luther King was assassinated, followed two months later with the killing of Senator Robert Kennedy. Civil unrest gripped the nation. Cities burned while an uncertain future loomed. During the summer of 1968, parts of Washington, DC burned and I can so clearly remember going down into DC to feed and give water to the firefighters who were trying to extinguish the flames.We also met and spoke with several newspaper reporters from The Washington Post and one morning I woke up to find my picture on the front page of this newspaper! I still have this edition of the paper as a reminder of those tumultuous days.

On another night, when several of us from Capuchin College were working downtown, we met some students from the University of Maryland. As we talked and worked together, one of the young ladies from the university asked us about ourselves. She obviously was not a catholic and didn't understand why we wore our brown habits. As I tried to tell her about ourselves and our way of life, she looked puzzled and asked me, "why would you want to do that? It seems like such a waste." To this day, I can still remember that conversation. Although I gave her some standard answer of wanting to serve God and other people, I felt the hollowness of what I told her. This was also what I was trying to sort out for myself.

This cultural landscape of the 1960s, found expression in a variety of ways. Music became a major avenue of expression. For example, Bob Dylan's song "Blowing in the Wind," seemed to perfectly capture the zeitgeist of the disillusioned youth who would push for social change. Released in 1963, when this folk singer was only twenty-two, this song asked deep, existential questions, "how many times must a man look up, before he can see the sky? The answer, my friend, is blowing in the wind." It's hard to believe that someone so young could convey such wisdom and depth of experience, but the climate of the 1960s was just right for a poetic artist like Dylan to emerge. People needed his words then, and we need them even more today. Another of my favorite groups which subsequently had a significant impact on my life, was Peter, Paul, and Mary. They too spoke to people about many issues in American society that were very troubling to people.

In a similar way, it was also a tumultuous period of time in the Catholic Church. The same kinds of upheaval began when Pope John XXIII convened the Second Vatican Council in 1963. He wanted to open up the church so it could minister to contemporary people who were looking and longing for renewal. In addition, he wanted to renew religious life so that these people who had dedicated their lives to God could find contemporary ways to preach the Gospel, evangelize others, and bring them to Christ. But renewing religious life in the 1960s proved to be a monumentally complex task. Those belonging to a wide variety of religious orders had to decide what was essential in their rule, and then translate this into present day realities. The problem was that most of the religious at the time had been shaped by the old regime at a very profound level, and many found that they could not think in any other way. They could modernize their clothes but they could not change the habits of their minds and hearts, which had been formed by a training that had been carefully designed in a different world and was meant to last a lifetime. For some, this was a time of great anguish. They saw a cherished way of life disappearing, yet nothing of equal value, in their opinion, had emerged to take its place.

Although Pope John XXIII called for the beginning of the Vatican Council in 1963, it took about two years for the results of the Council to be promulgated. Altogether, sixteen documents were produced on various aspects of church life. The Decree on the Appropriate Renewal of the Religious Life was promulgated on October 28, 1965. The Council Fathers wanted the renewal of religious life to involve two simultaneous processes: 1) a continuous return to the sources of all Christian life and to the original inspiration behind a given community and 2) an adjustment of the community to the changed conditions of the times.

And so, when I arrived at Capuchin College, our house of theology, in July of 1965, I was thrown into this religious milieu. It was a tumultuous time in religious life and the way in which most religious orders were asked to begin their own unique religious renewal was to have a series of community meetings so that everyone had an opportunity to share their ideas. Although this sounded easy enough, it ended up being very difficult because their were so many different ideas.

Capuchin College was a large monastery at the time. There were four years of students studying theology, several professors, a variety of friars involved in other ministries, as well as several elderly, retired priests. Altogether, there were around sixty of us. As a result, our community meetings were generally very lively and often difficult. Because there were so many of us, it was difficult to come to a consensus on any particular topic. At times, our meetings became very contentious and unkind. Many individuals held very stringent views on topics and obviously thought their positions were the correct ones. In addition, there were often serious conflicts between the young and the older friars. Those that had been in religious life for many years and were trained in an older understanding of how to live our Capuchin way of life, were often threatened by a discussion of possible changes. Because of this, they held tight to their position of mostly maintaining the status quo. On the other hand, most, but not all of the younger friars were hoping to implement some changes that allowed our Franciscan charism to speak to the realities of contemporary life in the 1960s. As our community discussions continued throughout the course of 1965, a real divide developed among some in the community.

For me, it was a time of optimism and hope. I knew that this year would be important to me because I realized that I had to make a decision about professing solemn vows for life. My hope was that some of the changes to our daily routine would give me more freedom to help me decide whether to remain in religious life or not. The fact that now there were over forty students in all four years of theology gave me the hope of making new friends and doing things with different people.

When I first arrived in July, 1965, several small changes made a significant positive impact on me. For one thing, many religious orders also had their houses of theology located in Washington, DC, near Capuchin College. Because of this, we had leagues in a variety of sports competing with other religious orders and then we were allowed to socialize together after our games. As soon as I arrived in DC that summer, I played for our baseball team against other religious communities. It was always an enjoyable time. Also, because our theology classes hadn't yet begun, our daily schedule on Wednesday and Saturday afternoons were free so that we were able to do some interesting things in the DC area. Often, several of us would ride our bicycles down into town to visit a lot of interesting places like the popular monuments and museums. This felt very freeing to be able to enjoy these things outside of the monastery. This helped me with the issues of confinement and isolation that had been so difficult for me these past three years in the novitiate and St. Mary's Monastery.

Another change became important for me that summer in 1965. During the previous year, I had learned to play the guitar and practiced regularly to improve my skills. With folk music on the rise in the 1960s, Friday evenings became fun and relaxing. Capuchin College, as well as many other religious communities were located very close to Catholic University. On Friday evenings, we were permitted to go down to the university to join many other religious groups to join in a sing-along in what was then called a "hootennany." These were also a lot of fun and allowed me to meet other religious in a relaxed atmosphere.

As the school year got underway in September, I discovered that I liked studying theology much more than philosophy. The material itself, although challenging, was very interesting to me. In addition, all of our books were now in English! This change was another result of the academic changes brought about by the renewal of religious life because of Vatican II.

Another positive change occurred because one of our young priests returned from his studies in Rome where he received his doctorate in theology and joined the faculty at Capuchin College. I liked him a lot. He was young, energetic, and enthusiastic. Everyone could tell how much he enjoyed teaching theology by the volume of notes he would give us for each class. His enthusiasm spilled over onto many of us and became very evident in the lively discussions we would have in class on various theological topics. He encouraged questions and wanted us to think for ourselves rather than simply regurgitate answers to a pre-programmed set of questions. I found this approach very refreshing. Furthermore, this young priest loved to play sports, especially basketball, and he would often join us on the basketball court during our free time. He was a good athlete too. Before joining the Capuchin Order, he played for his high school team.

Liturgically, it was also a time of major renewal and change. Probably the biggest one and most noticeable was that now the altar was turned around so that the priest celebrating Mass would be facing the people rather than have his back to the congregation. At the same time, the Mass and the Divine Office, which began to be called the Liturgy of the Hours after Vatican II, were also changed from Latin to English. It was good to understand what you were praying rather than trying to follow along using a prayer book.

Complimenting these liturgical changes, was the addition of changes to the music used during Mass. Previously, there were songs in both English and Latin and these were almost always accompanied by an organ. However, due to the changes encouraged by Vatican II, guitars and other instruments were now permitted. By now, there were several of us who were playing the guitar and gradually new music began to emerge from some very good catholic songwriters. We quickly learned these songs and our group often played during Mass. This too, was very refreshing to me.

As I mentioned earlier, these kinds of liturgical changes were extremely difficult for some of our older friars. They had been formed in a very traditional approach to celebrating Mass in Latin, with the priest's back facing the people and these changes were traumatic for some of them. It was like their world had been turned upside down. Because of this, our superior of the house only gradually implemented these changes.

Early in October, 1965, I began to see Fr. C. for spiritual direction. Each of us studying theology were supposed to be receiving spiritual direction as our journey toward making our final vows became closer. Because of my uncertainties of the last three years, I knew that I needed help. In the beginning, I met with Fr. C. on a weekly basis so that he could get to know me as a person. I shared my early family life with him as well as my early experiences of being in the high school seminary at St. Fidelis. Gradually, I told him about my difficulties in the novitiate and last two years in the monastery studying philosophy. I tried to be as honest as I could with him because I knew I needed help to figure out whether or not I should take my final vows. I talked a lot about my difficulties, my doubts about living religious life and the depression I had been feeling. I found it easy to share with him.

From the first time I went to Capuchin College in July, 1965, to begin my study of theology up until January 1966, I actually felt better than I had the previous three years. My depression had somewhat lifted, my headaches were fewer, and my stomach issues had partly subsided. Personally, I attributed these improvements to my new surroundings at Capuchin College, to the more interesting study of theology, and especially to the many changes brought about by Vatican II which gave me more of a sense of freedom. These, along with the liturgical changes that I found very uplifting, allowed me to feel better about myself going forward.

C. Feeling Trapped

As January and February of the new year emerged, I could feel myself slipping backward again. I realized that this was caused by the impending pressure to decide whether to take my final vows or not. My spiritual director, Fr. C. thought that there might be something going on inside of me psychologically that he wasn't equipped to handle. So, he wanted me to see a catholic psychiatrist, Dr. P. I also thought this might be helpful and began to see him on a weekly basis at the end of February. Dr. P. was an interesting character. Tall and thin and generally very quiet, he allowed me the time I needed to explain my situation to him as well as the religious life issues I was struggling with. After three or four visits with him, he thought that some anti-depression medication could be helpful to me and so I began taking this medication toward the end of March. He thought that if I felt better I would be able to make a more informed decision about my vows.

Although I found it easy to talk with him, I also felt that he had a preconceived bias toward me staying in religious life. Although he never directly said this to me, he would often give me spiritual reading to do as part of my therapy. For example, he wanted me to read sections of three books that seemed to be his favorites, and he thought these would help me find some answers to my questions about remaining in the monastery. These three books were *The Weight of Glory,* by C. S. Lewis, *The Way of Perfection,* by St. Theresa of Avila, and *The Living Flame of Love,* by St.

John of the Cross. These last two were written by two great Carmelite saints and I could tell by the way Dr. P. spoke about them and how he referred me to specific passages that he was very familiar with them. I found these readings helpful to a certain extent, but there seemed to be a distinct bias to them. Most of the passages I read and reflected on had to do with advancing in the spiritual life in relation to suffering certain crosses in life. In other words, Dr. P. thought if I could see my difficulties in living religious life as crosses that I needed to bear and align these with the cross of Jesus, that I could find a way of understanding my difficulties as invitations to grow in holiness. I knew that this is what I had been trying to do for the last three years and wondered if "spiritualizing" my struggles could actually bring me any peace. However, like the dutiful young friar that I was, I faithfully read the passages in these books and had some very interesting discussions with him about them.

As the days and weeks progressed toward the date of July 15, 1966— our final profession day—I found myself continuing to struggle both psychologically and emotionally. The depression became worse as well as my daily headaches and some digestive problems at times. Having talked with Fr. C., my spiritual director, about my struggle for the last eight months and Dr. P. my psychiatrist for the last four months, I continued to feel conflicted. Both of them thought I was a good candidate to take my final vows and although they did not say so directly, I could tell this was their preference for me. They both seemed confident that I could overcome these difficulties and find happiness in religious life. For my part, these last months of prayer, receiving spiritual direction, therapy, and medication, helped me to at least figure out that my two main issues were celibacy and living the daily routine of monastery life. I didn't think that the vows of poverty and obedience would be that difficult for me but I thought celibacy would clearly be a struggle. And living in such close quarters with others, as community life required, would certainly be a challenge.

Spiritual writer Rabbi Joshua Heschel said that "we are closer to God when we are asking questions than when we have the answers."[1] He believed that to be a Christian is *not* to be a person who knows all the answers. Rather, to be a Christian is to be a person who lives in the part of the self where the question is constantly being born.

I understand this idea much better now than I did in the spring of 1966. Most of us know the feeling of longing for answers. I know I

---

1. Zohar and Marshall, *Connecting with Our Spiritual Intelligence*, 15.

certainly did. For the last three years, I had been asking myself the question of whether I should stay in religious life or not? And if Rabbi Heschel was right when he said that "we are closer to God when we are asking questions than when we have the answers," then, I felt like I should be very close to God! However, this was not the way I was feeling. Because I had been struggling with my question for the last three years, I was essentially feeling trapped—unable to find a way out of my dilemma. Trapped within myself.

D. My Right Question

One day in prayer, as I continued to struggle with these issues, I began to wonder if I was truly asking the right question. Down deep, maybe what I was really looking for was someone to decide for me. Perhaps this was my real weakness. Maybe what I was looking for was validation to leave from someone else. Maybe if my spiritual director or psychiatrist affirmed my desire to leave, then I wouldn't have "to go into myself" anymore as Rilke said, to try and find the answer. Then, maybe I would begin to feel better, both physically and emotionally.

As I struggled with this new insight about myself, I began to read *The Drama of the Gifted Child: The Search for the True Self* by Alice Miller. She believed that the gifted child was not necessarily a child prodigy. The gifted child was the opposite of the daredevil who fears nothing, particularly what other people think of him or her. Rather, for her, the gifted child was the sensitive child, the good child who was anxious to please, to measure up, and not disappoint others. I knew this description certainly fit me. For the last three years, whenever I thought about leaving, guilt and shame would overwhelm me. The belief that if I left, I would be turning my back on God who had given me this vocation would make me fearful. The belief that if I left, I would be letting myself and others down, kept me tied up in knots.

1) "Monastery Culture"

It is often difficult to adequately describe the impact of a culture or subculture on a person. Many times, certain dimensions of life in a subculture are not articulated or spoken, but everyone knows they are present. Moreover, this belief is learned by everyone in the subculture at an early age. This was certainly true of the "culture of monastic life" in the 1960s. Once a person entered religious life, you were generally expected to stay. There was this feeling that only the good ones—the strong ones—persevered. The weak ones left. The strong ones offered their difficulties to God and found a way to work out their problems by staying in the monastery.

Furthermore, those priests who were tasked with the formation of seminarians and young religious, also possessed this same bias. They were there to try and help the young friars work out their problems within the confines of religious life, not to leave it. It was only as a last resort, that an authority figure would advise a person to leave. And then, only if there seemed to be a major problem. This "monastery culture" was always present to encourage people to stay in religious life, not to leave.

And so, at this point in the spring of 1966, I began to wonder if I was really asking the right question—should I stay in or leave religious life? Maybe my right question had more to do with *courage*. Maybe my right question had more to do with overcoming my weakness of wanting to rely on others to give me permission to leave. This is what I had to figure out. But I needed to hurry because July 15 was coming quickly.

The well known spiritual writer and monk, Thomas Merton, joined the Cistercian Order in 1943. He lived in a monastery called Gethsemani, in Kentucky from 1943 until 1968 when he died in Bangkok, Thailand where he had gone to give several conferences and retreats. The Cistercians, also known as Trappists, are probably the most strict religious order for men. They live a life of prayer and penance and speak only when necessary. Merton kept a journal of his days in the monastery which has been published as *The Intimate Merton*. It is a very interesting book because he shares with the reader his own personal difficulties and experiences during his years in the monastery which at times were fairly turbulent for him. However, it is not a journal where he wrote something every day. There might be gaps of days or weeks but when he did write, you get a very unique glimpse of what his monastery life was like in the 1940s through the 1960s. Most of these years were before the Second Vatican Council and so they come from a very traditional way of living monastic life. For approximately ten of these years during the 1950s and early 1960s, Merton was highly involved in the Cistercian formation program of the young monks. First of all, he was their novice master followed by several years as the director of scholastics which was the term used for the monks who were also studying to become priests.

At one point, after much prayer, reflection, and spiritual direction, one of the young monks who had been in the order for eight years, decided to leave. However, he was afraid to tell Merton because the young monk greatly admired Merton and didn't want to disappoint him. Finally, he got the courage to meet with him to talk about his decision. After Merton listened to his story, he simply told the young monk that he wanted him "to go in peace and remember to stay close to Our Lady."[2] Rather than being disappointed in the young monk who had decided to leave the monastery, Merton let him know that he was happy that he had carefully discerned his decision, and simply wanted him to be peaceful as he began another phase of his journey in life.

Even though I read this brief journal entry years ago, I have always remembered it, precisely because it was so different from my experience. Although this young monk might not have been struggling with the guilt and shame issues that I had, the way Merton handled this situation gave this young man the assurance that he was not disappointed in him or saddened by his decision. This kind of response gave the young monk the freedom he needed to go in peace.

For me, in my situation, I think it could have been very helpful if my spiritual director or psychiatrist—the only two people who knew I was struggling about my decision to take my final vows—could have somehow found a way to explore with me my fears of disappointing God, myself, and others if I left the monastery. Maybe that would have given me more freedom to cope with this issue. In addition, that might have given me a clearer path to try and understand myself better in relation to the issues of guilt and shame.

E. Final Vows

Having agonized about my decision for months, I decided to make my final profession. I didn't know what else to do. At the time, I was both mentally and emotionally exhausted. And because we were now beginning to see some changes in religious life because of Vatican II, I was more hopeful that other changes would also eventually emerge which would allow me to find more happiness and peace with life in the monastery.

Before our profession day, we again had to make an eight day silent retreat. In an unusual sort of way, I found these days more relaxing and

2. Merton, *The Intimate Merton.*

restful. Since I had already decided to make my final vows, I used these retreat days to try and rededicate myself to our Capuchin Franciscan way of life.

Profession days in religious communities are always big days of celebration. And so it was for me and my classmates. With twenty of us making our final profession, it was a day of hope for our entire province. We had the largest class ever to take our final vows and so St. Augustine Church in Pittsburgh, our province's headquarters, was packed with friars, family, and friends coming to celebrate with us. The ceremony itself was beautiful. The Mass, the singing and the homily were all very inspiring. When my time came, I approached the altar where our provincial was sitting. I placed my folded hands in his hands and promised to live in poverty, chastity, and obedience "all the days of my life."

F. "Alverno"

After our final profession day, we again were allowed a week's vacation. Again, my family and I drove back to our home in West Virginia, spending an enjoyable and quiet week there visiting family and friends.

Following the week's vacation, I went to Alverno for the rest of the summer. Alverno was a large old home which had been renovated into a type of monastery where the theology students went for the summer months. Tucked away in the mountains of western Maryland, it was a lovely place to live during the extremely hot days of summer in Washington, DC. The pace of monastery life was slower and more relaxed here where the students could go hiking along some beautiful trails in the woods or go swimming as well as doing some summer reading.

Before Vatican II, most of the major men's religious orders had some type of summer residence. These were the days when young men in formation were not permitted to be involved in any kind of ministry. The idea here was that you were a student first and this was your main job until after ordination. I always saw this as a huge detriment because this way of living was totally focused on oneself. For me, this was very unhealthy emotionally and psychologically. Since I was already an introspective person, this type of life style encouraged too much focus on oneself. Becoming involved in some kind of ministry would not only have been helpful to others but it would have been a healthier balance to our daily routine. It would have allowed us to "get out of ourselves" and become involved with other people. And what could have been wrong with that? Wasn't that what we were being trained for? But in those days before the decrees of Vatican II were promulgated and implemented, this was the dominant way that all men's religious orders trained their young religious. One of the reasons why the novitiate and my last two years of college at St. Mary's Monastery were so difficult for me was because of the isolation and confinement that I experienced. Everything in my daily living kept me feeling enclosed, with much too much introspection going on. For me, this was very unhealthy.

But all of this would soon change. Precisely after we returned from our week's vacation after making our final vows, several new changes were implemented as I began my second year of theology. Again, because of Vatican II, we were now allowed to become involved in some form of ministerial work.

By this time, there were four of us playing the guitar and so we formed a singing group. This became my new ministry. Over the next three years, we became rather well-known in the DC area in religious and church circles, and were often invited to play at a "folk Mass," using guitars for the music or to entertain a group of people of some organization in a parish or school environment. This allowed me to become less introspective and to feel less confined and isolated. I was very happy with this type of change in religious life brought about by Vatican II. This new involvement in some ministry was healthy for me both emotionally and psychologically.

It is very interesting today to look back over the years and see how religious formation programs have evolved. Today, working in some kind of ministry is central to every level of religious formation. Beginning in the novitiate, everyone is expected to be involved in some kind of ministry. The same would be true as young friars progress through their college years as well as their years of theology. No one today would ever think about having people in formation *without* being involved in some form of ministry. It is seen as an *essential* element in a formation program at every level. And yet back in the early 1960s when I was in formation, you were not allowed to be involved in any kind of outside ministry. In those years, it was seen as a detriment to one's vocation. How such major changes can occur over a period of fifty years is truly amazing when, like me, you have lived in formation programs in one very distinct way, and now see how it is so different. But from my perspective, things are so much healthier today than when I was living in the monastery.

Another major change that has occurred over the years is the movement away from confinement and isolation in living monastic life. While it is very true that the young men in formation today continue to need a certain amount of silence and solitude for prayer and reflection, it is also true that St. Francis wanted his friars to be out in the world ministering to people. This approach is much healthier today and it certainly would have helped me a great deal if things had been this way when I was in formation.

After spending approximately a month at our summer monastery at Alverno, we packed up and headed back to Capuchin College in Washington, DC to begin our second year of theology. I continued to enjoy my studies in theology and found them to be challenging. There were two other major changes that occurred during the Fall of 1966. First, a new superior was appointed for Capuchin College. Fr. D. was our moral theology professor. He was a wonderful friar and was very inspirational to me. He was a very kind, caring, and compassionate priest and everyone in the monastery thought it was such a blessing to have him as our new superior. He loved smoking his pipe and was a big Washington Redskins fan! Usually, personnel changes in our monasteries occurred every three years. These changes were the result of what was called "provincial chapters." In the Capuchin Order, as with many of the major men's religious communities at the time, a provincial chapter was held every three years. At these chapters, all of the friars who had made final profession came together to discuss and vote on many dimensions of monastery life. One of these discussions always involved electing friars who would lead the province for the next three years. The leader was called our provincial. This person, was joined by three other elected friars who served as provincial council members. One of the first things these four provincial council members did after the conclusion of the provincial chapter, was to make personnel changes in the province. It was this process that caused Fr. D. to be appointed as our new superior of Capuchin College. He would be my superior for the next three years.

It is important to understand and remember that these were very turbulent years in religious life. It was a time of change on many levels and the superior of a house was the person chosen to implement these changes. This, of course, brought the local superior much criticism. Some liked the changes and wanted them implemented quickly. Others were opposed to the changes and vigorously fought them. At times, there was a great deal of tension in the house.

Fr. D. was a very sensitive person who found himself caught in the middle of these battles. He was often called to be like a referee, trying to appease everyone. Eventually, this took a serious toll on his health. The first year he had this position, which was my second year of theology, he managed the situation fairly well. However, gradually, as his second and third year wore on, his emotional health began to fail. He was becoming more depressed. By the end of his third year as our superior, he had what I thought was a complete mental breakdown. Many of us were extremely worried about him. Finally, after no one had seen him for four or five days, several friars decided to go into his bedroom to see what was going on. They found him in his bed, very disheveled and depressed, almost unable to move. He was truly suffering and badly needed help. Because he seemed to be almost totally dysfunctional, they decided to call the provincial. Several days later, Fr. D. was moved to our novitiate monastery in Annapolis, to rest and receive the help he desperately needed. This resulted in a new superior being assigned to our community. The priest who had been our assistant superior became our new superior.

The second major change that happened at the beginning of my second year of theology in the Fall of 1966, was the renovation of our chapel. Before Vatican II, the priest said Mass in Latin with his back to the congregation. The friars stood, knelt, and sat in what were called "choir stalls," facing each other. Everyone always had their place, and because of the "age factor," you were always next to the same people. After we received permission from our provincial to renovate the chapel in accordance with the guidelines of Vatican II, work began in earnest. One of my classmates who had a construction background before entering the Order led this effort. The altar was moved down to be closer to the congregation so that the priest celebrant could now face the people while celebrating the Mass in English. Both of these changes were huge. Having the priest face the congregation and saying the Mass in English were major changes in the Catholic Church and monastic life and it stirred up a lot of emotions and controversy among everyone in the community. This, of course, led to many "interesting" community meetings. The other major change with regard to the renovations of the chapel involved the choir stalls. All of these were removed, and church pews were now inserted in their place, so that our chapel basically now looked like a regular small Catholic Church rather than a monastic chapel. Along with these two major changes, there were more minor ones as well. The entire chapel was repainted to try and brighten up the atmosphere and some of the older statues were replaced with more contemporary ones.

The third major thing that occurred because of these changes to the chapel was the fact that now anyone could come to our chapel and pray with us. This meant that members of other religious orders as well as lay people could now be a part of our praying community. This change was truly refreshing. Many people joined us for Sunday as well as daily Mass, and at times people would also join us in praying the Liturgy of the Hours, which previously had been called the Divine Office. Over the course of my last three years at Capuchin College as a theology student, I had the opportunity to meet many wonderful people, some of whom became life long friends. This was very healthy for me and helped me to be less introspective.

G. Minor Orders

From my earliest days in the seminary, we were always encouraged to keep our eyes fixed on the goal—becoming a priest. Every aspect of our lives was geared toward this. In an interesting way, the Church in the 1950s capitalized on this idea of keeping the goal of the priesthood constantly before us. As I was progressing through four years of theology, there were certain goals to be attained that kept the ultimate goal of ordination to the priesthood in clear focus. These were called "minor orders." The two major orders were to be ordained a deacon and then a priest. But beginning in my second year of theology, we began to receive what was then called the "minor orders" of acolyte and lector. Becoming an acolyte was the minor order that would formally acknowledge our position to serve Mass and be around the altar. Becoming a lector acknowledged the fact that we were now officially able to read the Scriptures. However, anyone could already do these things so there was no real practical impact on our lives when we received these minor orders. However, they were another way the church kept our goal of the priesthood clearly before us. We were making progress in attaining our goal. For some reason that is still not clear to me after all these years, receiving these minor orders did not dramatically impact my decision to stay or leave the monastery. I just accepted the idea that they were another step along the way.

With the change of thinking about the importance of being involved in some kind of ministry during our formation years, I began to see what the possibilities might be for me during my second year of theology in the Fall of 1966. One day, I noticed an announcement on our community bulletin board that a girl's catholic high school was looking for an eleventh grade religion teacher. The job description looked interesting to me and so I applied and got the job. The school, Holy Cross High School, needed someone to teach moral theology which was an extremely interesting and challenging area in the 1960s. Gone were the days when everything in moral theology was "cut and dried." Many moral theologians, as well as lay people, were looking for a new approach to understanding this area of theology. Just like it was such a tumultuous time in American society during the 1960s, this was also true in moral theology. Everything seemed to be up for discussion, from human sexuality to social justice issues. The teachings of the church were being questioned and considered by some at least, to be outdated. Of course, when Pope Paul VI issued his encyclical *Humanae Vitae* in 1968 upholding the traditional catholic position on birth control, this caused a lot of turmoil. Many lay people, as well as some moral theologians, were hoping that these conservative ideas on sexuality would be changed. When they were not changed, it caused much discontent among the faithful.

For me, teaching moral theology to eleventh graders was very challenging but also very rewarding. Essentially, I wanted to create an environment where the girls felt safe and could ask questions about any topic that interested them. Needless to say, we had many interesting discussions. Everything, from pre-marital sex to feeding the poor and taking care of the homeless were investigated. Topics like war and peace took front and center stage, mostly because the Vietnam war was raging at the time. A lot of questions on marriage and divorce provided a rich area for discussion as well as the moral authority of the church. I remember having a very lively discussion one day on why we have to accept and believe the teachings of the church on these issues. What authority does the church have over us that allows them to dictate what we need to believe and how we need to act? Why can't we simply decide on our own? These and many other topics came up for our consideration and I think that by the end of the school year in May, 1967, these teenagers appreciated the freedom to ask questions in an open and accepting way while also appreciating how complex some of these issues were. I think they also came to understand the role of the church in this area of their lives and how to go about forming their conscience on these and many other difficult topics.

For me, this experience of teaching juniors in high school was challenging. Preparing for class and leading our discussions not only made me study the issues more thoroughly, but also encouraged me to struggle to find ways of "translating" church teachings in this area of moral theology where I was being continually challenged. Also, I think it made my own study of theology more real and pragmatic. It made me get my "head out of the clouds" and try to find ways of making some of these church teachings relevant. And isn't this what I would be trying to do as a priest?

H. Toner Institute

By the end of my second year of theology in June, 1967, the idea of being involved in some kind of ministry became even more important for the summer months. No longer were the theology students assigned to our summer monastery at Alverno. Rather, each of us was given a summer ministry assignment and only at the end of this assignment could we go to Alverno for a few days, if there was time. My summer ministry was to be a counselor, along with two of my classmates, at the Toner Institute for Boys which my province staffed in a Pittsburgh suburb. This was a home for troubled high school teenage boys and our job was to try and help them in any possible way. Many of the boys came from very abusive backgrounds and families. Some had run away from home and were placed there by the court. Many of them had already been severely wounded in life, either sexually, emotionally, or psychologically. Mostly, we played baseball and other sports with them. Sometimes, we were the referees for their games. We ate our meals with them and we quickly learned that we were not going to cure these wounded teens. A lot of our time was spent just "hanging out" with them. We wanted to be there if, and when, anyone wanted to talk. For some of these boys they had never really had anyone who was very interested in them. Often, it was a new experience for them to be around adults who wanted to spend time with them and listen to their struggles and stories. We discovered if we were able to be present to them, to just be around and hang out, they would sometimes open up and share something about themselves. Moreover, we also quickly discovered that there were no easy answers, no quick fixes to their problems. But we were there to try and help in any way we could and hopefully give them a positive experience of "church people" as they liked to call us. We tried to let them know that the Catholic Church cared about them and was interested in their well-being.

Working with these troubled teenagers was a blessing for me in many ways because it gave me personal contact with wounded people. It helped me put into practice, on a concrete level, what I had been studying about the life of St. Francis. He wanted his followers to work with the poor and wounded people in life. People who were struggling and hurting. People who were marginalized and looked upon as social outcasts. It gave me a taste of what Francis of Assisi did when he kissed the leper. Working with these boys allowed me to catch a glimpse of what our Franciscan charism was all about, and I appreciated that.

In addition to this blessing was also the feeling of gratitude I had from being raised in a family and an environment which was more healthy and allowed me to have a better start in life. Although my family was not perfect, by any means, it nevertheless gave me the basis on which to build a healthy foundation.

Another blessing emerged because of this summer ministry experience. Because the Toner Institute for Boys was located in the suburbs of Pittsburgh, it gave me the opportunity of living in a small fraternity. Including myself and two other theology students, there were only three other friars living in this small monastery. The other three priests were working in other ministries. The dynamics of community life were very different than in our large houses of formation. I liked this atmosphere better because all six of us had to be involved and invested in making community life function in a healthy way. Your presence was important and relied on in everything from communal prayer time to cooking, cleaning, and recreation times. This experience was good for me because it encouraged a daily routine where the six of us had to share our lives and be there for each other.

I. Importance of Friendship

There was one other important thing that happened to me at the end of my ministry experience in the summer of 1967. I was packing things up and getting ready to head back to Capuchin College to begin my third year of theology studies. Before I left, one of my Capuchin priest friends invited me to go to his house with him for dinner. Excited about the prospect of a good home cooked meal, I readily accepted his invitation. As we set off, he asked me if I minded stopping by a convent for a few minutes so that he could see his sister who was a nun. Although I never knew that he had a sister who was in the convent, I said "sure, that would be fine." After fighting Pittsburgh traffic, we arrived at her convent where I met Sister L. She was young, probably about my age and I found her to be very pleasant and engaging. We spent about an hour there, sharing some ice tea and cookies. After this, we headed for my friend's house where we enjoyed a delicious meal. It was a lovely way to spend the day before I headed back to Capuchin College to begin my third year of theology.

Several days later, after settling in once again to monastery life, I wrote a card to Sister L., thanking her for her hospitality in welcoming her brother and me in a very gracious way. About a week later, I received a card from her, thanking us for coming for a visit and for having the opportunity to meet me.

This was the beginning of a friendship with Sister L. that lasted for over three years. Although we lived in different cities and hardly ever got to see each other, it was nevertheless an important relationship for me. However, because this was a long distance friendship and before the days of computers, cell phones, Facebook, and Skype, the way we cultivated our friendship was mostly through writing cards and letters. In those days, we weren't even allowed to make long distance telephone calls.

I believe that our friends are special graces that the Lord gives us in life. St. Francis de Sales believed that friends were gifts given to each other along the way—"bright mirrors of the steadfast, overflowing reality of God's eternal love."[3] To my mind, we don't just happen to run into people in our lives. Rather, the Lord is directing things so that we meet certain people and not others. And, among those that we meet, some will become very good friends who help us in life in so many ways and we do the same for them. Good friends help us to grow and mature. These are people with whom we can share our lives, both our joys and our sorrows, people who truly know us, whom we feel comfortable with and like to be with. But we can't do this with everyone. That is why they are "special graces." There is a touching story about a special friendship in the book *Tuesdays with Morrie*. Morrie had a good friend named Maurice Stein with whom he had been friends for over thirty-five years. At one point in the story, Maurice was going deaf. And Morrie, who was struggling with the advanced stages of ALS or Lou Gehrig's disease, was getting to the

---

3. de Sales, *Introduction to a Devout Life*, 177.

point where he was unable to speak and his friend, Stein, was unable to hear. TV personality Ted Koppel was interviewing Morrie and asked him what that would be like for their friendship. "We will hold hands," Morrie said. "And there'll be a lot of love passing between us. We've had thirty-five years of friendship. You don't need speech or hearing to feel that."[4]

In his book, *The Four Loves*, C. S. Lewis said that friends on our spiritual journey are envoys of the overflowing grace an attentive God lavishes on us. As such, they are not chance acquaintances but gifts given to us by God.

> Christ, who said to his disciples 'you have not chosen me, but I have chosen you,' can truly say to every group of Christian friends 'you have not chosen one another but I have chosen you for one another.' The friendship is not a reward for our discrimination and good taste in finding one another out. It is the instrument by which God reveals to each the beauties of all the others . . . They are, like all beauties, derived from Him, and then, in a good friendship, increased by Him . . . At this feast it is He who has spread the board and it is He who has chosen the guests.[5]

One of my favorite Scripture passages in the Old Testament comes from Ecclesiastes: "To everything there is a season, and a time for every purpose under heaven: a time to be born, and a time to die; a time to plant, and a time to pluck up that which is planted" (Eccl. 3:1–2). Somehow, in the summer of 1967, it was the right time for me to meet Sister L.

J. Third Year of Theology

Returning to Capuchin College in August 1967, I felt better than I had in a long time. My summer ministry at the Toner Institute for Boys and meeting Sister L. were both positive experiences for me and I felt ready to begin my third year of theology, Emotionally, I felt like I was in a better place and was hoping that this coming year of studies would be a good one. I was also encouraged by the fact that in October, my superior asked me to attend a conference in New York City with an older priest. I felt honored to be chosen to go to this weekend conference and my superior also gave me some indication that my province was thinking about having me go into formation work after I was ordained. The theme of the

4. Albom, *Tuesdays with Morrie*, 70–71.

5. Lewis, *The Four Loves*, 126–27.

conference was the future of religious life. The two of us took the train to New York City where we stayed at a monastery that belonged to the Capuchins of the New York province. It was my first experience to go to New York City and my first experience to stay in another Capuchin province's monastery. The friars there were very welcoming, and made us feel right at home. The conference itself was very good with several prominent speakers discussing the future challenges of religious life after Vatican II. Lively discussions followed their presentations and many ideas were shared. Over a hundred religious men attended from a variety of religious orders. Listening to these ideas was very interesting to me because I was still in formation myself. Some rather new ideas about living religious life styles were presented by some while others wanted to pretty much maintain the status quo. In addition, some interesting ideas about the meaning of living in a community in the future were discussed as well as looking at the meaning of living our vows of poverty, chastity, and obedience. I felt that I learned a great deal from this conference and the material presented offered a lot of information for discussion between the two of us on our train ride back to DC.

As I began my third year of theology in September 1967, I knew once again that this was going to be another year of discernment for me because the following May, 1968, we were going to be ordained deacons. And although I had already professed my final vows of poverty, chastity, and obedience, becoming a deacon reminded me in a very concrete way about the obligation of celibacy. Moreover, if anyone was going to be ordained a deacon, it was assumed that the person would continue on for ordination to the priesthood. Becoming a deacon offered us the ability to begin preaching. Personally, I was looking forward to this. I wanted to become a good preacher and help people understand how the Scriptures could become more meaningful in their daily lives. In this third year of theology, we had to take a course called "homiletics" which basically was the study of how to become a good preacher. In this course, we had to write sermons/homilies, and take turns presenting these homilies to our classmates and professor who critiqued our presentations. Getting their feedback was helpful to me. I always found it challenging to write not only what I hoped would be a meaningful homily but also to find ways to make my preaching practical, concrete, and down to earth.

K. Understanding Chastity and Celibacy

The idea of celibacy and my commitment to this way of life became the focal point of another period of discernment as my third year of theology began. But the topic of celibacy was always there in front of us from our earliest days in the high school seminary. In those early days, the concept of "custody of the eyes" was drilled into us. Whenever we were getting ready to go home for summer vacations, we were always warned about getting too close to girls because we had to "protect" our vocation. Be careful around girls was the mantra. "Avoid the near occasion of sin," we were told because girls might make you lose your vocation. And if you wanted to be a priest, you knew that celibacy was a major requirement. But this approach to the idea of celibacy was always very negative. We never heard much about the positive value of celibacy—about how living a celibate life style could give a person more freedom to live for God alone and free to serve others more generously.

One day as a sophomore back in the college seminary, I was talking to one of my friends not long before we went to the novitiate. We were both very aware of the fact that at the end of our novitiate year, we would take our vows of poverty, chastity, and obedience, and we were sharing ideas about how difficult the vow of chastity could be. We got into this idea of having "custody of the eyes" that had always been drilled into us. My friend told me that he just didn't buy into that idea anymore. Instead, he said he was now going "to admire the Lord's handiwork." I liked this idea very much! It made so much more sense to me. It gave me, even in this early stage of my understanding about celibacy, a more positive way of looking at women. It seemed much more healthy to me. He went on to ask me if I had noticed some very pretty girls who would come to the seminary on our monthly visiting days? He didn't know who they were, but he thought they were probably the sisters of some of the seminarians. Secretly, I told him that I too had noticed them. Together, we agreed that we were going to "admire the Lord's handiwork!"

Another early reminder of how difficult the celibate life style could be for me came to me in the form of a song. When I was a senior in the high school seminary in 1960, there were four of us who formed a little band. I played the drums in our group. Actually, we were never all that good, but we enjoyed getting together to play and sing some of our favorite songs. There was a song that I grew to like a lot which was called "Turn Around." I don't even remember how we discovered this song.

Nevertheless, it spoke about how quickly a child grows up and leaves home. Whenever we played that song, I always remembered thinking that studying for the priesthood would mean that I would never have a child. I would never get married and have a family of my own. While I intellectually understood this reality even before I went to the high school seminary, on an emotional level, this was becoming more real for me. Interesting how we can remember some things so vividly even after some fifty-eight years!

Trying to discern whether I could be happy living a celibate life style was always an issue for me each time we approached professing our vows. I know it was a huge issue for me at the end of my novitiate year and also before taking my final vows at the conclusion of my first year of theology. But in some ways, my struggle and uncertainty about celibacy became more acute during my years of theology. During these years, our Capuchin way of life became more open and not so self-enclosed. We were now involved in our ministries where we had many more opportunities to meet and work with women of all ages. Also, our chapel at Capuchin College was now open to everyone and many people came regularly to worship and pray with us where again there were many opportunities to meet people. In general, religious life was now more open and we could leave the monastery with our superior's permission, and participate in a variety of activities where again the opportunity to meet people and form friendships were more possible.

This kind of openness in religious life allowed me to meet several women during my years of theology that made the reality of a celibate life more challenging. During my second year of theology, there were a number of student nurses who came to our chapel every Sunday for Mass. They were lovely young women and I admired the Lord's handiwork! One of these young ladies who was dating a midshipman at the Naval Academy in Annapolis, at the time, came to me on a fairly regular basis for advice about her relationship. While I was happy to try and help her in any way I could, I was also very aware of how attractive she was. It was another reminder to me about celibacy—that I would never be able to pursue this kind of relationship with anyone. Then, in my third year of theology, I again had the opportunity to meet another very attractive young lady from Pittsburgh who was in graduate school at Catholic University and who came to our chapel regularly for Mass. Since Capuchin College was just up the hill from CU, I used to see her and talk to her all the time. She was another concrete reminder of what I was going to miss after ordination.

Certainly, the most concrete issue I had to sort out with regard to celibacy came about because of the friendship that had developed between Sister L. and myself. For me, at this point, it was not a question of leaving religious life and marrying her or anyone else. However, my relationship with her greatly affected the way I felt about myself—my self esteem. And even though we rarely saw each other, I nevertheless felt good about myself. I noticed that I seemed to be happier and not as depressed. And even though I had continued to take my anti-depression medication, I also knew that this friendship was helping me in other ways too.

In my young adult years, this friendship with Sister L. allowed me to experience what it was like for someone to truly care about me for the person I was—not for anything that I did. She helped me to feel good about myself as a person. Also, I suppose on some level, it helped me to understand that if I made the decision to leave, that developing this kind of relationship with someone would be possible for me. It took this idea out of the theoretical realm and made it real and concrete for me.

During my third year of theology, I continued to receive spiritual direction every two weeks. As ordination to the diaconate came closer, and ordination to the priesthood followed soon after, the focal point of my sessions was celibacy. I needed to figure out if I could make this type of life long commitment. Not only could I do this, but could I remain healthy emotionally and psychologically in living this kind of life style? Could I ultimately find happiness? What made this discernment more difficult was the fact that now I not only knew these young women but I also knew some older friars who were not very healthy emotionally and psychologically. They were obviously very unhappy guys and while I didn't know exactly what made them this way, they certainly frightened me. Was this because of celibacy? Did their vow of chastity contribute to their unhappiness? I had been reading a good deal about how our vow of chastity could impact our lives as religious, and living with several of these men made me more apprehensive. So, all of these issues revolving around celibacy became a constant topic of discernment that I was trying to figure out with my spiritual director.

As the winter of 1968 approached, I was feeling stuck. I didn't know what to do to gain anymore clarity about this issue. In one of my sessions with my spiritual director, he suggested that I also begin seeing Dr. P. again—the psychiatrist I had seen on a weekly basis during my first year of theology when I was trying to discern whether to make final vows or not. Reluctantly, I agreed to this but I wasn't convinced that this was going to help me very much. Up to this point, I had already received a great deal of therapy and quite honestly, I wasn't sure Dr. P. was the person I should be talking to about this. I remember thinking about how he tended to "spiritualize" everything and I was afraid he would do the same with this celibacy issue. I wasn't sure that seeing celibacy/chastity as a cross, a suffering that should be offered up to God was the right approach for me at this time. Moreover, I didn't know if the spiritual reading he previously suggested from the writings of C. S. Lewis or St. John of the Cross or St. Teresa of Avila, would be beneficial to me. I thought what I needed was someone to talk to who would explore ideas and listen to my concerns about celibacy, someone to truly listen to me and who had no preconceived ideas about it, someone who could be objective. However, having explained my concerns and hesitancy to my spiritual director, I basically followed his advice and agreed to see Dr. P.

Back in 1968, I don't think we understood celibacy and the vow of chastity in a very positive way. For most priests, celibacy equalled not getting married. Most of the emphasis was on sex. To live a chaste life meant that you had to protect yourself from sins of the flesh. We certainly had to watch out for those "particular friendships" with anyone, especially women. Our training always seemed to emphasize the dangers, the pitfalls, connected to chastity. "Watch out," "be careful," became the key warning phrases about living our vow of chastity. But this negative approach could also lead religious to suffer emotionally. Because of this negative approach, I knew many men who were severely wounded emotionally. It was like there was a whole dimension of a person's life that was underdeveloped.

In the 1970s, there was a study done about the emotional health of American priests. There were four categories that were used to implement this survey: 1) well developed; 2) developing; 3) underdeveloped; 4) mal-developed. The percentages of the first category, well developed, and the fourth mal-developed, were both relatively small. However, there was a relatively high percentage represented in the second category, developing, but the largest category represented in this survey was number three—underdeveloped. This meant that there were significant difficulties in the development of the emotional life of priests in the United States. The idea of conducting this survey was not to punish priests who were having difficulties emotionally, but to try and find ways and develop programs that would help them grow emotionally. And with regard to religious order priests living their vow of chastity, I think our training put us at a disadvantage.

Today, there is a much better understanding of chastity. Basically, I think it is a much healthier approach to understanding what this vow truly means. It is much more positive and it is not simply related to sexual behavior. This viewpoint helps all of us to understand the importance of chastity. I wish I had known these things and been trained in this way when I was struggling with this idea before I was ordained.

St. Augustine (354–430), as we know, had two conversions in his life, one in his head and the other in his heart. At age twenty-five, he converted to Christianity, at least intellectually. After years of experimenting with various pagan philosophies and ways of living, he was now convinced in his head that Christianity was correct. The rest of him, however, was not so sure. For nine more years, until he was thirty–four years old, he was unable to bring his moral life into harmony with his intellectual faith. It was during these years that he frequently prayed his infamous prayer: "Lord, make me a good and chaste Christian, but not yet."

It is important to understand that all of us, not simply vowed religious people, are invited to live chaste lives. But what does this mean? First of all, we don't hear or read very much anymore about this idea of chastity. For many people, living chastely is certainly counter-cultural and requires a tremendous amount of courage to go "against the grain," so to speak. Generally speaking, except for people in religious life who take the vow of chastity, the term is rarely mentioned. This is unfortunate. There is a richness to this concept that can add a wonderful dimension to our spiritual and psychological lives. However, for many people in our secular society, to live a chaste life is to be bound to the past, to be unenlightened, to be "out of touch," and to not truly understand the modern world.

For a Christian, sex always needs the protection of a healthy chastity. In the Christian view of things, chastity in fact, is one of the keys to a healthy sexuality. This, however, needs to be correctly understood.

It is important to understand that the concept of chastity itself is not the same thing as celibacy. To be chaste does not simply mean that one does not have sex. Nor does it mean that one is a prude. Basically, chastity is not even a sexual concept, although faults in chastity are often within the area of sexuality.

Chastity has to do with how we experience everything. It's about the appropriateness of any experience. Ultimately, chastity is reverence—and sin, all sin, is irreverence. To be chaste is to experience people, things, places, entertainment, the phases of our lives, and sex, respectfully, in a way that does not violate others or ourselves. To be chaste is to experience things reverently, in such a way that the experience leaves both them and ourselves more, not less, integrated.

Therefore, we are chaste when we relate to others in a way that does not transgress their moral, psychological, emotional, aesthetic, and sexual boundaries. This is an abstract way of saying that we are chaste when we do not let irreverence or selfishness ruin what is a gift by some-how violating it. Conversely, we lack chastity when we cross boundaries prematurely or irreverently, when we violate anyone or anything in any way, and somehow reduce what it is. Chastity is respect and reverence. Its fruits are integration, gratitude, and joy. Lack of chastity, is irrever-ence and violation. Its fruits are bitterness and cynicism. Wherever there is violence, disrespect, emotional chaos, lack of community, bitterness, cynicism, and sexual irresponsibility, there is a lack of chastity.

It would have been helpful to me back in the winter of 1968 to have understood chastity in this way as it relates to celibacy. With ordination to the diaconate fast approaching in May, 1968, and to the priesthood soon after, it would have given me another way of talking about this di-mension of religious life with my spiritual director and psychiatrist. But this understanding of chastity was not very well developed at the time.

L. Deaconate, Priesthood, and First Mass

In the Spring of 1968, I had to make a decision to be ordained a deacon or leave the monastery. With the encouragement of my spiritual director and psychiatrist, and because I didn't have the courage to leave, I decided to ask that my name be submitted to my major superior and the arch-bishop of Washington, DC, for acceptance to become a deacon. After the necessary inquiries, I was approved for ordination to the diaconate in May, 1968.

Becoming a deacon, was a happy day for me. At this point, I felt like I had made the best decision I could at the time and felt rather peaceful and contented. Candidates from many other men's religious orders joined us at the Basilica of the Immaculate Conception in Washington, DC for the diaconate ordination ceremony. However, this was a rather quiet day with mostly other religious order members attending and participating.

There was not a lot of fanfare surrounding this ceremony but there was a quiet joy among us. After the ceremony, all of us simply returned to our respective monasteries to continue our journey on to the priesthood.

Becoming a deacon was important to me because it gave me, as well as all my classmates, the ability to preach at Mass. Each of us took turns in doing this and I know that I loved the opportunity to reflect on the Word of God that would be used for the scripture readings for the day, developing an idea for preaching, and then trying to make the readings practical for our daily lives. Preaching was very important for me and I always worked hard to do a good job.

The established route to the priesthood called for men to be ordained at the end of their fourth year of theology. However, for reasons that were never clear to me, our Capuchin Order, as well as some other men's religious orders, were allowed to have their men ordained at the beginning of their fourth year of theology. Then, we had to return to Capuchin College to finish our theological studies. For that last year of theology, we were known as "simplex priests." This meant that we could celebrate Mass but we were not allowed to hear confessions. In order to administer the Sacrament of Reconciliation, we had to first complete our theological studies.

Our ordination to the priesthood was set for October 19, 1968. Since I had done my discernment leading up to the diaconate, I began to look forward to my ordination to the priesthood. The long journey that began in September, 1957, was finally coming to fruition. Basically, I felt good about this and believed that I was ready to receive this sacrament. My parents were also excited. Together, we spent most of the summer working with my home parish in Huntington, making arrangements for my first Mass there as well as the reception afterwards in the church hall. In addition, we had to find a place to host a dinner for family and friends after the reception. Finally, we had to put together an invitation list which was largely done by my mother. Completing all of these things, required a great deal of time, energy, effort, and cooperation.

However, before we were ordained in October, we received our summer assignments. Most of my classmates were assigned to a variety of parishes where they could function regularly as a deacon, preaching, baptizing and learning about parish life. However, I was asked to go to summer school at Catholic University to take several courses in the psychology department. The thinking was that these courses would be helpful to me in the future when I would be working in our formation programs.

I must say that I thoroughly enjoyed these courses at Catholic University. Having struggled so much during my years in the monastery, I found them to be very helpful to me personally. They gave me some insights into my own issues as well as prepared me for my future assignment. Since I had been studying some psychology on my own since my junior year of college, I found the information in these courses dovetailed nicely with what I had been reading on my own. In addition to going to summer school, I also had the opportunity to preach at Mass in our chapel as well as several parishes in the area. Needless to say, it was a very busy summer.

As our fourth year of theology began in September, most of my focus was on my ordination in October. We actually had to practice saying Mass so that we would know the rubrics and how to do things properly. Doing things like this, made the reality of ordination more real. And again, before we were ordained, we had to make another eight day retreat. This time was actually very good for me because it gave me time to really pray and reflect on what it meant to be a priest.

Finally, October 19, 1968 arrived. It was a beautiful, bright, sunny, autumn day. There were eighteen of us being ordained and we were the largest class ever in the history of our province. Naturally, all of us were extremely excited. Our journey to the priesthood, begun so many years ago, had finally arrived. St. Augustine Church in Pittsburgh was packed with friars, our families and friends.

Today, even after fifty–two years, the ordination ceremony continues to be very vivid in my memory. Mass was scheduled for 11:00 am and we were supposed to be in the sacristy at 10:30 am to meet the bishop of Pittsburgh who would be ordaining us. After putting on our vestments, the ceremony began with all of us, as well as many other priests processing into the church singing the entrance song led by the church choir. As the Mass began those of us who were going to be ordained, prostrated ourselves in front of the altar while the choir chanted the Litany of the Saints. This was part of the ancient ritual of the church, invoking the blessing of the saints on all of us. Following the scripture readings, the bishop preached a very uplifting homily on the meaning of the priesthood as servants of Jesus Christ. After this, with each of us kneeling in a line, the bishop approached each of us for the laying on of hands. In a very solemn moment, and in total silence, he placed his hands on each of our heads, invoking the Holy Spirit to come down on us, ordaining us to the priesthood. Following this, all of the priests in the church came forward in silence and each of them placed their hands on our heads, manifesting a continuation of the priesthood through the ages, and asking the Holy Spirit to bless each of us as we now shared the priesthood together. All of this was quite moving. Then, each of us approached the bishop's chair once again for the anointing of our hands with the sacred chrism oil. We each placed our folded hands into his where he made the sign of the cross over the palm of our hands with the oil and then our hands were wrapped in a blessed cloth. This too, was a very moving part of the ceremony because this cloth was then given to our parents at the end of the ceremony. I know that my mother kept this cloth for years because after she died in 2009, I found it among her personal belongings.

And now, since each of us were newly ordained priests, we concelebrated this Mass with the bishop and the other priests who were present. The remaining parts of the Mass were pretty much the same as any other Mass but there was one other "special moment" at the sign of peace. At this time, each of us went down to the congregation and gave the sign of peace to our parents, family members and friends. Everyone seemed especially happy.

As Mass concluded, we all processed out of church, went back to the sacristy to remove our vestments and maneuvered our way outside to the front of the church where everyone was gathering. It was a wonderful feeling to be congratulated by so many people. After being together for so many years in the minor seminary and then the monastery, most of us knew each other's parents as well as some other family members. Everyone was so gracious to us. After about a half hour of this, we all made our way to the reception in the church hall. There were light refreshments for everyone and much more time to visit with everyone in a leisurely way.

Gradually, in late afternoon, people began to leave the reception hall. Since my sister and her family lived in the Pittsburgh area, my family and friends went to her house to continue the festivities. It was nice to have this time with a smaller group of people because it gave us more time to visit with each other in a relaxed way. As the evening came to a close, everyone began to return to their homes and I went back to St. Augustine monastery to spend the night.

Laying in bed that night, I couldn't fall asleep. It had been such a momentous and exciting day and my mind would simply not calm down enough for me to sleep. I must have laid awake for over an hour, reminiscing about the entire day. I felt very happy and joyful and thankful to be a priest. I remember going over the entire ordination ceremony in my head as well as the day's events and all the people who came to celebrate this day with me. Moreover, I remembered going to the high school minor seminary as a young fifteen year old sophomore and how I thought this day would never come. In addition, I remembered all the very difficult times I had in the monastery, and wondering if I was ever going to make it to this day. But God had somehow brought me to this day and tonight I was just very thankful.

Because most of my classmates were from the Pittsburgh area, they celebrated their "First Mass" at their home parish the following day. But since my family had a six hour drive back to my home in West Virginia, my "First Mass" was officially scheduled for the following Saturday. However, one of my classmates graciously asked me and my family to join him the following day to concelebrate his First Mass with him and his family. It was a lovely ceremony and after going to another small reception for him and his family, we headed home.

Driving back home on our six hour trip, my parents and I mostly reminisced about the previous day. They spoke about how moving the ceremony had been and since they had never been to an ordination before, they both thought it was lovely. Then, we began talking about our plans for my First Mass the following Saturday and what remaining things needed to be done. Since most of the major items had already been completed, it was mostly a few minor things that needed to be done and we had a whole week to finish these.

I thoroughly enjoyed my week at home. For the most part, it was a quiet week, which is what I needed. In the morning, I celebrated Mass each day at our parish church and then tied up some loose ends in preparation for my First Mass on Saturday.

Saturday, October 26, the day of my "First Mass," was a beautiful autumn day. With friars, family and friends mostly arriving the previous day, I had an opportunity to visit with some of them in the evening. Four of my Capuchin priest friends were joining me to concelebrate the Mass which would make the day even more special. I had asked my close friend, who had been my spiritual director and theology professor, to preach the homily and he readily accepted my invitation. Several other friars from Washington, DC and Pittsburgh had also made the journey as well as my friend, Sister L. and her mother.

With all the preparations completed, Mass began at 11:00 am. Booklets that had the order of the Mass along with the accompanying songs had been printed and distributed so that everyone could easily follow along and participate. There was a joyful atmosphere among everyone as we entered the church for the opening song. As I processed down the aisle, people turned to greet me. Some of them, including several of my high school classmates in the ninth and tenth grades before I went to the seminary, waived and smiled. It was wonderful to see everyone and to have so many people who had been important to me, join me in this celebration.

After the scripture readings, my priest friend preached a very meaningful homily. He developed the idea of a priest as a servant taken from among the people, to give back and serve the people like Jesus had done. Then, relating this idea to me, as a newly ordained priest, he challenged me to live my life in this way as a servant of Jesus given to minister to his people. I remember thinking that this is what I wanted to do. This was the kind of priest I wanted to be. After the homily, we continued concelebrating the Mass with my parents, brother, and sister, and several other relatives bringing up the gifts at the Offertory. Then, after praying the Our Father together with everyone, the time for the Sign of Peace arrived. This gave me the opportunity to approach the congregation and give my greeting of peace to my parents, sister, and brother as well as many other relatives and friends. Following this, when it became time to distribute communion, I felt honored to be a priest and distribute the Eucharist to everyone. Finally, as the Mass concluded, we began to sing the final hymn and process out of the church. Again, I was able to give and receive the smiles and joyful greetings of so many people. This had truly been another memorable experience for me.

After Mass, everyone went over to the parish hall to receive my first priestly blessing which is very customary with a newly ordained priest. Light refreshments were served to everyone and a kneeler was placed in front of me. As my family were the first to approach, I felt honored to give them my first blessing. Following them, other people approached and it gave me a brief opportunity to talk with them and thank them for coming before I also gave them my blessing. This, too, was a lovely part of the day.

The final part of the day consisted of a dinner at a banquet hall in one of the local hotels. As the dinner was concluding, several people shared some reflections about me and the events of the day. Because these reflections were often humorous as well as personal, it was a joyful way to end the celebration.

The day of a newly ordained priest's First Mass is always something very special and meaningful. I know this was very true for me. And even though it happened over fifty-seven years ago, I can still remember that day most vividly. It's like no matter what happens in life, a newly ordained priest will always remember this day. It was something I have never forgotten.

M. Life in the Monastery after Ordination: 1969–1975

After I was ordained in October, I returned to Capuchin College to finish my fourth year of theology. Following this, my first assignment was to spend the summer of 1969 moving to Montreal, Canada to study French. Following these three months, I was going to spend the next year at St. Paul University in Ottawa, Canada. My goal there was to obtain a Master's Degree in theology and it seemed as though French would be helpful in fulfilling the requirements for this degree. Then, after completing this degree, I would be assigned to Capuchin College to teach theology at the Washington Theological Union and become the spiritual director to our theology students.

1) St. Paul University, Ottawa, Canada

Both the summer of 1969 as well as my year studying at St. Paul University was a lonely year for me. I didn't know anyone. When I went to Montreal to study French, I stayed in a large Capuchin monastery where everyone spoke French. However, although it was a large monastery, there were only six Capuchin friars living there and they were all involved in a variety of ministries. Sometimes, I wouldn't see some of them for days. There were no other young Capuchin priests there and so, I was mostly on my own for that summer.

Following this experience, I went to Ottawa to begin my year at St. Paul University. Here, I lived at another very large monastery that was owned by the White Fathers who were missionaries in Africa. Fortunately, there were two other English speaking student priests there who became friends of mine. Although all of us were students, we nevertheless did some enjoyable things in the Ottawa area during the course of the year. This, at least, gave me some companionship and a feeling of camaraderie.

In addition to this, I noticed one day right after classes began, that there was a request posted on one of the bulletin boards at the university for a priest to help out with Masses on weekends at one of the local parishes. I called the pastor of this parish and indicated my desire to possibly minister at his church. He asked me to come and meet him and his associate pastor which was also good for me. After our meeting, he asked me to come the next weekend to his church to celebrate two Masses. After doing this, and perhaps getting some feedback from his associate and some parishioners, I was offered the job of helping out at this parish on the weekends. Since I knew this would be good for me, I accepted his invitation. During the course of the year, going to work at this parish was very helpful to me because it got me out of my theological studies and into the world of real people. Moreover, I became good friends over the course of the year with the associate pastor who was himself having some difficulties with the pastor. They seemed to clash a lot about trying to implement some pastoral ideas about parish life and the associate would often bounce ideas off me to get another opinion.

Serving at this parish church regularly on the weekends also allowed me the opportunity to meet people and make some friends. Since they knew that I was from the United States, they often included me in parish functions and invited me to their homes for dinner. They were very welcoming to me and this also gave me more of a balance between my studies and being involved in parish ministry. Several people that I met there back in 1969, have remained life long friends.

My theological studies at St. Paul University were intense and difficult. It was an accelerated master's degree program that required a lot of reading, exams, and writing papers. Needless to say, it kept me very busy but I found it both interesting and challenging. As with most degree programs, some of the professors were better than others but I felt that this was a good program for me.

During the course of the school year in 1969, I only got to come back to the States for Thanksgiving and Christmas. This was difficult for me and I felt a great deal of loneliness. One of the dimensions of life that helped me through these feelings was my friendship with Sister L. Our correspondence enabled me to maintain a positive attitude that encouraged me to "see the light at the end of the tunnel." In contrast to this friendship, I hardly ever heard from anyone back in my community. This was a difficult reality for me to understand because it made me question the value of community life. I was away for almost a year and except for when I came back to the States for Thanksgiving and Christmas, I had very little contact with any of the friars in our Pittsburgh province.

2) Teaching Theology at the Washington Theological Union

After obtaining my Master's degree in theology in May, 1970, I returned to Capuchin College. My assignment was to work in our formation program as the spiritual director of our student friars who were studying theology and to teach courses in spirituality at the Washington Theological Union. Since I wasn't that much older than some of our students, I was apprehensive about my role as spiritual director. But the students seemed to accept me for the most part and each of them could go to anyone for spiritual direction. They didn't have to come to me. Another part of my assignment was to plan for retreats and days of recollection which I enjoyed because I was able to contact other religious men and women to share ideas. Even in 1970, it continued to be a pretty tumultuous time in the Catholic Church as well as in religious life. But over the year, I was able to meet with some other priests from different religious orders and together we helped each other develop programs for our theology students which we hoped would be beneficial to them.

Beginning to teach in a theological school was a daunting task for me. My assignment was to prepare courses in the area of spirituality. I can still remember the first two courses I offered for the first semester: *Spiritual Direction* and *Nature, Grace and Religious Development.* I had most of the summer to prepare for these and I worked diligently on them. However, at the time, courses in the area of spirituality were all elective courses and I really didn't know until the week before classes began, if anyone would sign up for them. You had to have at least six people in your class for it to be a "go" and there were a lot of elective courses that were offered in every area of theology. However, when I received my class list, I saw there were eighteen students who had signed up for my *Spiritual Direction* course. As a beginning new teacher, this was both exciting and scary. Except for teaching that religion course to the juniors at Holy Cross High School, I had no teaching experience. And, of course, as "the new kid on the block," I wanted to make a good first impression as a theology professor.

Another factor that played into my anxiety was teaching at the Washington Theological Union which had only been in existence for two years. Up until 1968, many men's religious orders had their own school of theology with their own professors. However, during these years, with all the changes going on in society, the church, and religious orders, the number of men entering religious life was dropping. Eventually, because of this, there were simply not enough theological students to justify the continuation of some religious orders having their own separate theology faculties. So, the thought was to try and form one major school of theology in the DC area, which would be open to all religious orders if they wanted to join. After a number of meetings were held between a variety of religious order superiors, the Washington Theological Union was born. The Capuchins decided to participate in this school of theology. However, because there was this one school of theology now, it meant that there was less need for professors. And so, while the required courses in theology were filled with established professors, the elective courses and corresponding professors would undergo some kind of weaning process in which those that were well subscribed to would be able to remain and those that were not would be eliminated. This was another reason that teaching at this school of theology was very challenging—and somewhat nerve wracking—for me. Basically, I had to prove myself to be a competent teacher.

The first day of class for me was both exciting and nervous. I knew I was well prepared but since I didn't have any experience teaching theology, I was also nervous to see if I could communicate my information in an effective way. Although I got through my first class well enough, it was not long before I began to get the feeling that I was losing the interest of the students. Then, one day my Capuchin priest friend who had been my spiritual director and had taught theology for a number of years, pulled me aside and told me that one of the Capuchin students who was in my class told him that my course was not very interesting. Of course, that hurt. However, he also asked me to meet with him so that he might be able to give me some pointers about how to make my material more interesting. After swallowing my pride and hurt feelings, I gladly accepted his invitation. During the following four days, I met with him several times to try and learn how I could improve. After reviewing some of my material, he gave me a number of suggestions that he thought might be helpful. So, I followed his advice and subsequently discovered that his suggestions were very helpful. During the first several weeks of my course, I also sensed that some of the philosophical ideas that I was trying to explain to the students were falling on deaf ears. They simply didn't seem to be interested in how philosophy impacted theology as it related to the idea of spiritual direction. At this time, there was a very intelligent, young Capuchin friar who was studying philosophy at Catholic University. So, I decided to ask him for his help so that I could make this part of my course more interesting. He graciously said he would be glad to help me in any way he could. I found his tutoring very helpful. Essentially, he taught me how to understand some important philosophical ideas that I needed for my course and then several strategies on how to convey these ideas to my students in an interesting way that would hopefully hold their attention. Over the following years, I was able to also use what he taught me in some of my other courses in spirituality.

With the help of these two friars, I could gradually sense the interest of the students again and their participation in class greatly increased. The rest of the semester seemed to go pretty well, and the reviews that I received from the students at the end of the semester were mostly positive. I learned from this experience that becoming a good theology teacher involved not just knowing your material well but also knowing how to connect with your students. It was a learning experience for me that greatly influenced the way I taught for many years.

3) "Settling In"

My first years after ordination were my "settling in" years. I was trying to settle into my role as spiritual director to our young friars studying theology. I was trying to settle into my role as a young priest beginning to teach theology which required a lot of work on my part. Part of the challenge was developing interesting elective courses that the students would choose to take. Then, once I had decided on a course, I had to read and study a lot myself in order to learn the material and make it interesting to the students.

Besides my teaching ministry, I also enjoyed working with our student friars. They were young and eager to learn. Part of my job was developing programs that would continue to help them grow spiritually, emotionally, and psychologically. Since this approach had largely been lacking in my own formation program, I was eager to incorporate these dimensions into any programs that I might develop. For example, since I was responsible for setting up days of recollection, I tried to get speakers who had a background in psychology as well as spirituality. One of the priests I invited to speak was a Capuchin from the New York province. He had degrees in both spirituality and psychology and he was also very humorous. Everyone seemed to enjoy and learn a lot from the two days of recollection that he conducted for us.

Another part of my ministry was to help out in several parishes on the weekends. I enjoyed this very much because this gave me the opportunity to work with people in a concrete way. Besides celebrating Mass with them on Sundays, I also went to the parish on Saturday to assist hearing confessions. Ministering the sacrament of reconciliation to people was something that I thoroughly loved because it gave me a chance to bring the mercy of God to others.

4) Painful Partings

Things were actually going fairly smoothly for me until the spring of 1971. I had pretty much settled into my assignment and felt relatively peaceful in the daily living of my life in the monastery. But that seemed to all come crashing down on me when my friendship with Sister L. ended.

In one of my graduate school courses at Catholic University, I will always remember a sentence of one of my psychology professors. In class, we had been discussing the importance of friendships and relationships in our lives and how important these are for a person's emotional and psychological health. He said, "if you have a friendship that is good, there is hardly anything better. But if you have one that ends, there is hardly anything worse." After my friendship with Sister L. ended, I could truly understand what these words meant.

Back in the twelfth century, St. Aelred of Rievaulx was a person who wrote a great deal about the importance of friends to help us grow in our spiritual lives. He encouraged people to choose their friends carefully because this person was to be a partner in the love of God—a kindred spirit. Perhaps this is why it is so painful when friendships don't work out.

Everyone has experienced broken friendships or friendships that haven't endured for a variety of reasons. No doubt each person has his or her own understanding of what went wrong to cause the friendship to deteriorate. Nevertheless, the pain endures, sometimes for a long time. These 'painful partings" can be gut-wrenching and can happen for a variety of reasons.

Even Jesus experienced the painful reality of people walking away from him and wondered if his apostles would also walk away. In chapter six of John's Gospel, Jesus is explaining how he will give himself to people as his own flesh and blood. But many of them could not accept his teaching. "This is intolerable language," they said. "How could anyone accept it?" Then John continues, "After this, many of his disciples left him and stopped going with him." Jesus even wondered if his closest friends would walk away. On a human level, how hurt and disappointed he must have been. He turned to the Twelve and asked, "What about you, do you also want to walk away? Simon Peter answered, "Lord, who shall we go to? You have the words of eternal life" (John 6:60–69).

When we loose a friend, for whatever reason, it is always painful. If we lose a friend because of sickness or death or perhaps because a friend moves away, there is always a profound sense of loss. However, when a friend walks away for no apparent reason or for a reason we don't understand, there is also an emotional wrenching that takes place that deepens the feeling of loss. I had been friends with Sister L. for over three years and although we lived in different states and rarely got to see each other, we were able to maintain our friendship through writing cards and letters. For me, Sister L. was certainly a "kindred spirit," a gift given to me along my journey, a "bright mirror of God's steadfast eternal love," as St. Aelred said. And I thought it was the same for her. For over three years, this friendship was an important blessing to me. The well known philosopher Aristotle connects friendship and happiness, and I could truly say this relationship brought me a lot of happiness. It also gave me energy and zest for living. Then, gradually, things began to change. The cards and letters came less frequently. As I began to realize all of this, I would write to her about these changes and asked her how she saw our relationship changing, but to no avail. For some reason, she would not answer me. Interiorly, I began to panic. I felt lost, abandoned, angry and sad. As I desperately searched for answers, I became more and more depressed. Over a period of several more weeks, the friendship ended. It took me many months to begin to work my way out of this depression. Clearly for me, this was a "painful parting." I could now totally understand what my professor in graduate school meant when he said, "when a relationship ends, there is hardly anything worse."

One of the most difficult aspects to this friendship ending was the fact that I didn't know why because for some reason she wouldn't tell me. I didn't know if it was something I had done or something completely out of my control. Several months later, after I had mourned the loss of this friendship, I was determined to try and discover the reason for our friendship ending. I decided to contact several people who knew both of us to see if they knew what was going on with Sister L. I shared with them about our friendship dissolving and while they felt bad for me about this, they went on to tell me that she had become good friends with a priest that had recently been assigned to the parish where she lived. Well, now at last I had an answer. Now, I understood the reason why our friendship ended. And although it was difficult at first to accept this reality, knowing the reason helped me to not blame myself and to let the healing process begin.

That was 1971. Forty-one years later in 2012, I decided to try and contact Sr. L. and talk with her about our friendship. I had not heard a word from her in those forty–one years, but I had been getting this feeling that this might be helpful to clarify some things for me. So, I used Facebook to find her, got her email address and wrote to her, asking if she would be willing to meet with me. She agreed to do this and we decided on meeting for lunch one day at a restaurant about halfway between Pittsburgh and Millersville, Maryland where I was living. I must admit that I was somewhat nervous and apprehensive before I got there. When she arrived, we greeted each other cordially and found a table in the restaurant. After talking about what each of us had been doing for the last forty-one years, I decided to ask her personally why she thought our friendship ended. She simply said, "I fell in love." When I asked her why she wouldn't tell me, she really didn't say very much or explain things very well, but went on to ask me for my forgiveness. I assured her that I had forgiven her a long time ago and I sensed that she felt relieved by my response.

Although people obviously change a lot over the years, it always amazes me how some of our experiences with them can be vividly remembered. Sometimes, those memories can also be healed. Maybe, it's the healing of these memories that bring us comfort and peace.

5) My Doctorate at Catholic University

Beginning in 1972, my superiors wanted me to get a doctorate in theology, so I began taking courses at Catholic University on a part time basis. At this time, almost every professor in the Washington Theological Union had obtained their doctorates and the long range plan for me was to continue teaching courses in spirituality. Because I was still teaching at the time, it took me three years to finish my course work and even though this caused me to be busier than ever, I found them to be interesting and challenging and I clearly enjoyed them.

After finishing my course work, it came time for me to choose a dissertation topic. This could be difficult because I also had to find a professor who would be willing to work with me and direct me. Initially, I wanted to do something on the theology and spirituality of Thomas Merton. He was a very influential Cistercian monk and spiritual writer in the 1950s and 1960s. I had read many of his books by this time and was greatly impressed with him and his writings. So, I set up an appointment with the chair person of the theology department to discuss this idea. After explaining my ideas to him, he sounded intrigued but ultimately told me that while he liked my plan, he didn't think there were any professors in the theology department who knew enough about Merton to direct me. So, he thought it would be best to choose another topic. Although I was disappointed about this, I also knew that it was very important to work with a professor who understood my topic very well because over the course of the next two or three years, I would be spending a lot of time with him or her. In addition, there were always stories going around among the doctoral candidates about the large number of students who had completed their course work but never finished their dissertation. I knew I didn't want to become another statistic in this category.

About this time, one of my classmates who had been working on his PhD in philosophy at Oxford University, was home for a break during the summer. In July, he came to Capuchin College for a visit and we began to talk about our doctoral programs and writing dissertations. At this point, he was almost finished with his. He was writing on the idea of faith in the writings of John Henry Newman who was a very influential Anglican priest who converted to Catholicism in 1845. My classmate went on to tell me that there was an expert on Newman teaching at Catholic University by the name of Fr. F. He suggested that I meet with him to see if we could come up with a viable dissertation topic for myself. Over the next couple of weeks, I met with Fr. F. on several occasions and told him that I would like to do something in the area of spirituality. He suggested that I read two books on Newman to see if he and his writings appealed to me. So, after doing this, I went back to Fr. F. to tell him that I liked Newman and then we tried to come up with a topic about Newman's spirituality that I could write about. During our conversations, I told him about my work as spiritual director at Capuchin College. Fr. F. thought I might like to write about Newman as a spiritual director during his catholic years. But, in order to do this, I would have to read twenty-two volumes of Newman's *Letters and Diaries* and discover from his letters how Newman directed others. Twenty-two volumes! I could hardly imagine doing this. However, in the final analysis, this is what I actually ended up doing. My dissertation topic became *John Henry Newman Spiritual Director, 1845–1890*.

N. New Assignment: St. Conrad Friary, 1975

In June, 1975 I received a new assignment. My provincial wanted me to go to St. Conrad Friary in Annapolis, to be the assistant novice master. Besides teaching the novices, he thought this would also give me more time to work on my dissertation. It would be a rather small community of about ten friars. When I received this assignment, I must admit I had some mixed feelings because this was the monastery where I had so much difficulty back in 1962 when I was a novice.

However, I ended up liking this assignment very much. I enjoyed working with the novices and I was able to find the time to continue working on my dissertation. I began reading the twenty-two volumes of Newman's *Letters and Diaries* as well as other books on his life and spirituality. Whenever I read something about how Newman directed someone in their spiritual lives, I would xerox the page and catalogue the material under a variety of topics. Needless to say, this was an extremely tedious project but it allowed me to eventually discover a way to formulate a plan to deal with this vast amount of material.

Working with Fr. F. as my dissertation director proved to be a challenging endeavor. He certainly was a Newman scholar but he was also extremely meticulous about my writing. It was amazing because when I finished a chapter, I would take it to him to review and each time I got it back, it would be filled with his famous red ink pen! Then, I would have to make his corrections and submit it to him again. Sometimes I would have to do this two or three times before he would approve a chapter. And remember, there were no computers in those days, so there was always a lot of work involved in re-typing everything. However, I always remember what Fr. F. told me when I first spoke to him about being my director. Because I had to ultimately defend my dissertation before a board of three professors, he told me that if it got approved by him it would also be accepted by my three examiners. Interestingly enough, this was the way it worked out.

Besides working with the novices and writing my dissertation, several other factors made these enjoyable years for me. The Naval Academy is located in Annapolis, and on Sundays I would often go to a small chapel there to celebrate Mass. This gave me the opportunity to meet families serving in the Navy and Marines, some of whom became life long friends.

Another factor which made these days pleasant for me centered around what is called the Third Order. Most religious orders have opportunities for lay people to incorporate the spirituality of their founder into their lives. In our case, that would be Franciscan spirituality. Individuals who joined the Third Order are called Secular Franciscans or Third Order Franciscans. So, the novice master and I wanted to try and increase the membership of the group that had been coming to St. Conrad's. Since there was a regular group of people coming to Mass on Sundays, we invited people to come to the friary to explore the idea of becoming Secular Franciscans. Because a good number of people came to the meeting to see what was involved, we established a regular schedule of classes to explain some dimensions of Franciscan spirituality to them. This aspect of my life at St. Conrad's was extremely meaningful and life giving to me.

During these years, it became clearer to me that my parents were having a lot of difficulties in their relationship. This became even more obvious when I went home for several days each year. My father had made several bad business decisions and his drinking had become more of a problem. This was painful for me to see them going through this and not really being able to help. Fortunately, I had become friends with a family in the Annapolis area who were always very welcoming to me. Whenever I needed to talk, I usually visited them to share my worries and concerns about my parents. They were always there for me as a wonderful support.

O. Director of Pine Lane Retreat Center: 1977

In 1977, I received another assignment. About a mile from St. Conrad's, my province had a retreat house called Pine Lane. It was on a beautiful piece of property overlooking the Severn River. A wonderful, elderly Capuchin priest had been the director of this retreat house for a number of years. He died suddenly one day and because my province was undecided about whether to keep this retreat house operating, the provincial asked me to go there and be the director until a final decision was made. Even though I had no experience with this kind of ministry, I agreed to do this.

Since I was technically the director of Pine Lane, I didn't actually have to conduct these retreats all the time. Rather, groups of people would schedule the use of this facility and often bring their own priest.

An interesting dimension of this ministry for me was the fact that I lived alone in a very small house behind the retreat house itself. This was a new experience for me and one that I thoroughly enjoyed. Ever since I went to the seminary back in 1957, I had mostly lived with large groups of people. Living by myself and also interacting with the retreatants gave a nice balance to my days. After approximately eight months into this ministry, my province decided to sell this piece of property and so, I was out of a job!

Part Three

Why I Left the Monastery

6

Being in the Wilderness

"Only when we are no longer afraid do we begin to live"

(DOROTHY THOMPSON)

ALTHOUGH I HAD NOT completely finished writing my dissertation, I was asked to return to Capuchin College in Washington, DC in 1978 to resume teaching at the Washington Theological Union. However, this time, rather than being the spiritual director for our students, I was asked to be the assistant superior. Several things happened during these years that had a major impact on me. First of all, I was asked to teach a summer school course on Franciscan spirituality at St. Bonaventure University in Olean, NY. Located in the foothills of the Adirondack Mountains, this was a beautiful area. The Franciscan Institute was located here, and friars from different provinces conducted research projects on Franciscan spirituality at the Institute. Every summer there was a Master's degree program offered that attracted students from all over the United States as well as from several other countries. I was asked to teach a course on Franciscan Spiritual Direction. Teaching here was a wonderful experience for me. Meeting so many Franciscan priests, brothers, and religious sisters was invigorating. We also prayed and ate together which gave me an opportunity to get to know many of the students personally. I enjoyed teaching here in the summer school program for three summers.

Among the students that I met during that summer of 1978 were three Sisters of St. Clare from Ireland. Over the course of the summer, I was able to spend time with them, and I became very fond of one of them, Sr. M. and I thought she also had feelings for me. Sometimes, we would have opportunities to talk and share ideas about our Franciscan way of life as well as her life in Ireland. That was very intriguing to me and as summer school was ending, I told her that I hoped we could stay in touch. She said she would also like to do this too. After she returned to Ireland, we began corresponding with cards and letters because again, there still were no computers or mobile devices. Over the ensuing months, I could tell that my feelings for her were growing and at some level within myself, this raised the whole celibacy issue for me again.

Over the next three years, I had the opportunity of going to Ireland where I had a chance to see Sr. M. The first time, in the spring of 1979, I received permission to travel to Rome to attend an international conference on John Henry Newman, the subject of my doctoral dissertation. On my way, I stopped in Ireland to see her. Then, in the summer of 1980, I was asked to conduct several seminars on Franciscan spirituality in Dublin and during these days, I was also able to visit with her. It had been two years since I first met her at St. Bonaventure and over this period of time, my feelings for her intensified. Finally, in 1981, because I was once again in turmoil about staying in or leaving the monastery, I asked my provincial if I could go to Ireland for several days to visit her. Because he knew I was struggling, he granted my request.

The second major factor that had a profound impact on me during these years was something that happened in our community at Capuchin College. Since I was the assistant superior in the house, the superior and I were charged with the day to day operations of our house of theology, as well as developing programs that would promote the religious, spiritual, and psychological health of everyone. During the spring of 1979, we began to hear rumors from some of the friars that there were a number of students and non-students who were involved in gay activity. Several stories said that some friars were going out very late at night and no one seemed to know why or what they were doing. Others said that homosexual activity was also going on in the monastery. With this kind of information, we called our provincial to let him know what might be going on and especially to ask his advice on how we should handle this issue. After discussing a variety of options with him, he told us to conduct an investigation to try and get at the bottom of this. So, my superior and I began talking with many of the friars about what they knew about these behaviors and activities. After doing this for several weeks, we did discover that there were several friars who were engaging in these gay activities. We reported our findings to the provincial as he requested and he said he would "take it from here."

However, nothing happened. After asking us to conduct this investigation, he didn't do a thing. He never backed us up and never told us why. Of course, the superior and I were "personas non gratis." We were now the bad guys in the community. Although we never divulged any information to anyone except the provincial, we felt like we had stirred up a hornet's nest. We were the ones causing problems in the community because we had obediently done this investigation. There was so much anger at us and tension in the house that it seemed like you could cut through it with a knife.

This experience was definitely extremely painful for me and the worst thing in the community that ever happened to me living in the monastery. And it certainly took its toll on me. Not only was this gay behavior against our vows but the way it divided the community was devastating. Rather than trying to live the Gospel life and our Franciscan spirituality in the community, we were now living in this kind of toxic community atmosphere.

For me, I was personally devastated. This experience certainly "burst my bubble" with regard to living monastic life. I suppose that I was somewhat naive about what to expect or hope for in living in a community, but from now on, I realized how difficult it could be. For some people, it might all look wonderful from the outside but living it from the inside made me question the value of living in a monastery.

The third factor that had a major impact on me during these years was the fact that my father died on July 30, 1980. I can still remember it so well. I was still teaching summer school at St. Bonaventure and conducting final exams, when a friar knocked on my door saying I had an urgent phone call. It was my superior telling me that my father had died. Since it was the day before the end of summer school, I finished giving my exams and started making phone calls to my sister and brother. After discussing some things with them, we decided to meet in North Carolina where my father had been living to make final arrangements for his funeral. My plan was to be the celebrant at his funeral Mass and preach the homily. I was supported and strengthened by the fact that four of my brother priests traveled to North Carolina for the funeral. Things seemed to go smoothly enough until I began preaching. After a few sentences, I broke down completely, and one of the other priests carried on for me as best he could. After this, I was able to get through the rest of the Mass.

These three issues: 1) meeting Sr. M. at St. Bonaventure; 2) the experience of investigating the gay activity in our community; 3) my father's death, threw me once again into emotional turmoil.

A. The Storm Inside Me

Although my parents separated and divorced in the mid 1970s, my father's death was traumatic for me. After he moved to North Carolina, I didn't know exactly where he was living and so I had very little contact with him. It felt like he didn't want any of us to find him or be in contact with him. But over the years, after he had made several bad business decisions, he seemed like a broken man. It was like his own very troubled family life caught up with him and he didn't know how or have the skills to deal with those complicated issues.

After my father's funeral in July 1980, I headed back to Capuchin College to begin teaching once again. Fortunately, by now, I was well known in the Washington Theological Union and had a very good reputation as a teacher. Over the previous five or six years, I had the opportunity to develop a number of courses that were well received by the students and I always had a significant number of theology students signing up for my elective courses.

So, while the intellectual part of my life was feeling successful, my emotional life was in turmoil once again. A couple of months after the semester began in September, I could feel myself spiraling downward. I began to feel pretty much the same way I did in the novitiate before professing my first vows and then three years later my final vows, and again before I was ordained a deacon. Again, I knew I needed help.

But where to get this help? From my teaching, I knew of a Carmelite priest, Fr. P., a psychologist, living in the area. I called him and asked him if I could come and talk with him about becoming my spiritual director. He agreed to see me and I began to talk with him on a weekly basis. It took several months to try and explain to him my struggles over the years as well as the current level of turmoil that I was experiencing. He was a good listener and encouraged me to talk and explore the issues that were difficult for me. With him, I had a sense of freedom. This felt very different than my experience with the psychiatrist I had seen during my years as a theology student. With Fr. P. I never got the feeling that he had any preconceived ideas about me staying in or leaving religious life. I genuinely felt that he only wanted what was best for me.

1) Year's Leave of Absence

After working with Fr. P. on a weekly basis for about four months, he told me that he had received a new assignment from his superiors and that he would be leaving the DC area. This felt like a real loss for me and it was particularly difficult at this time because I was trying to decide whether to take a year's leave of absence. This is the procedure that religious are encouraged to take when they are thinking about leaving but are not sure. What happens is that the person leaves the community for a year, gets a job, and lives on their own. This allows the person to explore life in a different environment while continuing to live their vowed life. Then at the conclusion of this year, the person is better able to make an informed decision.

Before Fr. P. left the area, he told me that he thought taking a year's leave of absence would be beneficial to me. Because I was in such emotional turmoil, he thought this would give me the opportunity to have a different perspective on the issues I was struggling with and to understand myself better since I would be living in a different environment. But since I continued to feel a tremendous amount of guilt and shame about leaving, he wanted to refer me to another psychologist who was a layman and who was supposed to be particularly good with these two issues. He told me that he had worked with this psychologist for a fairly long time and encouraged me to continue my therapy with him. This is how I met Dr. L.

To say the least, Dr. L. was a very interesting character. At the suggestion of Fr. P., I began to see him on a weekly basis. Going to him for counseling for more than a year, was probably the most difficult and at the same time, helpful thing I had to do up to this point. At first, I really didn't like him very much. Talking with him was not like what one might think of a therapist. He was not a "warm, fuzzy" person at all. I used to tell people that he was "tough as nails." Although he, too, was a good listener and gave me time to talk about my issues, he never then hesitated to tell me directly what he thought. He was constantly challenging me and often I would leave his office very upset and angry. But, at the same time, although he had his own approach to counseling, I also had the feeling that, in a strange sort of way, he was good for me—that he was there to help me.

I spent the first several months talking to him about my family and how those dynamics impacted my life. After listening to me share what it was like for me growing up in my family, he felt that those family dynamics were pretty unhealthy. He thought that my father was a very wounded person emotionally because of his own troubled family life and because of this, my dad was unavailable to me emotionally as a child. My father didn't know how to talk about his feelings and consequently, I never learned how to do this either. Nevertheless, I had a need to please him in order to gain his love and approval. Although my father traveled a lot because of his work, I always remember that he used to be home on Fridays and liked watching the Friday night boxing matches on TV. Because I wanted to please him, I would watch this program with him.

Although my mother was a much warmer person by nature than my father, she was also more quiet and reserved. Dr. L. thought she might have been depressed for a fairly long time. With all the difficulties she and my father had around my dad's job changes and subsequent moves, I could understand how this was true. However, because my dad traveled a lot, my mom was always there for us. With her, I will always remember how much she liked the TV shows "I Remember Mama" and "Life is Worth Living." Again, I would try to watch these programs with her.

Dr. L. had an interesting way of understanding and explaining family dynamics. His basic idea was that children in a family are always trying to "get the goodies," as he called them. The "goodies" of course, are the love, approval, and attention of their parents. Kids need this, he thought, in order to grow and mature emotionally and psychologically. In our family, my sister, who is a year and a half older than me, was "daddy's little girl." She certainly had a special place in his heart. In fact, he used to affectionately call her "toots." We used to tease her about this. My brother, who is two years younger than me, tended to be the mischievous child who couldn't sit still for very long. He always got a lot of attention because of this—probably more than he wanted! I was the middle child who somehow fell into what Dr. L. called the "good little boy syndrome." For me, being a good little boy was my way of "getting the goodies" that I needed, the love, approval, and attention of my parents. From a very early age, I somehow learned that if I always did the right thing, always did what pleased others, always tried to be perfect, that other people would think that I was a "good little boy." Of course, while being this way was not always bad, for me it carried over into my teens and young adult years, and significantly impacted my decision to go to the seminary, enter religious life and become a priest.

In one of our sessions, Dr. L. told me that he thought I was one of the angriest people he had ever met. Needless to say, I was stunned by this statement! He clearly thought I had a major problem with anger and went on to explain what he meant. Although this idea was puzzling to me at the time, I gradually came to understand what he meant. Although I knew my father could become very angry, I had always worked hard to control my anger. I was actually afraid to become angry and never learned how to express angry feelings in an appropriate way. At times, when my Dad became very angry, my brother and I would get yelled at. Experiencing this, made me afraid of showing anger, and so I stuffed these feelings because I always thought that in order to "get the goodies" from other people, I always had to appear to be nice. Showing anger would mean that I wasn't a nice person, that I wasn't being perfect. I always felt that I couldn't have people see me this way because then they wouldn't like me very much. Again, the "good little boy syndrome" was hard at work.

Secondly, Dr. L. thought I was very angry at our provincial for not supporting my superior and me after we conducted our investigation into the gay behavior issue in our house of theology. He thought I *should* be very angry at him because of this. It was like we had been betrayed and I had carried around this unresolved anger for three years. So, he wanted me to go and talk to my provincial about this and tell him how I felt. I must say that even the idea of doing this was really scary for me. In my wildest dreams, I couldn't ever imagine doing this. However, after arguing with him about this and voicing my opinion, he nevertheless thought it was very important for me to do this. I can still vividly remember calling my provincial on the phone and asking him if I could come to Pittsburgh to talk with him. He agreed and so we set up a time that fit into his schedule. When I arrived, we took a walk in the courtyard in the middle of the monastery. Even though I was almost shaking in my boots, so to speak, I told him how angry I was at him for not supporting our findings about the gay activity in our house after he told us to investigate this. When I asked him why, I didn't think he really gave me a very good answer. He just said, "I didn't want to rock the boat."

At the time, driving to Pittsburgh and confronting my provincial about this, was probably one of the most difficult things I had ever done. Some people might think that this would not be a big deal, but for me, it was a major accomplishment. And although I strenuously objected to doing this in the beginning, I could understand how important and helpful it was for me to do this in the end.

Thirdly, Dr. L. said he thought I was extremely angry with my community. I certainly knew he was right about this. Maybe more importantly, I really didn't know how to react to this. In the monastery, we had always been taught to "love one another," and to forgive any offenses you might experience with regard to your brothers in the community. But this was certainly easier said than done. Living on a daily basis with guys who were angry at me was very difficult. Once again, I just stuffed these feelings because I didn't know what to do about them or how to appropriately express them. Stuffing angry feelings over a period of time, usually leads to depression which I knew I was feeling at this time.

Fourthly, Dr. L. thought that I was angry at myself because of my inability over the past years to decide on whether to stay in or leave religious life. At the time, I wasn't sure how accurate this was, but I was hoping that I would gain more clarity about this as we continued to work together.

One of the major reasons that Fr. P., the Carmelite priest who had been my spiritual director, wanted me to work with Dr. L. was because he was reported to be very good assisting clients with issues of guilt and shame. These two emotions had tied me into knots ever since I was in the novitiate—seventeen years earlier. After discussing these issues with Dr. L. for about seven months, I came to better understand why they were so problematic for me. Dr. L. thought these two issues were such a problem for me because of my psychological make up which was also reinforced by the "culture of religious life" and the Catholic Church. For me, this over-riding, deep seated need I had to always please others, to be perfect, and to always have people think the best about me, wouldn't let me pay attention to what I really wanted to do in life. And whenever I even tried to consider what I might want to do, these feelings of guilt and shame would overwhelm me and then I would "shut down" because of how uncomfortable I would feel. So, I tried to just bury these thoughts and feelings about leaving as a way of protecting myself.

Then, following on the heels of this essential way of perceiving myself came the "culture of the Catholic Church and religious life" in the 1950s and 1960s. The idea that the priesthood and religious life were put on such a high pedestal as being the best vocation in life, that only a few were "chosen" and that this was the best way of "saving your soul" and getting into heaven reinforced my need to stay.

Because of these dynamics, Dr. L. thought I had been trapped emotionally—for years. Later on, he told me that when I first came to see him, I was in "pretty bad shape" and came close to a mental breakdown. He thought that this kind of emotional entrapment kept me constantly in emotional turmoil through the years. Dr. L. was never one to "pull his punches," so to speak, and always told me *directly* what he thought was going on. In my case, he thought I should have left a long time ago. In fact, he thought I should have never gone to the seminary or entered religious life in the first place, and that I certainly should have left in the novitiate. In addition, although it was pretty much unknown to me at the time, he thought I entered religious life because of my deep seated need to please others.

Dr. L. also told me that he thought all of these interior dynamics were the cause of my depression that I had struggled with for years. He felt that in my striving to live my religious life as best I could, that I was like trying to stuff a square peg into a round hole. He believed that the daily strain of living religious life kept me in constant emotional turmoil. Essentially, Dr. L. told me that he thought I never had the emotional or psychological freedom to truly make a free choice.

A final topic that we discussed at length was the issue of celibacy. Dr. L. felt that meeting Sr. M. at St. Bonaventure University was the catalyst that brought all of my issues to the surface again. She was, he thought, someone who concretized for me what another way of life might look like. Although at this point, we had never talked about leaving and getting married or anything like that, Dr. L. thought that developing a friendship with her allowed me to experience emotionally what another way of life might feel like.

In the spring of 1982, I began to seriously consider taking a year's leave of absence. After discussing my issues for the last three years with Fr. P. and Dr. L. as well as constantly praying about all of this, I began to allow myself the freedom to at least consider this option. Now that I had what I thought was a better understanding of my issues, I began thinking about finding a place to live and getting a job if I left. I knew from talking to other guys who had left, that my province wasn't going to help with very much financial support.

One of the organizations in the church that I had been involved with was called the Teams of Our Lady. This was a group of married lay people who were dedicated to growing spiritually as married couples. Each team was comprised of six couples and a chaplain who was a priest. We would meet once a month at one of the couple's homes for Mass, dinner, and then a discussion about a specific topic on married spirituality. I had been the chaplain to my Team for about six years and we knew each other very well. In the spring of 1982, I shared with them my struggles and the fact that I was seriously thinking about taking a year's leave of absence. They were basically very supportive. I asked them for help in finding a place to live and getting a job. About a week later, I received a phone call from one of the couples saying that I could stay with them. They had a room in their basement that I could use until I could afford a place on my own. This answered the first question I had about finding a place to live.

Next question on my agenda in order to be able to leave, was how to find a job. Along with putting the word out to friends, I also began looking for jobs in the "want ads" section of the local newspaper. One day, amazingly enough, I saw an advertisement for a job as a personnel director at a large construction company in the DC area. If anyone was interested, they were directed to call the president of the company. When I looked at his name, I realized that I knew him. About ten years before this, he and his wife belonged to another Teams of Our Lady group that I was also the chaplain for. Although I hadn't seen him in about eight years, I decided to call him. Fortunately, he remembered me and invited me to his office for lunch and an interview. Long story short, he offered me the job about ten days later. Of course, I accepted this position, and actually felt like the Lord was leading me and guiding me through this difficult process. Providentially, I believe the Lord led me to look at that advertisement in the newspaper that day and get this job. So, my second basic question had now been answered.

After finding a place to live and getting a job, I finally made my decision to take a year's leave of absence. I decided to do this during the Memorial Day weekend in May after the semester ended. So, I called my provincial and informed him of my decision. Although he was verbally supportive, I could tell from his voice that my decision saddened him. However, he didn't offer me any monetary support and I decided not to ask him for anything since I already had a job. But later on, I regretted this because some kind of monetary assistance would have been very helpful.

As I began packing my things and preparing to leave, I felt overwhelmed with all kinds of questions and emotions. On the one hand, I knew the time had come for me to leave because I realized that I just couldn't do this anymore. And yet there was a sense of regret in me, a kind of sadness at leaving a way of life that had been an essential part of my life for over twenty-five years. And, as difficult as some of these years had been for me, they were nevertheless formative years, enabling me to become the person I was.

Probably the most dominant and consistent feeling I was experiencing as I was packing to leave the monastery was fear. Fear of the unknown. While I knew I had received a very good education and was a good teacher and preacher, I couldn't help but wonder if these assets could be transferred into the secular world. And if they could, how could I best do that? I had lived in the monastery for so long, I wondered if I could make these kinds of changes in a healthy way. Along with these emotions and questions, there was this inevitable, nagging question as to whether I was doing the right thing.

On the other hand, I also felt a sense of relief because I had finally made this decision which had been so difficult for me. There was also a sense of anticipation and excitement as I left. I realized that there would be many new challenges that I had to face and perhaps new difficulties, but I was hopeful that I could handle these in a positive way.

As the day for me to leave the monastery approached, my plan was to pack the monastery car quickly and have one of the friars drive me to my brother's home over the Memorial Day weekend. He lived about fifteen miles from the monastery and I thought it would be important and helpful to me if I could be around his family for several days. I knew their love and support would be good for me before I moved my things to the home of the couple who had offered me a room.

B. Life After Leaving the Monastery—Early Years

After a relaxing Memorial Day weekend at my brother's home, I moved the few belongings that I had to Arlington, Virginia to take up residence with the couple that had graciously offered me a room. When you live in a monastery for as long as I did, with a vow of poverty, you don't accumulate very many things so the actual move was easy. I quickly discovered that there were so many things to learn about every day living "in the world." I was forty years old at the time, and never had a bank account, never wrote a check, never had much money in my pocket, never even bought ordinary household items, and certainly never bought a car.

Maybe the most challenging and necessary thing for me to do quickly was to buy a car because I had to shortly begin my job. But I had no credit and no history of buying anything. When I told the car salesman this, he looked at me in amazement! Fortunately, the husband of the couple I was staying with offered to co-sign a loan for me to buy a car, so that was very kind of him and helpful to me.

Living life outside the monastery walls was challenging for me in many ways. For years, I lived by a pre-planned schedule. The events of every day were centered around community prayer times as well as many community activities. Now, I was on my own. My time was my own. And while this felt freeing on the one hand, it also required me to balance my time living in the world. For anyone who has never lived in a monastery or any other enclosed lifestyle, this might not seem like a big deal, but to me after living for twenty-five years in the monastery, it required a new way of thinking and a substantial adjustment.

My new job as the personnel director for this large construction company involved a steep learning curve. Not only did I have to learn about the company, but more importantly, what were the responsibilities of the personnel director. I found that the people working there were encouraging and helpful to me. In fact, somehow the word had gotten around about my background, and many of my fellow workers found this very intriguing. We had many interesting conversations about what it was like to live in a monastery. But, more importantly, several vice presidents of the company took me out to lunch and explained what they thought about the role of the personnel director and what they expected from me. This, along with the conversation I had with the president of the company when I came for my interview, helped to orient me in the right direction.

After I left the monastery, I continued in therapy on a weekly basis with Dr. L. And although the province gave me no financial help when I left, they did agree to continue paying for my therapy for which I was grateful. For a while, I went to therapy twice a week, once for individual counseling and the other for group counseling. Both of these were helpful to me in adjusting to life outside the monastery.

The men in my group counseling sessions as well as Dr. L. encouraged me to begin dating. I really didn't have much desire to do this because I wanted to wait and see what Sr. M. was going to do. I knew how much I cared for her, and I wanted to give this relationship a chance. However, they thought it was better for me not to "put all my eggs in one basket" so to speak, and that beginning to date someone now would be healthy for me. After arguing with them and Dr. L. for several weeks about this, I decided to take their advice.

After working for several weeks as the personnel director, I discovered that the company had a Toastmaster's group. This group of people are interested in, and dedicated to, developing a person's public speaking skills. Each week, members of the group took turns writing and delivering a talk that would be critiqued by the other members. In this group, there was a lady that I found attractive and I decided to ask her to go out to dinner. It was a nice evening. But I must admit that I felt somewhat awkward. However, since this was a first date, our conversation flowed rather smoothly as we talked mostly about our family histories and work experience. Although it was a pleasant evening, I didn't pursue this relationship.

My group counseling colleagues continued to encourage me to date more than one person in order to gain more experience. So, mostly in order to appease them and get them off my back about dating, I asked another woman to go skiing. However, she turned me down. Now I thought I would at least wait for Sr. M. to make her decision.

During this time Sr. M. and I continued corresponding with each other. She was having her own struggles in religious life and had been thinking about taking a year's leave of absence, but I also knew that this had to be her own decision. In my heart, I knew how much I cared for her and was hoping that she would take this leave of absence so that we could freely test our relationship to see if there was a future for us to be together. She too was very conflicted about taking this step but decided to do so in mid 1982. First, she went to England to work in a college library and then decided to come to the United States in the spring of 1983. While I was very happy that she decided to take this step, I also knew that this decision was immensely difficult for her. It meant leaving her family, her religious community, her country, and everything that was familiar to her. Although her father had died in 1962, she was still leaving her mother and eight siblings, as well as extended family and friends. This was truly a momentous step for her and one for which I was truly grateful.

After living for many months in the basement room of my friend's home, I moved into my own apartment. This also was completely new to me. It was the first time I had ever completely lived on my own. Besides the effort it took to furnish this new place, it also required another period of adjustment. On the one hand, I was happy to have my own place, but I also got pretty lonely at times. At this point, I had very few friends that I could do things with, and spent many lonely days on my own. Gradually, I became more accustomed to my new life style and actually felt that learning how to be by myself in the monastery helped me to deal with these lonely feelings.

When Sr. M. decided to come to the States in Spring 1983, fortunately she was able to stay with the same friends who had given me a room after I left the monastery. I had already moved into my apartment the previous summer. My friends graciously welcomed her. In addition, several of the couples who were in my Teams of Our Lady group, needed assistance taking care of their small children and they asked Sr. M. if she would be interested in doing this. Since she needed a job, she accepted their invitation. This was her first work experience in the United States.

After Margaret settled into her new surroundings in the U.S., we began to see each other regularly. This was an extremely happy time for me. I grew to love her deeply and I knew she felt the same way about me. One day, during one of my therapy sessions with Dr. L., he surprised me and said he would like to meet her. I wasn't sure exactly why he wanted to do this, but after asking Margaret and she agreed, we went to several sessions together. I think he wanted to see us together, to see how our personalities meshed and to see how we interacted with each other.

We decided to get married in late December 1983. The event was a small gathering of people but one that was very meaningful to us. After the ceremony, we had a reception at the home of one of our friends, and for our honeymoon we spent a few days at a friend's condominium in Bethany Beach, Delaware.

In January 1984, Margaret interviewed and was hired at a large Pension Fund where my friend was the Administrator. She stayed with this company for thirty–one years! During her employment with this company, she received numerous promotions and eventually became Assistant to the administrator. She excelled at this company and loved her work. We always felt that the Lord was guiding her in finding this position so many years ago.

1985 was a year I wanted to forget. First of all, I was 'let-go' from my job as personnel director at the construction company. I can still vividly remember this. It actually happened on Good Friday. I was called into one of the vice president's office who told me I was being "let go" because the company was downsizing. Whether that was true or not I didn't know. All I know is that day was my own Good Friday experience. Driving home that day, I worried about telling Margaret because we had just purchased our first house. It was a small townhouse but one that we could call our own. Furthermore, I wondered what I would do now. When I shared this news with Margaret, she was very understanding and she tried to comfort me and calm my fears.

1) Andrew

The most devastating thing in our lives occurred on August 30, 1985. Our son, Andrew, was stillborn. And Margaret almost died too. It was exactly one week before her due date and she was in the shower getting ready for work. All of a sudden she called out to me because she was bleeding. I rushed in and brought her back to lay down on the bed and immediately called 911. The ambulance came quickly and rushed her to the hospital with me right behind them. They immediately took her to the emergency room where the doctor performed a sonogram. He told us he could only hear one heart beat. When I asked him if that meant that our baby had died, he just shook his head and said yes. Both of us were in shock! Both of us were devastated. The doctor told us that he thought Margaret had developed a condition called acute pre-eclampsia where the placenta breaks away from the uterine wall, cutting off the supply of oxygen to the baby.

But not only did we lose our son, Andrew, Margaret was seriously ill and in critical condition herself. When all of this was happening, the emergency room physician had a nurse call her regular obstetrician who quickly came to the hospital. They couldn't stop the bleeding and so her obstetrician immediately called a physician at Johns Hopkins Hospital in Baltimore for a consultation. Together, they worked on developing a plan. But in the meantime, we were told that Margaret still had to give birth to Andrew even though he had died. I couldn't believe that she had to go through the agony of childbirth after the baby died, and when she was seriously ill herself. I thought they might do a C-section because maybe this would have been quicker. In any case, the doctors gave her a medicine called pitocin to induce labor and speed up her contractions. It was sheer agony for her and for me watching her and holding her hand while she went through this birthing process. Finally, after Andrew was born, they laid him on Margaret's chest for a few minutes so she could see him. Then, the nurse handed him to me and I just sat down in a chair with him and cried like a baby. They didn't rush me. I held him close to me for a long time. There he was fully formed and developed. But I was still in shock. I couldn't believe what happened that morning.

Eventually, one of the nurses came to me and ask if she could take him from me. Reluctantly, I gave him to her and tried to focus again on Margaret. They were giving her blood and trying to stabilize her. It was "touch and go" throughout that day with her obstetrician and the blood specialist physician working together. At the end of the day, they admitted her to the ICU unit of the hospital where they could monitor her very closely. Because she remained in critical condition, she stayed there for several days before being transferred to a regular room. Altogether, they gave her twenty-one units of blood and blood plasma. She remained in the hospital for nine days.

The following days were almost a complete blur for me. I felt like a robot just going through the motions. Most of my time was spent at the hospital with Margaret. But we still had to bury Andrew. I could hardly even think about that. Fortunately, one of our friends made some arrangements and contacted our parish priest who put together a short grave side ceremony. By this time, the news had gotten around to some of our friends and several of them showed up at the cemetery for the service. All I can remember is walking over to the hearse, picking up Andrew's body in the small white coffin, and carrying him down the hill to his place of burial. There, we had the brief funeral ceremony. But because Margaret was still so ill, the plan was for several of her women friends to have a prayer service in her hospital room at the same time, so that she could be a part of the service in this way.

This has always been the saddest day of my life. She was just a week away from her due date. All of our hopes and dreams came crashing down on us. I was so angry I just wanted to scream—at God, at somebody—at anything. But I needed to be there for Margaret. Gradually, after being in the hospital for nine days, she was allowed to come home. For the next week, we simply tried to be there for each other and began to mourn the loss of our son.

One of Margaret's wonderful, compassionate nurses at her obstetrician's office encouraged us to attend a meeting of Compassionate Friends. This organization was founded to help people who have lost a family member, begin the healing process. Margaret and I went to several meetings and found it helpful to share our story while listening to others. In the following years, after I became a psychotherapist, bereavement counseling became a focus of my practice. I gave many talks at gatherings and conferences of our local chapter of Bereaved Parents USA, to try and help others who had also lost a child. More recently, in 2014, I wrote a book called *Don't Be a Waster of Sorrows,* to help others and also to continue my own healing process.

I don't think I have ever gotten over Andrew's death. Although both of us have mourned his loss, there is a part of us that died that day with him. In an interesting way, several things remind me of him instantly, even after all these years. Maybe, this is my mind trying to hang on to him; maybe this is my way of never letting go of him; maybe this is my mind playing tricks on me. No matter. Hearing certain songs, seeing the name Andrew, and butterflies are all very meaningful to me. It has been amazing to me how often over the years, and under all kinds of circumstances and situations, how I have seen a butterfly pass by and sometimes stop. It's like my way of staying in touch with him.

Margaret and I were hoping to have a large family—perhaps four or five children. But, that was not meant to be. Between the years of 1986–89, she had two miscarriages which were also difficult to accept. However, our daughter Colleen was born in September, 1990 and we were thrilled. Margaret was forty–one at the time and we were afraid to try and have more children because of possible pregnancy and genetic problems. And although we were older parents, we felt very blessed to have our daughter. She has been a delight to us through the years.

Emotionally, loosing Andrew threw me into another period of depression. I was extremely angry at God and constantly asked why this had to happen. And, although I knew there were no answers to this question, there was a part of me that felt like God was punishing me for leaving the monastery and the priesthood. It was like in my head, I knew this wasn't the case, but in my heart I felt that it was. It took me quite a while after his death to get past this way of thinking and feeling and to work my way out of this depression. Even to this day, I still sometimes struggle with this feeling.

Losing my job and losing Andrew made 1985 extremely difficult for us. Eventually, Margaret felt like she wanted to go back to work. For me, after I lost my job in April, 1985, I had to find a job. At the time, I didn't really know what I wanted to do. So, I began to do some networking and talking to friends to see if they might have any leads to help me find a job.

It also gave me some time to think about how I could best use my gifts and talents. In the monastery, I had always done a lot of spiritual direction and counseling. I liked this kind of work and decided to look into this type of career. One day, a friend called and said he knew a person in Virginia who had his own counseling center. My friend encouraged me to call and talk with this gentleman. So, I did this and discovered that he was a licensed professional counselor. Towards the end of our conversation, I asked him about the requirements for obtaining this kind of license. He outlined for me what was necessary and encouraged me to look into this. He also said that if I could become licensed, he would offer me a position at his counseling center. Armed with this information, I contacted the Virginia state board of professional counselors and I discovered that I had already taken the number of required courses and fulfilled their internship requirements. All I needed to do was to pass the state's licensing exam. Long story short—I passed the exam and began my career as a professional counselor in Virginia.

I enjoyed this work very much but it was a sixty mile round trip commute each day. We lived in Maryland and Margaret's job was in Maryland, so I began to think about how I might begin my own counseling practice near our home in Maryland. As I looked into this possibility, I quickly discovered that Maryland did not license professional counselors, so I was stuck unless I went back to graduate school, got another degree, and then obtained a Maryland license. This was even difficult to think about because I already had five graduate degrees and couldn't see myself studying for another one. It seemed like I had spent half of my life in school! Without having made a firm decision at this point, I continued working in Virginia, commuting daily, praying for guidance, and continuing to discuss this situation with Margaret.

One aspect that added to my uncertainty was the fact that I knew very well how incredibly difficult it would be to try and develop a counseling center practice in a totally new environment. How would I become known in the area? How would I get clients? Did we have money for renting an office and furnishing it? Could I develop a referral base? Having discussed these issues with several people who already had established practices, I realized it would be a daunting task. Nevertheless, I thought I wanted to be my own boss and have my own counseling center.

When I was in the monastery at St. Conrad's near Annapolis, I had developed a network of friends who mostly came to our monastery for Mass on Sundays. Among these people was a friend who was also a pediatrician who had his own practice. One day, I decided to talk with him about my thinking on this issue and while he confirmed my fears about the difficulties involved in starting my own practice, he also said that he would try to help me by referring clients to me. This was very encouraging to me and gave me a renewed sense of hope.

While all of this was going on, I began checking out the requirements for licensure in the state of Maryland. This was extremely important because not only was it required by law but it was also necessary to qualify for payment from insurance companies. I discovered that the quickest way to become licensed in Maryland was to get a master's degree in social work and specialize in the clinical tract which focuses on becoming a therapist rather than doing strictly social work. So, this meant going back to school. Again! As I was pondering this decision, which was very distasteful to me, I realized there was really no other way if I wanted to eventually open a practice in Maryland. Reluctantly, I realized that I had to bite the bullet and do this.

Part of the registration process in the school of social work at the University of Maryland, was to submit my transcripts of the courses that I had already taken in my other graduate degree programs. Fortunately, they accepted some of my courses which reduced the amount of time it would take me to finish this program. I was pleased about this and eventually became licensed in Maryland.

After passing the state licensing exam, I began to search for an office to rent. Through another contact, I found a doctor who was trying to rent out his office on a part time basis. I will always remember that I began renting this office for a half day on Friday afternoons and gradually increased my time as I acquired more clients. During this process, I developed a brochure detailing my practice objectives and created business cards and began calling on doctors' and dentists' offices to introduce myself. I mention this because this was extremely difficult for me to do, because basically I am a rather introspective and quiet person. But I had to push myself to do this if I wanted to get my practice off the ground. At the same time, I also tried to get my face in front of as many people as I could by giving talks on a variety of topics and conducting seminars on personality growth and spiritual development. After doing these things for about eighteen months, I was able to finish with my clients in Virginia and spend all of my time at my practice in Maryland. I felt very fortunate in being able to accomplish this and eventually I was able to hire four other therapists to work for me.

Becoming a psychotherapist was a great career choice for me. I think that it helped to satisfy my desire to try and help people. This was one of the major reasons I entered the monastery and became a priest. Counseling opened a path for me to utilize my personality and the skills that I had acquired in the monastery and transfer them to the secular world. In addition, another part of my career involved becoming an adjunct professor at the Washington Theological Union where I had previously taught while I was still in the monastery and also in the graduate school of the pastoral counseling program at Loyola University in Baltimore. Finally, one other dimension of my counseling career involved being the school counselor at our parish elementary and middle school for seventeen years. I would spend one day a week at the school and I also enjoyed this work very much.

2) Writing for My Dispensation

When I left the monastery in 1982, I had every intention of remaining in the Catholic Church. So did Margaret. Although there were things I would like to see changed, I realized the church had been an integral part of my life for years, and I knew that I just didn't want to throw that away. However, what the church made me go through in order to get my dispensation from my vows and the obligations of the priesthood, was enough to test anyone's faith. For me, it was truly an onerous process. In fact, I knew several guys who had left the monastery and refused to seek a dispensation because it was so tedious and degrading. The process was also extremely painful emotionally. I had to drag back up to consciousness so many difficult events and memories, that I found myself asking if this was really worth it.

To my mind, it never had to be so difficult and painful. As I was going through the many steps, it felt like the church was punishing me for leaving and they were determined to make this as difficult as possible. It began with a basic questionnaire I had to complete, with all kinds of personality issues and family issues that I had to write about. Then, they needed someone in the monastery who knew me well to fill out another lengthly questionnaire as to how they saw me in religious life and stating why this person thought I had valid reasons for leaving. Thirdly, I had to ask my psychologist to write another lengthly document to get his opinion of me psychologically and emotionally. Fortunately, Dr. L. was willing to do this which I think helped a lot. Then, my original questionnaire was returned to me asking for more clarification about certain issues along with a request for more information. There seemed to be no end to it. They made me jump through so many hoops! This whole process took months and I became very angry.

Why did the church have to treat me this way? For just wanting to leave this way of life and begin another one. I remember one of the questions asked if my leaving was going to cause scandal to anyone? Can you imagine this type of question today after all the scandals caused by gay priests engaging in homosexual activity? And what about the scandal caused by hundreds of pedophile priests abusing thousands of children and teenagers? And what about the scandal of bishops trying to cover up this behavior? Moving guys like this around from parish to parish knowing that they were pedophiles. And what about the scandals in the hierarchy with a person like ex-cardinal Theodore McCarrick, Archbishop of Washington, DC? What kind of harm did these guys do? What about their scandal? And all I wanted was to leave religious life in an honorable way and get my dispensation. To my mind, what they put me through was so unnecessary.

Part Four

What I Learned from Living in the Monastery

7

Finding My Way Home

> "Midway this way of life we're bound upon,
> I woke to find myself in a dark wood,
> Where the right road was wholly lost and gone . . .
> It is so bitter it goes nigh to death."
>
> (DANTE)

I LEFT THE MONASTERY thirty–eight years ago. Since then, I have had time to reflect on and learn from my experiences of living in the monastery for twenty-five years. For me, leaving the priesthood and religious life was the most painful and difficult decision I ever had to make. In recounting my story about what I went through to make this decision, I hope to create a path for others to find freedom. My hope is that my struggle will be helpful to others who are also struggling to make important decisions in their lives. After all these years, I now have a better perspective and understanding of what I went through and why I struggled so much.

For me, I have learned that it is one thing to leave a place, like the monastery, but it is quite another to "let go" of a way of life. Because I entered the high school seminary at such a young age, when I was fifteen, I had been formed in certain ways of thinking, feeling, and living life that are not easily changed. In some ways, I have continued to struggle with these ideas through the years.

The one thing I knew when I left the monastery in 1982, was that I didn't want to leave an angry and bitter person. I had lived with enough men in the monastery who were unhappy, depressed, and angry and I knew for sure that I didn't want to end up like this. Similarly, I also knew other men who had left and were very bitter about the Catholic Church and religious life and I knew I didn't want to be like this when I left. But I had to work at this. There were plenty of reasons why I could have been angry and upset about a variety of things, but I knew that these kinds of feelings would just eat away at me if I let them. Consequently, I needed to resolve these issues and feelings before I left.

A. Coming Home to Myself

Famous author and holocaust survivor Elie Wiesel describes a very poignant conversation in his book *Night*. One day when he was twelve years old, Elie asked his father to find him a master who could guide him in his studies of the Kabbala. His father told Elie that he was much too young to be studying the Kabbala. So, Elie found his own master—Moche the Beadle, an old man who lived humbly and was very poor. One day, when Moche saw Elie praying, he asked him, "why do you pray?" Somewhat surprised by the question, Elie quickly answered, "I don't really know why I pray." However, after that initial question, Elie and Moche would often get together to talk about their Jewish faith. During their conversations, Moche explained that every question possessed a power that did not lie in the answer. "Man raises himself toward God by the questions he asks Him," Moche was fond of saying. "This is true dialogue. Man questions God and God answers. But we don't understand his answers. We can't understand them. Because they come from the depths of the soul, and they stay there until death. You will find the true answers, Eliezer, only within yourself." Then Elie asked Moche, "and why do you pray?" He replied, "I pray to the God within me that He will give me the strength to ask Him the right questions about life."[1]

Although I read this statement over thirty-five years ago, it is still something that I have never forgotten. Moche wasn't praying for any particular need or person, but only for the strength to ask the right questions about life. He knew that if Elie did this, he would find his own answers within himself.

---

1. Wiesel, *Night*, 13–14.

The first thing I have learned from my years in the monastery is the importance of asking the right questions in life. Why? Because our questions give direction to our lives. They influence the choices that we make in life. This was certainly true for me in going to the seminary. When I went to the high school seminary at age fifteen, my "right question" that I was asking myself was what does God want me to do with my life? Closely aligned with this question was how can I best love and serve him and at the same time save my soul and go to heaven while avoiding going to hell? Because I was a young teenager at the time and was struggling with many developmental, personal, religious, and family issues, I believed that God was inviting me to be a priest. But was this really the right question for me at the time? Only time would tell.

However, what I didn't understand very well at age fifteen, is that there are various seasons to our lives. Because I wasn't old enough to have very much life experience, I didn't understand the developmental process by which we change, grow, and mature. And, these healthy changes can have huge implications for the questions we ask and the choices we make.

B. A Second Journey

The human soul is like a fine wine that needs to ferment in various barrels as it ages and mellows. The wisdom for this is written everywhere, in nature, in scripture, in spiritual traditions, and in what is best in human science. And that wisdom is generally learned in the crucible of struggle. Growing up and maturing is precisely a process of fermentation. It does not happen easily and without effort.

1) No Short Cuts

What I have come to understand is that maturation is a lifelong journey with different phases, human and spiritual. It has many challenges and setbacks and there are no short cuts. We can struggle with different forces at various times in our lives. However, we are always struggling and doing battle with something, but the forces that we struggle with bring us change with the years.

On reflection, I have learned how important it is to ask the right questions in life but to also realize that as we change, grow, mature, and gain more life experience, our questions can also change. But because

I didn't understand all of these human dynamics at the age of fifteen, I found myself stuck and tied up in knots. So, the right question that I needed to ask myself became how could I understand myself and the human journey I was traveling?

In the summer of 1976, I began to prepare a new course I was going to offer in the Washington Theological Union. The course was *An Introduction to Christian Spirituality.* I had been thinking about developing this kind of course for several years because a survey was done among the students and they were asking for this kind of basic course in spirituality. However, in order to teach this course, I had to study extensively and read several authors on developmental psychology and Christian spirituality. As I was studying several developmental psychologists, I discovered that the works of Carl Jung were very helpful. And, from a more contemporary perspective, I found Daniel Levinson's book *The Seasons of a Man's Life* and Eric Erickson's *Childhood and Society* to be very helpful. Among the classic Christian spirituality authors I studied were the writings of St. John of the Cross and St. Teresa of Avila. Several contemporary authors such as Thomas Merton and psychiatrist Gerald May were also very enlightening.

My idea in developing this course was to try and understand how we grow and mature as a person psychologically and then to see how this developmental process impacts our growth spiritually. When I taught this course for the first time in the spring of 1977, it was very well received by the students and proved very helpful to me. For the first time, I began to clearly understand the various stages of our lives and the changes that we go through as we develop psychologically and how these changes affect the growth of our spiritual lives.

Then, in the spring of 1978, I got the invitation to teach in the summer school program at St. Bonaventure University where I met Margaret. These three things had a huge impact on me and they ushered in a third vocational crisis.

2) Crisis as Opportunity

Up until this time, I had always understood my difficulties in religious life as a negative thing which always heightened my level of anxiety. Basically, I was afraid to even allow myself to think or pray about staying in or leaving religious life. Whenever, I tried to do this, I would immediately shut down and not allow myself to go there because it became so un-comfortable. Actually, the fear and anxiety became so great that I only allowed myself to ask the question about what I had to do in order for me to stay in the monastery. What haven't I done yet? What else could I do? There was like this voice inside of me constantly saying "you have to stay, you haven't tried hard enough." However, what these questions did to me was to completely shut me down emotionally. I couldn't allow myself to even think about leaving because I thought this was always go-ing against what God wanted from me. Consequently, as I was growing and maturing through my young adult years, I continued to be conflicted emotionally. Somehow, it never dawned on me to look upon my crisis as a positive thing.

3) Orphaned Voices

Around midlife, many people undergo what is called a "second journey." Because of the tremendous upheavals that a person experiences at this time in their lives, a second journey gives people the opportunity to evalu-ate and reflect on their lives and then to possibly make some changes or adjustments where this might be called for. I wondered if my midlife issues would lead me into a second journey, and if so, where it might take me.

Gradually, I began to entertain the overwhelming "right question" confronting me. It seems as though I had been circling around it for a long time, but now it felt as though I had walked right into the middle of it. For me, it was a dangerous thing to do because entering the heart of this type of question usually means, as Rilke once told his friend Kappus, "living on into the answer."

Author Christine Painter said that "while we must venture far to find our "true self," it is also always with us."[2] With this idea in mind, I began to ask myself if I was being invited to enter a new passage in the spiritual life—the journey from my false self to my true self? In some way, these were the same thoughts, feelings, and questions I had experienced in the novitiate before I took my first vows and after my first year of theology before my final vows. At the time, it was difficult for me to understand these issues and so, I mostly buried them. Now, I knew I had to deal with them. To embark on this task is dangerous because, depending on how

2. www.goodreads.com/christine/painter/the-soul-s-slow-ripening.

it is navigated, it can radically affect one's alignment with oneself, with God, and with the world.

As I reflected back on this period in my life, I came to understand the importance and meaning of the "second journey." Seeing my issues in this way helped me to understand that my crisis was an opportunity to calmly look at my life and to possibly make some changes where they might be needed. It gave me a chance to possibly re-direct my life.

4) Whittling Away

There is an old Carolina story I like about a country boy who had a great talent for carving beautiful dogs out of wood. Every day, he sat on his porch whittling, letting the shavings fall around him. One day a visitor, greatly impressed, asked him the secret of his art. "I just take a block of wood and whittle off the parts that don't look like a dog," he replied.

In down home language, this story describes the movement of growth I'm referring to. With all the love and discernment we can muster, we gently try to whittle away the parts of ourselves that don't resemble the True Self. However, in "spiritual whittling," we don't simply discard the shavings. Transformation happens not by rejecting these parts of ourselves but by gathering them up and integrating them. Through this process, we can reach a new wholeness.

For the last seven years, I had been studying the writings of Thomas Merton, so that I could teach a course on his understanding of theology and spirituality. Merton envisioned much of the spiritual life as whittling away our false self in order to become our True Self. He called the struggle for authenticity a "contemplative crisis" and insisted that no one can avoid it, that eventually we all "get the treatment." According to Merton, "one's actual self may be far from "real," since it may be profoundly alienated from one's own deep spiritual identity. To reach one's "real self" one must, in fact, be delivered from the illusory and "false self" whom we have created."[3] With the help and encouragement of Dr. L., I began to seriously look at the illusions and false selves I had created. How could I whittle these away? Again, Merton said, "we are not very good at recognizing illusions, least of all the ones we cherish about ourselves."[4] Gradually, I took time to probe and reflect. Bit by bit, I encountered

3. Merton, *The New Man*, 63.

4. Merton, *New Seeds of Contemplation*, 34.

patterns of falseness, wounds, and cherished illusions that came together to form my false selves.

C. Naming My False Selves

In her book, *The Soul's Ripening,* Christine Painter also said that "we can only become something new when we have released the old faces we have been wearing, even if it means not knowing quite who we are in the space in between."[5] My "second journey" involved confronting these hardened patterns that I had spent a lifetime creating. These are the patterns that oppose the life of the spirit and obscure our true spiritual identity. Overcoming them means allowing God to transform even our most prized illusions about ourselves.

As this inner picture of what happens deep inside us came together for me, I realized that a major pitfall of human life was believing that these rigid ego patterns or masks are who we really are, and that there is nothing beyond the ingrained patterns we live out every day. I wondered if this was what I had done? Had my masks gotten stuck to my face?

As these insights began to sink in over time, I began to see how these false selves and the identity of the True Self wrestle for primacy in the human personality. Furthermore, in order for the ego to relinquish its control position, my hardened structures had to be cracked open. If I could do this, then this process could open a way for the gradual shift of centers from the ruling needs of the ego toward my True Self, or the core of God within me.

Most of us may like to think that we are individuals living out our own unique truth, but really, more often we are people who have been formed by family, society, church, job, friends, and traditions. All of these entities have a part to play in our development but sometimes our life becomes a matter of simply playing out the various roles for which we have been programmed. We need our outer roles and identities, of course, but we also need to live them *authentically,* in ways that are true to our own unique and inner self. When we live exclusively out of the expectations thrust on us from the outside, rather than living from the truth emerging from within, we become trapped by our false selves.

Existentialist philosopher Soren Kierkegaard wrote that the "ultimate thing" is "whether you yourself are conscious of that most intimate

5. Painter, *The Soul's Ripening,* 35.

relation to yourself as an individual."[6] This "ultimate" recognition is a necessary part of growing up. And at some point, if we are to continue to grow, we must begin to differentiate ourselves from the roles we play. Often, we do this "when the roles that felt good initially now feel empty," notes author Carol Pearson.[7] As I was working my way through the difficult days of trying to decide whether to stay in the monastery or leave, I remember feeling that a lot of my roles were feeling empty. Slowly, as I probed my life, I began to see how much of me was embedded in my false selves.

During the final months of 1981 and leading into 1982, I began a process of "naming" and "owning" my false selves. It was a very painful time for me because it required many weeks of looking within and reflecting on my life with a kind of brutal honesty. In addition, my psychologist, Dr. L., "held my feet to the fire," so to speak, and never let me revert back to my old patterns of thinking and behaving. He was tough to say the least but I also felt that he was often right on target in his explanation of things. Slowly, I began to trust him.

On reflection, I don't necessarily think that my false selves are particular to me. In my work as a psychotherapist, I have found that we human beings are more alike than different. And if each of us looks closely at ourselves, we might find that some of my false selves might also find a home in others—at least to a certain extent. Nevertheless, my task was to look closely at myself and name the patterns that were unique to me. And over the years, I have learned that the following false selves were the major ones that kept me feeling trapped and paralyzed, unable to decide whether to stay in religious life or leave.

1) Being a Pleaser

Back in the 1950s, I can remember my relatives always praising me because I was "such a good little boy." Maybe it was because I was the middle child in our family. Maybe it was because I somehow learned at a very early age that if I portrayed myself in this way, I "got the goodies," the attention, approval, admiration, and love that all children crave.

Somehow through these early years, I got a strong message that would follow me into adulthood. Be pleasing, do what's expected, no straying

---

6. Kierkegaard, *Purity of Heart*, 187.

7. Pearson, *The Hero Within*, 62.

outside the lines, don't rock the boat. Then, in 1957, I took this personality to the high school seminary where I followed the rules scrupulously. Five years later, when I entered the monastery, I began to "spiritualize" this way of being because I believed that this would lead to holiness. This way of living would be pleasing to God and enable me to gain eternal life.

Over a period of some very formative years, I learned how to please, how to adapt myself to the expectations of others, and live out their projections of what a "good boy" should do and be. I became very good at perceiving what I thought others wanted me to be. One time, when I was still living in the monastery, I remember visiting the home of a good friend. During the course of our conversation, I remember him talking disparagingly about a social justice issue that I supported. "I can't imagine how anyone could support such a cause," he said. "Can you?" I swallowed. I hesitated. My Good Little Boy wanted to please him and gain his approval. "No," I said weakly. "I suppose not." Later, I felt angry at myself and sad at how I had compromised myself.

2) Waiting to Be Rescued

During the years of my struggle to decide on staying in the monastery or leaving, I have come to understand that another reason why I stayed for so long was because I was afraid of making the wrong decision. I was looking for help outside of myself rather than trust my own ability to make a good decision. In a sense, I was waiting to be rescued by someone rather than taking responsibility for myself. Every time I thought about leaving the monastery, I was afraid of making the wrong choice and that if I decided to leave, God would somehow be disappointed in me and would punish me. In addition, my family and friends would also be upset and disappointed. Basically, I didn't trust myself and then the guilt and shame that I would begin to feel would set in and make me shut down on even thinking about leaving. After experiencing these feelings, I would begin to think of reasons and what more I could do to stay in the monastery.

Through my twenty-five years of living in the monastery, I wanted to make the right decision but fear kept me very confused. Maybe I was looking for my spiritual directors and psychologists to give me permission to leave—to say that it was ok. Gradually, I came to understand that I had to do it myself and that with God's grace, I would be able to make my own decision.

3) The Martyr Syndrome

From my earliest days in the monastery, I was taught to die to myself, so that I could serve God and other people in a more complete way. This is what was expected of you and the emphasis was always on holiness. In other words, the more you could do this, the holier you would become. As a result of this emphasis on dying to ourselves and serving others, it was easy to fall into the martyr syndrome. Long suffering and driven, a good religious never stops. He is ruled by a duty-at-all-costs mentality and gives unceasingly to the point of his own spiritual and emotional bankruptcy as well as his mental exhaustion. Feeling the need to meet everyone's demands, he buries his own needs and becomes the victim.

This is what happened to me as I tried to be a good religious. Living out the reality of this martyr syndrome meant that I always tried to do my duty and be responsible for following the rules. However, what I learned about this way of living is that I buried my own feelings and hardly ever had any of my own needs met. In doing this, I developed what I like to call "back burner" anger. When I was growing up, I remember times when my mother was preparing dinner and when a dish was almost cooked, she would move it to the back burner where she could keep it warm. There was a knob on the stove which was called "simmering," and she would turn the knob to that position. This is the way I would feel when I was living out the reality of this false self. Unable to say "no" to a variety of requests, like being invited to preach somewhere or to take on the role of becoming a spiritual director for another person, I would bury my feelings because I felt I "should" or "ought" to do this in order to be a good religious. But often, I would become angry—mostly at myself—and begin to "simmer." I would bury my own feelings and continue to move on.

Another thing I learned from being overly responsible and always focused on doing my duty was that it was difficult for me to relax and just have fun. Life becomes a relentless chore, with few moments of spontaneity and laughter. Interestingly enough, even before I entered the monastery, I somehow had the reputation of being the "responsible one," and the daily routine of religious life fostered this. Guys would often tease me and say, "you need to learn how to relax and have some fun." For some reason, it was difficult for me to allow myself to "waste time" and have fun. Over the years, I have worked on relaxing and having fun because this kind of behavior can put us in touch with our true Center, the place where, as Meister Eckhart observed, God and the soul are "eternally at play."

I have also learned that the important thing is *balance*. I believe that a healthy sharing of ourselves is important, but so is caring for ourselves and taking time for relaxation. Being a martyr distorts the virtuous ideal of giving to others by crossing over into the victim posture and a self-denial that squelches our true self and the creative life in our soul.

4) The Tin Woodman

In Frank Baum's book, *The Wizard of Oz,* we find the Tin Woodman, the character who had no heart. He represents the part of us that is cut off from our feelings. In the story, Dorothy found the Tin Woodman, completely rusted over, standing with his axe uplifted. She ran for an oil can and gave him a good squirt. Released at last, the Tin Woodman told Dorothy that he had once been a real person with a real body, in love with a young woman he planned to marry. The Witch of the East found him and caused him to cut off both legs. He replaced these with tin. Then he cut off his arms and again replaced them with tin. Finally, his entire body had been cut away and replaced with tin. He was no longer covered in warm flesh but was trapped in an unfeeling armor.

Reading through my journal, I came upon an entry that read like the voice of the Tin Woodman. "When I see something beautiful, can I allow myself to just savor the beauty and spend some time with it?" And a stern voice in me says, "How wasteful—what if you don't get everything done?" I ask, "can I allow myself to feel the pain of a broken relationship?" "No," the voice says. "Stifle it and pretend it never happened." So I ask, "what about the anger inside? Can I let myself feel it? " And the voice says, "it's not nice to be angry." Then I ask, "when I'm scared or hurting, can I open my soul and let someone look deep inside of me?" And again the voice says, "keep a stiff upper lip. Bury it."

In my years of being in therapy with Dr. L. in 1981–82, I came to understand how being in the monastery for twenty-five years somehow fostered my becoming like the Tin Woodman. It became one of the more destructive false selves that became a part of who I was. When we are cut off from our feelings, we become afraid of them. Perhaps early in our lives, when we risked expressing them, we were met with anger or punishment. So, gradually we built an ego structure in which we separated ourselves from our feelings and avoided deep self-disclosure, even to ourselves.

Anger has always been a difficult emotion for me. I have always been afraid of anger and early in my life, I learned to bury this feeling. This was because of my father's anger. Consequently, I never learned how to express my anger appropriately. And in the monastery, we were never taught about what to do with anger. In fact, the good religious was expected not to become angry in the first place and so, I buried my angry feelings for years. To this day, I can remember times in the monastery, when I would become upset and angry at someone or some situation. But I didn't know what to do about it. If it was a person who was making me angry, it was immensely difficult for me to go to that person and talk to them about the situation. Just telling them that what they were doing was making me angry was so hard that I rarely took the risk of doing it. Instead, I just buried the angry feelings and moved on. But I was seething inside. The fear of my anger and the fear of the person not liking me anymore kept me immobilized.

In a similar way, it was even difficult for me to express healthy, positive feelings. For example, during my years as a theology student before I was ordained, I became friends with Sister L. But I was afraid of these good, healthy feelings and then, when the friendship ended, I felt angry, sad, and depressed. However, for some reason, I just buried these hurtful feelings because I was embarrassed about them and felt that I should be able to handle these feelings myself.

5) The Turtle

Another false self that I needed to understand and struggle with was the "turtle." When turtles are afraid of something, they instinctively retreat into their shell in order to protect themselves. This is the pattern of retreating from life and protecting ourselves from rejection and uncertainty by withdrawing into our shells. For me, it was my response to fear and uncertainty. Because of my fears and uncertainties about leaving the monastery, I withdrew into my shell and made myself stay with the "tried and true." For many years, it was safer for me to stay in the monastery, rather than venture out into the unknown. It was scary for me to risk leaving the monastery and dealing with the implications of doing this. Like family therapist Virginia Satir said, "most people prefer the certainty of misery to the misery of uncertainty."[8]

8. Quoted in "The Family Networker," 13, 30.

Albert Einstein said that the most important question in life was whether the universe is friendly. It was difficult for me to leave the monastery, step out into the world and trust that I could find the world friendly. When I was growing up, I always thought I wanted to be a pilot. I even developed a plan. First, I would join the Air Force, learn to become a fighter pilot, and then after that career, I would become a pilot for a major airline. In fact, in the summer of 1960, after finishing high school at the seminary, my family moved to the Chicago area. Although I was only there for that one summer, I had a chance to join a flying club and took several flying lessons. I loved it. However, after that summer, I went back to the seminary and then my family moved to California. My dream of becoming a pilot faded. Many years later, after I left the monastery, when I was in my sixties, I took flying lessons again and fulfilled my dream of becoming a pilot. Some dreams just take a long time to fulfill.

Over the years in the monastery when I thought about leaving, I wondered if I could leave and still become a pilot. But, I didn't trust myself enough. Like a turtle, I retreated into my shell and played it safe. I was afraid to stick my head out of my shell and risk something different, something new.

6) Embracing the Leper

Philosopher Soren Kierkegaard pointed out that courage isn't the absence of despair and fear but the capacity to move ahead in spite of them.[9] I have now learned that I lacked this kind of courage in those earlier years.

In Arthur Miller's play *After the Fall*, there are several memorable lines that speak to the dilemma of our false selves: "I had the same dream each night—that I had a child, and even in the dream I saw that the child was my life; and it was an idiot, and I ran away. Until I thought, if I could kiss it . . . perhaps I could rest. And I bent to its broken face, and it was horrible . . . but I kissed it. I think one must finally take one's life in one's arms."[10] In a similar way, there is a moving description in the life of St. Francis of Assisi kissing a leper. Being a Capuchin Franciscan, St. Francis' spirituality has always meant a great deal to me. As a young man, Francis writes about his conversion experience. "The Lord granted me to begin my conversion, so that as long as I lived in my sins, I felt it very bitter to see the

9. May, *The Courage to Create*, 3.
10. Miller, *After the Fall*, 24.

lepers. But the Lord took me among them and I exercised mercy towards them."[11] One day, when he was out riding his horse over the Umbrian plain in Italy, he saw on the road before him a leper in his torn uniform. His first impulse was to turn and flee as fast as he could. But there were the words he had heard within himself, so clearly before him—"what you used to abhor shall be to you joy and sweetness . . . So, Francis sprang from his horse, approached the leper, placed his alms in the outstretched wasted hand—bent down quickly and kissed the fingers of the sick man. Francis saw this as a mighty victory over himself.[12]

Sometimes, the leper is ourselves. In naming the many patterns of my false selves, that is exactly what I needed to do: bend down and kiss the leper within me. Kiss those false selves within me. In a sense, I needed to show myself mercy. Only by confronting our false selves and embracing them can we liberate the True Self.

D. The God in My Gut

Certainly one of the most important things I learned in my twenty-five years in the monastery was how terribly important it is to have a correct understanding of who God is. This may sound strange to say for a person who had been living and praying in a monastery for such a long period of time. However, this played a major role in my life for so many years and in so many ways.

A wonderful, Jesuit priest, Pierre Teilhard de Chardin (1881–1955), was both a scientist and mystic. He spent many years ministering to the people in China. Chardin used to ask why so many sincere, good people did not believe in God. His answer was empathetic, not judgmental. He felt that they must not have heard about God in the correct way. His religious writings are an attempt to make belief in God more palatable for those who, for whatever reason, are struggling with it.

When I was growing up, our faith was an important part of our family. We went to church every Sunday, participated in the sacrament of reconciliation, and sometimes attended the parish mission. However, despite all of this, for some reason, I "got it backwards" about God's love. Somehow, for reasons that I still don't completely understand, I grew up feeling as though I had to earn God's love. I thought I had to "become

11. Jorgensen, *St. Francis of Assisi,* 37.

12. Jorgensen, *St. Francis of Assisi,* 37–39.

good" first, and then God would love me. Somehow, I grew up and missed the message that God loves me unconditionally. That no matter what I do, His love is always there for me.

This is what I have come to call the *principle of creative love.* This is the belief that we are *loved first,* independent of what we do or accomplish. His love for us actually creates the love within each of us that draws us out of ourselves to love one another. Like myself, many people think we have to earn God's love, that we have to become good first and then as a kind of reward, God will love us.

The belief that there are no conditions attached to God's love for us is almost too good to be true. It's so different from the way we humans usually love others. Even though we try not to, many of us put conditions on the way we love. Some of these conditions might sound something like this. "I will love others who love me." "I will love others if I like them." "I will love others who are nice to me." "I will love others who agree with me." "I will love those whom I like to be around and do things with." There are so many pre-conditions to our loving others that sometimes we are not even aware of them.

Religious writers and psychologists say that our understanding of who God *really* is for me personally is usually a very complex process. Most of us have an intellectual understanding of who God is for us as well as what I call a *gut image* of God. Intellectually, from our faith, we know that God is all knowing, all loving, all powerful, and that God became human in the person of Jesus. However, we also have an image of God that is deep within us. This image of God in our gut is so important because this is the God we relate to and pray to. This is the personal God who gives direction to our lives.

Several years ago, there was an interesting survey conducted about the predominant ways that teenagers thought about God. A variety of images were listed and the three images most often checked was seeing God as a policeman waiting to catch them doing something wrong, a wooden totem pole, who was totally disinterested in them, and a friend that they could talk to about their life. The implication was that these images were foundational for teenagers in developing their relationship with God. It affected everything from their prayer life to the ways they lived their everyday lives. In a similar way, the way each of us experiences God—the God in our gut—will have huge ramifications for our everyday lives as well.

So, where does this image of God come from and why is it so important? Some of our understanding of who God is for us personally can come from our faith, our parents, our teachers, our religious educators—even from things going on in our churches and culture. The reality is that most of us have at least an incomplete understanding of who God truly is and because of this we are constantly invited to refine our notion of God to make our understanding more personal and biblical. If our understanding of God is someone who is angry with us or punitive, then it might be much like the God of the Old Testament. Or, if our understanding of God is like a loving father, like we read about in the story of the prodigal son in the New Testament, then it would seem that his love and forgiveness is without limits.

During the 1950s, when I was a young teenager, there seemed to be a heavy emphasis on sin, what we used to call "fire and brimstone." Priests often preached on sin and the importance of avoiding serious sin so that when you die, you avoided going to hell. I know now that image of God had a profound impact on me.

When I went to the seminary in 1957, I believed that God truly loved me and manifested this love through dying on the cross for me. I wanted to go to the seminary and become a priest so that I could love him in return and to also bring other people to know him and love him as well. At the time, I didn't think my gut image of God had much fear in it. But somehow, after I entered the monastery in 1962, as a novice, fear became more predominant. Whenever I thought about leaving the monastery that year, I would become afraid that if I left, God would be terribly disappointed in me. This judgmental God would be mad at me. I felt like I was letting God down and would say to myself how could I leave when Jesus had done so much for me through his passion and death. At times, there was also the fear of God punishing me if I left. Then, during my last two years of college in the monastery, 1963 to 1964, these thoughts and feelings grew into the problem of scrupulosity. I began to feel that sin was everywhere in my life, and that God was very unhappy with me because of my sins. By 1980, when I once again seriously thought about leaving, the feelings of guilt and shame became more dominant. I felt extremely guilty about leaving and that God would be so disappointed in me. All of these ideas were part of the image of God I had in my gut during my years in the monastery. They wrecked havoc in my life.

In 1980, as I began to better understand this image of God in my gut during my last two years of therapy before I left the monastery, I also began to see more clearly what this image had done to me. At the same time, I also knew that if I wanted to leave the monastery and not be tortured by guilt, I had to work on this image. I knew that I had to try and correct this image. But how would I do this?

Since those days back in 1980—and even up to the present day in 2020—I have tried to do five things to correct this image of the God in my gut. It continues to be a work in progress.

1) Reading the Gospels

For many years after I was ordained in 1968, spiritual direction was a major part of my ministry. If I was directing someone and realized that they had a faulty image of God, I would encourage them to read the Gospels. One chapter a day, reflecting on the person of Jesus they saw in that chapter, so that this person could see what God is truly like. It doesn't take long to do this each day, but over time I had seen this helping people gradually change their poor, wrong, or incomplete image of God. And even though I had done this myself through the years, I began to incorporate this even more into my own prayer life in order to correct my own understanding of who God is for me.

2) "That's My Boy!"

As an assistant professor of spirituality in a graduate school theology program, I have had the privilege of attending graduation ceremonies. One year, I was participating at a commencement ceremony when Bob received his diploma. Bob was well known and liked at our school. He was an openly gay man and was a respected minister in the Metropolitan Community Church. Comfortable with his orientation, he founded the Gay and Lesbian Center on campus, and worked very well with many organizations at the school.

On graduation day, I remember seeing his father for the first time. He wore dark jeans and a black leather biker jacket with a bandana that covered his forehead. He was very muscular and looked like he could have been a bouncer at the local bar. As I watched him and his wife file into their reserved seats, I couldn't help but wonder what it must have been like for this gay man to grow up in his family.

The ceremony proceeded without incident. Names were read and diplomas were distributed as the graduates filed across the stage. The time came for Bob's row to rise and approach the platform. Bob ascended the stairs and as the dean called his name, his dad rose from his chair with his fist outstretched and shouted "that's my boy!" You could almost hear the audience gasp as they reacted to Bob's father's exclamation.

Clearly, this was a proud father who genuinely love his son. But what those in attendance that day didn't know was the interior struggle that his father had gone through to come to a point where he could accept his son for who he was. In the beginning, the reality of Bob being gay was immensely difficult for this "biker dad" to accept. For months, he struggled to accept this. Finally, with the help of a therapist, he came to understand that Bob's sexuality was only a part of who he was as a person.

As I reflected back on that day, I remembered what happened at the baptism of Jesus when a voice came from heaven saying "you are my son, my beloved, in whom I take great delight" (Mark 1:11). In the eyes of the Father that Jesus knew, we are all daughters and sons of the divine. Each of us is beloved. What a wonderful thought. This is the kind of God we have. Our God "delights" in us. No matter who we are, or what our beliefs are, we are all held in the sacred radiance that delights in our beauty and giftedness. God gazes upon each of us and is both moved when we suffer and delighted when we flourish. Before the face of our struggles, anguish, and pain, God's eyes are moist. In the radiance of our beauty, God beams with boundless pride. This is what Bob's father felt when he shouted, "that's my boy!" That's my beloved. And in him, I am so delighted. Over the years, this has been the image of God that I have tried to develop and pray to. I imagine the Lord saying the same thing to me. "That's my boy!" That's my beloved. In him, I am well pleased.

3) God Hugs Us

The third thing that I have tried to incorporate into my own prayer life came from the writings of St. Hildegard of Bingen who lived in the twelfth century. Her writings have been re-discovered in recent years and she wrote about having what she called a "still point." This is the place within each of us that represents the Center, the quiet core where God's Spirit dwells in us. "Do you not know that . . . God's Spirit dwells in you" (1 Cor. 3:16)? Sometimes we don't seem to know it. Yet in some holy place within, God lives and moves and has being (2 Cor. 6:16). And it's at this center of our being where we are deeply and profoundly known and loved by God. It is here that we attach ourselves to God. And it is also here that God attaches to us. Ultimately, St. Hildegard says that this still point, this center of ourselves is a love meeting, an embrace. She writes, "God hugs you. You are encircled by the arms of the mystery of God." God's hug. What a wonderful image. Now, when I pray, I begin by imagining God hugging me. This image of the God in my gut has made praying for me much more simple. Maybe all we need is to allow ourselves to be hugged.

4) The Vulnerability of God

Back in the 1970s, when I was teaching theology at the Washington Theological Union, there was a new way of understanding the nature of God that some theologians found very beneficial. Although some doctrinal issues were involved in this new understanding, this idea was very appealing to me. This new way of thinking about God was called "process theology," and one of the early proponents of this idea was a German theologian by the name of Jurgen Moltmann. He posited the idea that God possessed two essential natures—what he called the "antecedent" nature of God and the "consequent" nature of God. The antecedent nature of God was the part that was unchanging. God was all knowing, all powerful, and all loving. God would always be this way. However, the consequent nature of God was changing as our lives changed and evolved. The idea here is that God loves us so much that His very nature is affected by the reality of our lives as human beings. In other words, this part of God's nature is changed by the "consequences" of what happens to us in life.

Moltmann argued that God "experiences" our suffering and grieves with us. Our soul is so intimately connected with God, he said, that it's impossible for the Divine Being not to share our anguish. When I began to study this way of thinking about God back in the 1970s, it was appealing to me because of my struggle and anguish with regard to staying in or leaving the monastery. It was very comforting to me to believe that God understood my pain and my dilemma. He was not a God "out there" somewhere who was unaffected by my struggle. Rather, He was a friend who understood my depression, my fears, my uncertainties. His very nature was affected as a consequence of what was happening in my life.

Did God suffer? Was God capable of pain? Did God enter into our pain and powerlessness? Was God vulnerable? Most of us are used to understanding God as all powerful and invincible. But I was discovering the vulnerability of God, the God who knows pain and oppression, who enters deeply into our wounds.

But this way of thinking about God and relating to Him really took root in me when our son, Andrew, was stillborn in 1985. My wife and I were devastated. How could a loving God allow this to happen to us? Was He punishing us because both of us had left religious life? This old way of thinking about a mean, angry, and punishing God quickly came back to me. I went through a long period of depression and was angry with God. For me, the old way of thinking about what we called the permissive will of God made no impression on me. Then, slowly, I began to think about this idea in process theology where God is truly affected by what happens to us. When I cried, He cried. When I was angry, He was angry. When I was depressed, He was depressed. Gradually, I became less angry at God and less depressed. Nevertheless, although this happened over thirty-four years ago, I still have an immense sadness in me. A part of me died that day with our son.

Over the years, this way of thinking about God and relating to Him has helped me understand and develop a more positive image of the "God in my gut." Not only does God "delight in me," and "hug me," but He also "cries with me."

5) Mercy

Finally, a fifth way of correcting my faulty image of God came to me from another Capuchin priest friend. Sometimes, we hear something from someone that makes a huge impact on us. In one of his homilies on mercy, he said that Jesus *is* the mercy of God. In fact, he said that when he died and met the angel at the "pearly gates," his only word would be *mercy*. This idea has taken root in me over the years and has become a way that I try to relate to Jesus. Even though I left the monastery thirty-eight years ago, Jesus will always have mercy on me because He *is* the mercy of God.

E. The Swampland of the Soul

For over thirty-eight years, I have been unable to write about my experiences in the priesthood and religious life because I felt ashamed. These feelings of guilt and shame locked hold of me back in 1962 when I was a novice in the Capuchin Order and has lasted for these last fifty-eight years. They were particularly acute during my twenty-five years in the monastery. They dominated my life and kept me tied up in knots, unable to make any decisions about the direction of my life. Even when I wanted to leave religious life, I felt frozen because of these feelings of guilt and shame. Psychologically and emotionally, I felt paralyzed. Finally, after all these years, I have decided to tell my story in the hope of helping myself and others who also might be struggling with guilt and shame in trying to make their own decisions.

Shame can wear many faces. Bob was the sort of man who lived close to the edge, smoking, drinking, fighting, and driving fast cars. He was there, wherever the edge was. At sixty-three, he had been married four times and had made and lost two fortunes. He sat in my office looking very uncomfortable. In response to my questions about his past, he told me that he had grown up on a ranch in the Midwest. His father had been a cowboy, his mother the only daughter of the town banker. He had been close to his mother. His older brother, a robust and fearless child, had been close to their father. Their father had loved him, he said, and looked away.

I looked at him sitting there, large and competent and reckless looking. His hands, resting on his knees, were scarred from a lifetime of outdoor work. They were a man's hands. Why then did I have this feeling, this fleeting sense of him as a frail little boy? Following this hunch, I asked him what he knew of his own birth and early childhood. He told me that he had been born prematurely. For the first two or three years of his life, he was sickly and had absorbed a great deal of his mother's attention, worry, and time. His father's frustration had built until in one violent argument with his mother, Bob overheard his dad say, "if that little runt was one of the animals, I would have put it out to starve." Bob went on to say that in some way, he had always felt this.

His father's resentment toward him remained unchanged even after he had grown strong and made himself physically tough. "My dad was not a forgiving man," he said. Sometimes, his father would not speak to him or acknowledge his presence for weeks, acting as if he were not there at all. He never knew why. It had not been an easy childhood and at fifteen Bob had left home.

Annoyed with my questions, he asked me why all this was important. I told him that people's attitudes toward themselves sometimes made it easier or harder to stay healthy and so it was good to understand as much as we could.

Bob then went on to talk about his self-destructive tendencies. He told me that he had "pushed death" for as long as he could remember, and described years of hard living and numerous injuries. Even as a child, he said that he had been accident prone and this had diverted even more of his mother's attention toward him and fed his father's resentment. He did not understand why this was so because he was well coordinated and a good athlete. "I always felt like I was no account, like I was no good," he told me. His many successes, in business or in sports or with women, had not eased these feelings but just covered them over. "Fooled them all," he said grimly. "Perhaps," I responded, "but it must have been hard to feel okay, because you could never be sure just what you needed to do to be okay." He looked at me puzzled. "Were you supposed to live to please your mother, or die to please your dad?"

My remark shocked him. Silently, he had often wondered if he had lived recklessly in order to win his father's approval or to prove himself the tougher man. This put a new spin on it. "From the moment I was born, I was a real thorn in his side just because I was there. Nothing I did made a difference. He didn't want me anyhow."

I reminded Bob that despite his many brushes with death, the broken bones, the accidents, the risks he took almost daily, he was still here. I asked him what he thought had brought him through all this? "Luck," he said quickly. I shot him a skeptical look. "No one was that lucky," I said. He sat there for a while with his thoughts. Then, in a choked and almost inaudible voice, he told me that he himself had always wanted to live. I could hardly hear him. "Can you say that any louder?" I asked. Unable to speak, he just nodded. Almost in a whisper, he said, "I feel ashamed."

My heart went out to him. In a shaking voice, he said, "something in me wants to live." His eyes were fixed on the rug between his boots. "Say it, Bob" I thought. "Say it until it becomes real." I wondered if I dared to push him a little further. "Do you think you could look at me and tell me that?" I asked him. I could sense the struggle in him. Had I gone too far? He had never confronted his father. Most likely, saying such a simple thing out loud went against a lifelong pattern. Perhaps he would not be able to free himself even this little bit. With an effort he raised his eyes, his voice still choked but no longer inaudible. "I want to live," he said evenly. We stared at each other for a few moments but he did not drop his eyes. I smiled at him. "I want you to live too," I said.

Confused and caught between his mother's commitment to his life and his father's wish that he would disappear, Bob had felt ashamed and had ridden the fence between life and death all these years. Before this, he could never talk about this with anyone. And now, by giving voice to this debilitating feeling, he was beginning the process of finding some emotional and psychological healing. Shame thrives on silence. It hates to be exposed.

It has helped me to understand that there is a difference between shame and guilt. This can best be understood as the difference between "I am bad" and "I did something bad." Shame is about "who we are," and guilt is about "our behavior." So, whenever I thought about leaving the monastery, I not only thought I was doing something bad but that also I was a bad person. However, I have learned that both of these emotions can have huge implications for a person's life.

Susan was plagued with self-doubt. But it made no sense. She was a straight A student through college and the seminary. She was a beloved associate pastor at a thriving congregation. Her parishioners found her bright and articulate, personal, and caring. Any yet, a basic fear all but paralyzed her when she was asked to preach, facilitate a meeting, or teach an adult education course. An inner voice of self-doubt eroded her ability to speak in front of people. This critical inner voice constantly said to her "who do you think you are? You've got nothing worth saying to these people. You're a fraud. And surely this time, they will see it."

After working with Susan for several months, I asked her one day, "where did you learn this way of talking to yourself?" And then she remembered. When she was thirteen years old, she took first place in a school speech contest. She rushed home, eager to share her triumph with her father. Her dad, however, was in one of his "moods." As she bounced into the den waving her trophy, her dad just scowled and said, "who do think you are? Don't be throwing that trophy in my face. You got nothing to say. Never did. Nobody wants to listen to you." Susan was cut to the bone. She fled to her bedroom. Then she threw the trophy in the trash.

Susan's father had shamed her into believing that she was a bad person who couldn't do anything right. And this kind of shame is one of the major barriers to accepting and loving ourselves. In Jungian circles, this kind of shame is often referred to as the "swampland of the soul." When we feel ashamed like Susan did, we struggle to believe in our own goodness, talents or gifts. Sometimes, we can even have what I call "shame tapes" rummaging around in our heads. These are the messages that make us feel like we are "never good enough." When these tapes start playing, they often say things like, "what will people think? You can't *really* love yourself yet. You're not pretty enough, skinny enough, or talented enough. I'm going to pretend that everything is ok. No one can find out about this part of my life. I'll change to fit in if I have to. Who do you think you are to put your thoughts, ideas, beliefs, or writing out in the world?"

Shame is often referred to as "the master emotion." When we experience shame, it can paralyze us and force us to silence our stories. It's that warm feeling that washes over us, making us feel small, flawed, and never good enough. It is basically the fear of being unlovable and over time it can convince us that owning our own story of who we are will lead people to think less of us. Shame is all about fear. We're afraid that people won't like us if they know the truth about who we are, where we come from, what we believe or how much we are struggling.

In a sense, shame works like termites in a house. It's hidden in the dark behind the walls and constantly eating away at our infrastructure, until one day the stairs suddenly crumble. Only then do we realize that it's only a matter of time before the walls come tumbling down.

There are three things that are needed to enable shame to grow out of control in our lives: secrecy, silence, and judgment. When something shaming happens and we keep it locked up, it festers and grows. It consumes us. What we need to do is to have the courage to share our experience with someone. Talk about it with someone. Why? Because shame happens between people, and it heals between people. If we can find someone with whom we can share our story, we need to tell it. Shame loses power when it is spoken.

F. "There's a Crack in Everything. That's How the Light Gets In"

Thomas Keating, another Cistercian monk and spiritual writer says that "the greatest accomplishment in life is *to be what we are*, which is God's idea of what He wanted us to be when he brought us into being . . .

Accepting that gift is accepting God's will for us, and in its acceptance is found the path to growth and ultimate fulfillment."[13]

The problem for me was that in all my years in the monastery, I never heard a talk on human growth and development. There was never a sense that our greatest accomplishment in life was *to be what we are*, that each of us was a unique gift and in developing this gift of ourselves, in cooperation with God's grace, we would become holy. It was like we lived in a vacuum where our personalities should not be taken seriously. Everyone was somehow the same and if we were perfect enough, we would all become holy.

The biblical mantra that was consistently preached to us in a variety of ways over my years in the monastery was "be perfect as your heavenly Father is perfect" (Matt. 5:48). Intellectually, I knew that this was not possible for any human person, and yet this ideal of constantly striving for perfection was the ideal to strive for and it shaped my everyday existence. My understanding of this idea of perfection along with my lack of knowledge about personality development, almost did me in!

Since those days in the monastery and as a result of my twenty-four years as a psychotherapist, I have learned a great deal about this idea of perfectionism and the harm that it can cause in a person's life if it is not explained in a healthy way.

So often, many people feel the need to be perfect in order for them to love themselves or for other people to love them and that somehow they forfeit that love if they ever fall short of this ideal. There are few emotions more capable of leaving us feeling bad about ourselves than the belief that we don't deserve to be loved. But God doesn't stop loving us every time we do something wrong, and neither should we stop loving ourselves and each other for being less than perfect.

Several years ago, the well known author, Rabbi Harold Kushner, wrote a book entitled *How Good Do We Have To Be?* In this work, Kushner emphasizes the fact that no one is perfect. Yet many people, he says, measure themselves and others against impossibly high standards. But the result is always the same—guilt, anger, disappointment, and depression. A healthier approach, Kushner maintains, is to learn how to put our human shortcomings into proper perspective. We need to learn how to accept ourselves and others even when we, and they, are less than perfect.

13. Keating, *The Heart of the World*, 69.

Over the years, I have learned seven things about perfectionism that have been important and helpful to me.

1) Perfectionism is found, in varying degrees, in many people. We twist ourselves into knots, doing things to gain the approval and love of others. It would be much healthier if we could let go of what people think and accept ourselves, warts and all.

2) The quest for perfection is exhausting. We need to be gentle and compassionate with ourselves, particularly when we make mistakes. No one is perfect. We need to stop holding ourselves to ridiculously high standards in a quest to prove our worth to others. We are already enough. Compassion toward ourselves leads to compassion towards others.

3) Having the courage to let others see *who we really are*, to see those parts of ourselves that are not perfect, can be very healing. When we are our authentic selves, we end up connecting with others on a deeper level. Don't we love the company of people who are *real* and comfortable in their own skin?

One of my clients told me one time that she had always worked very diligently at *being good enough*. For her, it was the golden standard by which she decided what to read, what to wear, how to act, how to spend her time, where to live, and even what to say. Even *good enough* was not really good enough for her. She said she had spent a lifetime trying to make herself perfect. Now, she was simply exhausted and depressed. What she needed was to understand that she was human. She had always feared that she would be "found out."

4) I have also learned that becoming more human is what lies beyond perfection. This is what I didn't understand very well during all my years in the monastery. The reason for this is because perfection is only an idea. For most experts and many of the rest of us, it has become a life goal. However, the pursuit of perfection may actually be dangerous to your health. For example, the type A personality for whom perfectionism is a way of life, is associated with heart disease, high blood pressure, and other illnesses.

5) The fifth thing I have learned about perfection is that it is an idea, something that is learned. No one is born a perfectionist, which is why it is possible to recover. A friend once told me that he is a recovering perfectionist. He said that before he began his recovery, he always experienced himself and everyone else as always falling short. Who he was and what he did was never quite good enough. The same for other people.

He said that he felt like he was always sitting in judgment on life itself. Perfectionism is the belief that life is broken.

Sometimes, perfectionists have had a parent who is a perfectionist, someone who awarded love and approval on the basis of performance and achievement. Children can learn early that they are loved for what they do and not simply for who they are. To a perfectionistic parent, what you do never seems as good as what you might do if you just tried a little harder. The life of such children can become a constant striving to earn love. Of course, love is never earned. It is a grace we give one another.

6) I have also learned that it is important to understand the difference between healthy striving as a human being and perfectionism. Perfectionism is not the same thing as striving to be your best. During my years in the monastery, I didn't clearly understand this difference. Perfectionism is *not* about achievement and growth. Rather, it is the belief that if we look perfect, act perfect, and live perfectly, we can minimize or avoid the pain of blame, judgment, and shame. It's like a twenty ton shield that we lug around thinking it will protect us, when in fact, it's the thing that is really preventing us from taking flight.

7) One final thing that I have also learned about perfectionism is that it is also not self-improvement. At its core, perfectionism is about trying to earn approval and acceptance. Most perfectionists were raised being praised for achievement and performance—grades, manners, following the rules, people pleasing, appearance, sports, etc. My thing as I was growing up was being a "good little boy," being good in sports, and behaving properly in school. I can still hear my mother telling us as children that not everyone can get good grades in school but everyone can behave properly. Somewhere along the way, we adopt this dangerous and debilitating belief system. "I am what I accomplish and how well I accomplish it." For me, without even realizing it, I fell into this trap as I was growing up. Then, when I entered the monastery, this idea became even more embedded within me. *Please, Perform, Perfect.* Healthy striving is self-focused—*how can I improve?* Perfectionism is other-focused—*what will they think?*

Ultimately, I have learned that perfectionism is more about *perception.* We want to be perceived as perfect. However, this is unattainable. There is no way to control another person's perception, regardless of how much time and energy we spend trying.

Research shows that perfectionism actually hampers success. In fact, it is often the path to depression, as it was for me, or anxiety, addiction, and life paralysis. This term *life paralysis* is an important concept to understand because it refers to all of the opportunities we miss because we are too afraid to try anything that could possibly be imperfect. Furthermore, it is also all of the dreams that we don't follow because of our deep fear of failing, or making mistakes, and disappointing others. It's terrifying to risk when you're a perfectionist. Your self-worth is on the line.

Some years ago, one of my patients shared his story with me about being a perfectionist. He said that long before he went to medical school, he was trained to be a perfectionist by his father. As a child, when he brought home a ninety-eight on an exam, his father responded, "what happened to the other two points?" Tim adored his dad, and his entire childhood was focused on the pursuit of the other two points. By the time he was in his twenties, he had become as much a perfectionist as his father was. It was no longer necessary for his father to ask him about those two points. Tim had taken over that for himself. It was many years before he found out that those two points don't matter. They are not the secret to living a life worth remembering. They don't make you lovable or whole.

Fortunately, life offers us many teachers. One of Tim's was his good friend, David, who was an artist. One day they were talking and Tim happened to mention that his driver's license was coming up for renewal and that he needed to take a written test on the traffic laws. The DMV had sent him a little booklet. Tim studied it for days. During those days while Tim was memorizing the meaning of the white curb and yellow curb, David would try to persuade him to join him for a walk or go to a party or go out to dinner. Tim told him he couldn't take the time. He had to study. In the end, Tim received one hundred per cent on the test. Feeling triumphant, he rushed into David's studio shouting his good news. David looked up from his painting with an expression of great kindness. "Why," he said, "would you want to do that?"

It was not the response that Tim had expected. Suddenly, he understood that he had sacrificed a great deal to get a hundred on a test that he had only needed to pass in order to drive. He had spent hours studying for it that he could have spent in much wiser ways. He had learned many things that he did not even want to know! But Tim, being a perfectionist, really felt as if he had no choice. If his father could not approve of him with anything less than one hundred percent, he could not approve of himself with less than one hundred percent either. Even on a written driving test.

However, eventually Tim came to understand that this entire experience was not really about driving. It was not even about grades. It was about needing to deserve love. Fortunately, his friend David did not play by these rules. He didn't even know the game.

It has helped me to understand how freeing it is to know that we don't have to be perfect to be loved. That we don't need to get one hundred percent on so many dimensions of life. Moreover, we can truly love others because they are not perfect either. In other words, it's okay to be human. And perhaps this is really the more difficult challenge. Maybe this actually requires more courage. Appreciating our own humanness and the humanness of others, we realize that each of us is a work in progress. Each of us is like an unfinished symphony. Perhaps one word in our English language that we probably don't use very often is the word *yet*. But I have found this to be very important in understanding who we are and who we are trying to become. I have learned that it can be very helpful and probably more accurate to add the word *yet* to all our assessments of ourselves and each other. Bill has not learned how to be compassionate . . . *yet*. I have not developed courage . . . *yet*. I am not as kind as I would like to be . . . *yet*. This way of looking at life can change everything. It allows us to become less perfectionistic, less critical, less judgmental, about life itself. If life truly is a journey, a process, then all judgments are provisional. We can't judge something or someone until it is finished—even ourselves. Each of us is a work in progress. We are not finished . . . *yet*. No one has won or lost until the race is over.

It has been over thirty-eight years since I left the monastery. Since then, I have tried to live authentically and become the person God created me to be. I have come to believe that deep down, all of us want to stop pretending and love and accept ourselves "warts and all." So, I am no longer beating myself up for not being perfect. My focus now is to become more human.

There is a line from Leonard Cohen's song "Anthem," that serves as a reminder to me when I get down on myself for not being perfect. The line says, "there is a crack in everything. That's how the light gets in."[14] For a long time, I ran around trying to spackle all the cracks, trying to please, perform, pretend, and be perfect. Trying to make everything look just right. This line in the song helps me remember the beauty of the cracks—like the messy house, my imperfect manuscript, and the things

14. https://genius.com/leonardcohen.

that I forget to do sometimes. These things remind me that my imperfec-
tions and shortcomings are not inadequacies. They are simply reminders
that we are all in this together. Imperfectly, but together.

In his book, *Living an Examined Life*, James Hollis talks about how
each of us is part of a great mosaic.

> Each of us has a gift, the essential gift of being who we are, with
> all the flaws, shortcomings, mistakes, and fears of which we are
> all so aware . . . We are all here to be ourselves . . . And our gift
> to the great mosaic of the world is our uniqueness. Each of us
> has something to bring to the mosaic of time that is unfolding in
> and through us whether we are aware of it or not.[15]

Again philosopher Soren Kierkegaard said, "don't forget to love
yourself."[16] Sometimes, it helps to wake up in the morning and tell ourselves, "today I'm going to believe that showing up is enough."

G. Imprisoned By My Ideals

Outside, the rain came pouring down. It was a dismal, windswept Belfast
winter day, and as the mourners left the church and began to trudge to
Milltown Cemetery, hundreds of black umbrellas popped open. The coffin was wrapped in a bright Irish tricolor flag, and for a moment it seemed
to float, borne along on that dark tide, like a raft on an unquiet sea.

> "We cannot keep pretending forty years of cruel war, of loss,
> of sacrifice, of prison, of inhumanity, has not affected each and
> every one of us in heart and soul and spirit," Dolores Price's old
> friend, Bernadette Devlin, said when the mourners reached the
> grave. "It broke our hearts and it broke our bodies. It changed
> our perspectives, and it makes every day hard."[17]

The other graveside oration was delivered by Eamon McCann. He
spoke of Price's contradictions, and said that he had loved her for forty
years. "If Dolores had a big fault, it was perhaps that she lived out too urgently the ideals to which so many others also purported to be dedicated,"
McCann said. "She was a liberator but never managed to liberate herself
from those ideals. The mourners huddled under their umbrellas as the

---

15. Hollis, *Living an Examined Life*, in Well for the Journey, May 7, 2018.

16. https://brainyquote.com/lists/authors/top_10_soren_kierkegaard_quotes.

17. Keefe, *Say Nothing*, 331–32.

rain pounded the sodden ground. "Sometimes," McCann said, "we are imprisoned within our own ideals."[18]

For years, this was the way I felt—imprisoned within my ideals, unable to liberate myself from them. I went to the seminary in 1957 as an idealistic teenager, and left the monastery twenty-five years later feeling like "a candle had been blown out inside of me." And yet, when I left, a part of me mourned the loss of an ideal that I had pursued for twenty-five years. Sometimes, it's difficult to get free of earlier ideals that have helped to shape the person we are.

In Mitch Albom's book, *Tuesdays with Morrie,* Mitch writes about a conversation with Morrie about what is expected of us in life versus what we want for ourselves.

> "Have I told you about the tension of opposites?" Morrie asked.
> "The tension of opposites?"
> "Life is a series of pulls back and forth. You want to do one thing, but you are bound to do something else. Something hurts you, yet you know it shouldn't. You take certain things for granted, even when you know you should never take anything for granted."
> "A tension of opposites, like a pull on a rubber band. And most of us live somewhere in the middle."
> "Sounds like a wrestling match," Mitch said.
> "A wrestling match." Morrie laughed. "Yes, you could describe life that way."
> "So which side wins?" Mitch asked.
> "Which side wins?"
> Morrie smiled at Mitch, the wrinkled eyes, the crooked teeth.
> "Love wins. Love always wins."[19]

Should I stay in the monastery or leave? This was the tension I had experienced for years. This was the tension of opposites that felt like an "inner slavery," and kept me feeling trapped emotionally and psychologically. For over twenty-five years in the monastery, I had been immersed in living the ideals of St. Francis. During these years, I had constantly been encouraged to deepen my Franciscan spirituality. What would happen to these ideals? What would happen to me if I left the monastery? They had become so much a part of me that I wondered if I could still incorporate these ideals into a new way of life.

18. Keefe, *Say Nothing*, 331–32.
19. Albom, *Tuesdays with Morrie*, 39–40.

During the winter of 1980, when I was once again struggling with these ideas, I began to talk about these tensions with my psychologist, Dr. L. Once again, I was feeling trapped. On the one hand, I had met Margaret and felt a strong attraction to her which made me want to leave and yet on the other hand, I continued to feel a lot of guilt and shame when I thought about leaving. This kind of tension clouded my thinking and dominated our discussions.

Ultimately, Dr. L. encouraged me to stay with this tension of opposites and not to be afraid of them. For years, I had run away from them because they created so much pain and confusion inside of me. But he insisted that I pay close attention to these feelings because he thought the answer I was seeking was somehow contained within this tension.

Over the next year, I came to discover that we have within us a deep longing to grow and become a new creature, but we also possess an equally strong compulsion to remain the same—to burrow down in our safe, secure places. The truth is that we are a patchwork of light and dark, torn between what Quaker writer Thomas Kelly called "the enchantment of our own little selves," and "the God-possessed will."[20] Part of my struggle was understanding that our journey in life often involves change which can often lead to growth. I just needed to trust the process. That is why Dr. L. encouraged me to stay invested in the process of trying to sort things out and not run away anymore.

Part of this "sorting out" process for me was understanding that there is also another healthy tension in life that involves the process of "letting go versus clinging." For most people, this is never easy. Letting go of something in life isn't one step but many. It's a winding, spiraling process that happens on deep levels and then, only gradually. But to be successful, we must start at the beginning by confronting our ambivalence.

Sometimes, it seems that at the moment of our greatest possibility, a desperate clinging rises up in us. It was scary for me to even think about leaving the monastery. It was safer to hold onto the self and the way of life I knew. In my thinking about making a change, I would often catch myself trying to "save" my old way of life. In the words of Daniel Day Williams: "We fear it is all we have. Even its sufferings are familiar and we clutch them because their very familiarity is comforting . . . Yet so long as

---

20. Kelly, *A Testament of Devotion*, 63, 58.

we aim at the maintenance of this present self, as we now conceive it, we cannot enter the larger selfhood which is pressing for life."[21]

One morning in my library, I looked up the word *clinging*. I discovered that it comes from the Anglo-Saxon word *clingan*, which means "shrink." Sure enough, there is an undeniable connection between clinging and shrinking. When I thought about this idea in relation to our human journeys and our spiritual lives, I began to understand how clinging can create a shrinking within the soul, a shrinking of possibility and growth. My need to cling to "how it was" was overpowering.

"In human beings, courage is necessary to make being and becoming possible," wrote Rollo May.[22] It takes courage to stop clinging to my former ways of thinking and living. It takes courage to become who you are. Thomas Merton said for most of us it was cowardice that kept us "double-minded" and hesitating between the world of myself and God.

I have also learned that the opposite of courage isn't only fear but security. When Jesus invited the rich young man to "go, sell what you have . . . and come follow me" (Mark 10:20), I wonder if he meant to go and sell your security. Stop clinging to your old ways of thinking and living. Let go, trust, and launch out into the deep of yourself.

In some ways, I wonder if security could be a denial of life. I suppose that's true in the sense that total security eliminates all risk. And where there is no risk, there is no becoming; and where there is no becoming, there is no real growth. The real spiritual sojourners—the ones who touch the edges of life as well as the center—are people who risk, who stop clinging, who let go.

Years ago, a friend who volunteered at a shelter for abused children shared a story about courage with me. He said that one day he met a little boy named Billy. He had been horribly wounded and was reluctant to go beyond the security he had found in his room. The day of the Christmas party he shrank against the pillow on his bed and refused to leave his room. "But aren't you coming to the party?" my friend asked. He shook his head.

"Sure, you are," another volunteer said, standing beside my friend. "All you need is to put on your courage skin." Billy's eyebrows went up and the look in his eyes seemed to indicate his interest. "Okay," he finally said. While my friend watched, this other volunteer helped him don an

21. Williams, *The Spirit and Forms of Love*, 206.

22. May, *The Courage to Create*, 4.

imaginary suit of "courage skin," and off he went to the party, willing
to risk going beyond the secure place of his room. Sometimes, when I
am overwhelmed by the challenge of living authentically and living the
deeper self in me, I remember Billy and take heart.

Courage comes from the French word *coeur*, which means "heart."
In order to travel from clinging to letting go, we have to "take heart." If
the heart is the seat of the will, then this is the place that God awakens,
the place where the gentle uprooting takes place.

During the spring of 1981, I slowly began to understand how these
ideas could help to free me from the feeling of being imprisoned in my
ideals. Rather than seeing all of life as a black or white or an either or idea,
I began to think more in terms of both/and. Rather than understanding
that I could only live my ideals while living in the monastery, I began to
think how I could continue to live them if I left the monastery. After all,
I had incorporated these ideals into my life for twenty-five years and no
matter where I lived, they would continue to be an important part of who
I was and who I wanted to continue to be. This change in focus helped to
free me from the feeling of being imprisoned in my ideals. It also helped
to free me from the belief that I could only live out my ideals while living
in the monastery.

From this vantage point, I began to think about what striving for
holiness might look like for me if I left the monastery. How could I incorporate prayer into my life? How could I live a life of service to others?
How could I live my life outside the monastery and still strive to be a
blessing to others? All of these ideals had been foundational to me for so
many years and it was important and helpful for me to begin to view my
life in this way. And, in the final analysis, maybe what I really needed to
do was to be more like Billy. I needed to put on my courage skin.

One more interesting thing happened to me during the months of
1981 as I tried to free myself from the feeling of being imprisoned in
my ideals. This internal struggle somehow allowed me to go back and
remember what these ideals had meant to me and how they drew me to
the monastery in the first place. I recalled the excitement and enthusiasm
of those first days in the novitiate, when I had been convinced that I had
embarked on the road to holiness; the beauty of the liturgy; the holiness
of some of my brothers in religious life; the kindness of some of my superiors; and the grief and sorrow that I had felt when it had become clear to
me that I had to leave. I realized that the Order had itself been undergoing a painful period of transition. For the first time in years, I allowed

myself to feel the attraction of the ideals that had propelled me into the monastery and kept me there in the first place. In a curious sort of way, these memories brought me some peace and for that I was grateful.

H. Held Hostage By Fear

For over twenty-years, we lived in Maryland near the Chesapeake Bay Bridge which stretches some 1.3 miles across the Bay. Over the years, I have had a number of clients who were deathly afraid to drive across the bridge. The problem was made worse due to the fact that if you didn't drive across the bridge to get to the other side, it was about a three hour drive to go around a different way. For some of my clients, the fear was so great that they were almost paralyzed. If the fear was so strong and there were no other available drivers, the person could actually pay a driver to take them across to the other side.

From my years in the monastery and my work as a psychotherapist, I have learned that fear can be an unbelievably powerful force in our lives. I know it was for me. It kept me feeling trapped for years. But my fear was not something from the "outside." Mine was an inner slavery that made me feel paralyzed—stuck—unable to move. And I know now that I paid a heavy price for this. Because of my own struggle, I have learned how important it is for people to try and handle their fears head on and not run away from them.

Each one of us can be afraid of things in our own way. If you are not afraid to drive across bridges, it can be difficult to understand how anyone could be so afraid of doing this. And—how much courage it takes for a person to be able to accomplish this.

Much of what I have tried to do as a psychotherapist for over thirty years is to help people become free from what entangles them. This is so important because only people who are not enslaved by something or someone can trust themselves and follow their own goodness.

Over the years, I have learned that for me, and probably for many of us, the slavery that keeps us from following our own goodness is not something outside ourselves, but rather an "inner slavery." What we believe about ourselves can hold us hostage. We can feel trapped by ideas of worthlessness and lack of self-esteem. We can feel enslaved by notions of victimhood or entitlement. This kind of slavery is a story about the fear of change, about clinging to beliefs, places, and behaviors that can be hurtful because letting go of them will mean facing something unknown. However, the choice is never simply between slavery and freedom. Ultimately, we must always choose between slavery and the unknown. In the final analysis, this may be the more difficult thing to do.

The inner slavery that held me hostage for years was fear. In struggling to decide whether to stay in the monastery or leave, I had to ultimately decide to face these fears or remain trapped. During my therapy sessions of 1980–81, these fears became the focus of my discussions with Dr. L. It was extremely important for me to face these fears because for years they caused me so much stress that I would simply shut down emotionally. I wouldn't really allow myself to stay with these thoughts about leaving because of the turmoil they caused inside of me.

My fear of going back on my commitment to God was paramount. After all, I had taken my final vows and felt that if I left, I would be disappointing God. It was like there was this voice inside my head that kept saying, "how could you do this, after all he went through for you by being nailed to a cross?" In my lowest moments, I even felt like I would go to hell if I left. These kinds of thoughts also greatly affected my prayer life. We were always taught to incorporate what was going on in our lives into our meditation periods. This was important so that we could make our prayer life real and practical. But for me, if I tried to do this, I just became anxious and upset.

Another dimension of my inner struggle was my fear of the disapproval of others. Because my old "good little boy syndrome," was so strong, I was afraid that I would be letting other people down, disappointing them. Fortunately, I enjoyed a very good reputation as a priest and religious, both inside and outside the monastery, and I feared that if I left the monastery, people would look down on me and would choose not to be friends with me anymore. However, this only happened to me with a few people. Most were very accepting of my decision. Now, some forty years later, I can understand how unfounded this fear was, but at the time it was a major part of my struggle.

Fear of the unknown was also a dominant source of anxiety for me. After being in the monastery for over twenty-five years, I worried about what I would do, how I would manage living "in the world" again with all the unknowns this would generate. I think for most people, the unknown is always difficult to handle constructively. Most of us are more comfortable dealing with what we know. For me, living in the monastery was what

I knew and although it was difficult to deal with at times, it generally didn't generate the same level of anxiety that dealing with the unknown did.

The unknown is a real part of everyone's life. It is something that everyone struggles with. From my own life experience, and from those who have shared their lives with me, I have learned that dealing with the unknown can keep you tied up in knots, afraid of trying anything new which can be very limiting in life. It can hinder you from exploring new destinations. It can make you stay in a job that you are unhappy with or keep you in a relationship or a friendship when it is much better to move on. It can keep you in a monastery when you want to leave. If you let it dominate your life, it can keep you from growing in a variety of ways.

I. Finding Freedom

What we believe about ourselves can hold us hostage. This is important to understand because I have learned that a belief is much more than just an idea. Our beliefs are a powerful force within ourselves and greatly affects the way in which we actually experience ourselves. For example, if people have been severely wounded emotionally or psychologically, they often grow up with negative beliefs about themselves which causes them to struggle with self-esteem issues. They feel as if they are never quite good enough, that people don't like them because of their perceived beliefs about themselves that they are not talented and can never do anything right. Freeing ourselves from these beliefs we have about who we are and ways we have been persuaded to fix ourselves, can be extremely difficult.

From my earliest days in the minor seminary in 1957, and certainly through all my twenty-five years in the monastery, we were taught to be obedient. "Follow the rules and do what you are told," kept us safe and feeling that we were good seminarians and good religious. We were taught that we were sinful people with fallen human natures, and that the way we knew that we were following God's will was by being obedient to our superiors. Of course, these ideas took on added importance in the monastery because obedience was one of our three vows. However, the downside of this way of thinking was that over time, these ideas taught us to distrust ourselves—to distrust our ability to know what was best for ourselves. For me, this belief played an important role in trying to decide whether to stay in religious life or not. I was never really taught to believe in myself, in my own goodness or in my ability to know what was best for me. I discovered that learning how to trust myself was so important in my struggle to find interior freedom.

Often, finding this kind of interior freedom is not about doing things differently. It's about changing our beliefs about ourselves. It's about discarding the old ways we have come to understand who we are and trusting in ourselves enough to believe in our own goodness. This new belief, this new way of thinking about ourselves can lead us to freedom.

One of my clients, Marsha, had been raised in a very abusive family and had been severely wounded emotionally and psychologically. Her self-esteem was so damaged that she hardly trusted herself to make any kind of decision with regard to her future. At the same time, her mother was locked in a world of her own. She trusted no one, and was afraid to leave the house. She had been this way ever since Marsha could remember.

When Marsha came to see me as a young adult, she was locked in a web of fears that dominated her life. She told me she was becoming more like her mother which frightened her even more. At first, I encouraged Marsha to speak about herself, to describe her family to me and to elaborate on her fears. I took this non-directive approach in the beginning, fearing that she was too fragile to be challenged directly. But after about six months of this kind of therapy, I decided to modify my counseling approach because she seemed to be stuck. Just letting her reminisce about her life didn't seem to be helping. Additionally, she had told me several things in our conversations that led me to believe that she might be stronger than she thought.

So, I decided to try a new approach to help her cope with her fears and find some interior freedom. I had used this approach with several other clients and they seemed to respond favorably. I was hoping this would also be the case with Marsha.

Essentially, this new approach would allow me to be much more direct with her in order to gradually help her see that she was a stronger woman than she thought she was. So, I no longer allowed her to talk about her fears because this simply encouraged her to wallow around in them. Instead, I told her that for the next four weeks she was simply not allowed to be afraid. And, like my other clients that I used this approach with, Marsha became very angry and upset with me. She looked at me with confusion, unable to imagine what I meant. Carefully, I explained to her that I had observed that her first reaction to just about everything was fear and that when people had one reaction to everything, that reaction became suspect. In short, I didn't believe that all her fear was objectively real although I realized she thought it was.

Like I expected, she did become angry with me, telling me that I was not very compassionate and did not really understand her. "No," I said. "I believe that after all these months, I do understand you very well. But these fears that have so little to do with who you are as a person has gotten in the way of your growth." Calmer, she asked me again what I was suggesting that she do. She reminded me that she experienced fear many times every day. "I know," I told her, "and I am proposing an experiment." I suggested that whenever she felt fear that she think of it as only her first response to whatever was happening. The most familiar response, as it were. But then I encouraged her to look for her second response and follow that. "Ask yourself, if I was not afraid, if I were not allowed to be afraid, how would I respond to what is happening?" She was reluctant, but she agreed to try.

At first, Marsha had been discouraged to notice how many times she experienced fear every day. But gradually, she was surprised to find that often she could step beyond her initial stab of fear with some ease, and then she had a wide variety of different reactions to the events in her life. It had never occurred to her to challenge her fear in this way before.

After a few months, she even began to wonder whether this belief she had about her fears was actually true. For the first time, she questioned if this fear that had been her life's constant companion was just a kind of habit, a knee jerk response to life that she had learned years ago from her mother. Over the next few months, whenever she felt fear, she would stop and ask herself if it were true, looking closely to see if she really was afraid. Surprisingly, she often discovered she was not.

Looking at her fears in this way, enabled Marsha to gain some interior freedom so that she could begin to trust herself. No longer held hostage by fear, she began to feel more confident in her ability to make good decisions for herself. She had begun to change this fundamental belief about herself that had dominated her life for years.

This was the kind of freedom that I was striving for in the spring of 1981. I realized that my decision to remain in the monastery or leave, had to be made freely without any preconceived beliefs about knowing the will of God as given to me by my superiors. I had to make my own decisions, trusting in my own goodness, that I had the ability to decide the right way for myself.

Through my own struggles and working with many clients over the years who have felt enslaved by their fears, I have learned that in order to become who God truly wants us to be, we need this kind of interior freedom. Sometimes, this effort takes a long time. But that doesn't matter. It may be the most worthwhile way to spend our time.

J. Buy a Plant

When a person enters religious life, one of the first lessons they are taught is that basically it is a life lived for others. It is a life of service, of caring for other people in a variety of ways. Almost immediately, the religious person is invited to live a life long journey in which we were taught to die to ourselves, to die to our own selfishness, so that we can serve the needs of others. We were taught that sacrificing our own needs, desires, and wants leads to holiness.

We also know that Jesus was truly a caring person in so many ways. Whether he was healing, curing, forgiving, touching, praying, spending time with others, going out of his way to visit someone, and ultimately dying for us, he was willing to forget about himself so he could genuinely care for others.

During all my years living in the monastery, I don't think I ever heard a talk about the need to care for ourselves. This was certainly true in the 1950s, 60s, and 70s. The emphasis was always on what St. Paul said in his Letter to the Galatians: "I have been crucified with Christ, and it is no longer I who live, but Christ who lives in me" (Gal. 2:20). If we were able to do this, and die to ourselves, we were living the essence of monastic life. Fortunately, in more recent years, there is now a better understanding of the importance of learning how to take care of ourselves, so that we can continue to minister to others. Through my own struggles, I have learned how vitally important it is to do this.

Before I retired several years ago, I had a plant in my office. It was in one corner of the room and over the years, it became a conversation piece for many of my clients. They would often ask how it was doing. Was it thriving? How was it growing? Did it take much time to care for it? Over the years, I have also learned that every client comes to counseling because in some way they live in a psychological environment that makes growth difficult. Emotionally speaking, they are trying to find a way to grow and thrive like my plant. They are trying to learn how important it is to take care of themselves.

Sarah was a remarkable woman who was referred to me because of depression and anxiety. The owner of a successful interior design firm, she was on friendly terms with many very creative people. Yet she had come because of a deep loneliness and a long string of self-destructive behaviors and relationships with men. She was a large woman of great warmth and humor and had a wonderful laugh. Yet, below the surface of this outward upbeat personality, there was a definite sadness.

Born in Ireland of a socially prominent Catholic family, she was raised in a traditional home in which she had felt safe and protected. As a young girl, she attended Catholic schools and traveled with her family to many wonderful places. It had been a pleasant and comfortable life.

"When did all this change?" I asked her. Painfully, she told me about an evening when she had left her boarding school on an errand and had been raped at knife point. She had received very little honest understanding and support from her overwhelmed parents or her church, who dealt with her shame by covering over it with silence. Shortly afterwards, she had left Ireland and moved to the States to live with an aunt.

Although this happened twenty-three years ago, the rape had left her deeply wounded, vulnerable and shamed. She became unable to set personal boundaries or take control of her life. She took whatever came her way and tried to make the most of it. In addition, she didn't really believe that she could change things. However, at work, she was powerful and extremely competent, making shrewd decisions and running a successful business in a highly competitive field.

For more than a year, we talked about her experience which opened many old wounds but also allowed some healing to begin. It also allowed us to explore some negative conclusions she had drawn about herself and about life. After some months of this, we began to examine how she lived her own life. For many years, she had spent her life without knowing how to grow emotionally or how to work through all these feelings. I told her that she had very little experience in knowing how to care for herself. Then, I suggested she begin a practice to enable her to learn this. "Did I mean meditation?" she asked. "Not exactly," I said. "But a plant." She laughed and said she didn't think she could keep a plant alive. But that was just the point. Although she was doubtful, she agreed to try.

Over the next several months, Sarah struggled to keep the plant alive. Her task was to pay attention to it every day, noticing what it needed to thrive and then responding to those needs. At first, it was touch and go. Her plant suffered from over indulgence, followed by periods of neglect, much like Sarah herself. "Listen, more carefully," I encouraged her. "If you really pay attention, it will show you what it needs."

Sarah's plant was tenacious. Despite some difficult times, it would recover and continue to grow. Sarah began to admire its resilience and she began to see something of herself in it. She spoke to me about its strength and ability to continue to grow despite some difficulties. Gradually, she got better at recognizing its needs.

At about this time, Sarah began to consider making some changes in her life. The demands of her work were enormous, and she had very little time for herself. Building on a new trust in her own judgment and her ability to know what she needed, she sold her business and opened a design school. Then, she met a good, kind man and began dating him. Over the next several months, as she moved into this new life and this relationship, she no longer felt a need for our sessions.

A few years later, I received an invitation to her wedding. She and her husband are now settled in their first home. Proudly, she showed me pictures. Her yard was enormous. When I commented on its beauty, she smiled and said, "I planted it myself."

What I have learned over the years, is that the way we tend to care for a plant may be the way we tend to take care of ourselves. Plants grow and thrive when they receive what they need—water, the right amount of sunlight, plant food at times as well as careful pruning. Humans grow and thrive when their physical, emotional and psychological needs are satisfied. When this kind of foundation occurs, the person is set for growth.

When I went to the seminary at the age of fifteen, and then entered the monastery at the age of twenty, there was never any consideration of what each of us needed to thrive. There was never any talk or discussion about our emotional and psychological needs. In fact, all the way through my formation years in the monastery, I never heard about the difference between a need, a want, or a desire. It was like the human part of us was dismissed yet somehow we were expected to grow and mature into healthy adults.

Healing requires a certain willingness to hear and respond to life's needs. Sarah had never listened to her needs. In fact, she did not know how to take care of herself emotionally and psychologically. My plant was a better teacher of this sort of thing than I was. Sometimes, the most unexpected things can become like a co-therapist.

What I didn't know at the time but learned later on was that in order to care for others, we first need to learn how to take care of ourselves. I am reminded of the announcement that a flight attendant gives to the passengers in an airplane right before take off. "If the cabin loses pressure, the oxygen masks will fall from above. Put on your own mask first before you try to help the person next to you." I have learned that we need to care for ourselves first so that we don't burn out, and then we can allow our caring to overflow to others.

K. "The Ragged Meadow Of My Soul"

When I left the monastery in 1982, I could identify with the words of the poet E. E. Cummings when he said that life can be like walking inside "the ragged meadow of my soul."[23] At this point, I tried to believe that I could find my way "home" through this ragged meadow.

1) From Brokenness to Healing

Teilhard de Chardin, Jesuit priest, paleontologist, and philosopher, asked for this kind of healing on his journey when he prayed, "in all those dark moments, O God, grant that I may understand that it is you who are painfully parting the fibers of my being in order to penetrate to the very marrow of my substance."[24] I thought that this deep and beautiful prayer could help me learn to trust that inside of me there is a loving, divine power that heals and guides.

I found something breathtakingly hallowed about this truth: that in the midst of my struggles, God was drawing me to wholeness and healing. I prayed often for the faith to believe, to see that in my experience God was parting the fibers of my being. I also struggled to trust that the whirlwind I was riding was a sacred opportunity—that it wanted to take me somewhere. But where? I didn't know at the time.

As I trudged through this "ragged meadow of my soul," on that day in May, 1982 when I left the monastery, I continued to pray that "inside of me there is a loving, divine person that heals and guides." I certainly realized that I needed healing. One thing was very clear to me. I knew that I didn't want to end up an angry and bitter person. I had known men in

23. Cummings, *A Selection of Poems*, 80.
24. de Chardin, *The Divine Milieu*, 89–90.

the monastery who, for whatever reason, had ended up this way and this frightened me. Moreover, I had known some friends who had also left the monastery and they too were angry and bitter about religious life and the church in general. I wanted to try and find a healthier way for myself.

2) From Bitterness to Mellowness of Heart

My journey over the years has taught me that if I wanted to find a healthier way to heal from my brokenness, it would involve several things. The first thing it involved was what theologian and spiritual writer Ronald Rolheiser called "mellowness of heart." But what does that mean? Webster defines mellow as "well aged and pleasingly mild," and "made gentle by age or experience." Since I left the monastery, I have learned how important this was for me in order to find healing.

Pope Francis spoke about this kind of mellowness of heart on the occasion of John Henry Newman's canonization Mass on October 14, 2019, when he read a quote from one of Newman's sermons describing the holiness of daily life. "The Christian has a deep, silent, hidden peace, which the world sees not . . . The Christian is cheerful, easy, kind, gentle, courteous, candid, unassuming; has no pretense . . . with so little that is unusual or striking in his bearing, that he may easily be taken at first sight for an ordinary man."[25]

T.S. Eliot said that "the last temptation is the greatest treason, to do the right deed for the wrong reason."[26] This describes a major challenge in Christian discipleship. We must do the right things, but we must also do them for the right reasons. Why is this important? Because I can will and do the right things for the wrong reason. For example, I can do a selfless act for others, but be manipulative in that supposed generosity; I can die for a cause and simply be acting out of my own hurt or out of infantile grandiosity; and, I can be a warrior for truth mainly because I become energized through conflict. I can do all kinds of good things out of anger, guilt, grandiosity, or self-interest. Moreover, like the older brother in the story of the prodigal son, I can be scrupulously faithful for years and years, but with a bitter heart.

The older brother in the story was angry and bitter. On the surface, it seemed that his devotion to his father lacked nothing. After all, he had

25. Catholic News Agency, October 14, 2019.
26. Eliot, *Murder in the Cathedral.*

never left his father's house, had done all of his required work and had kept all the commandments. But he was complaining about the celebration being given for his younger brother who was returning home after his loose living and squandering his part of the inheritance. However, interestingly enough, the older brother was not *inside* his father's house. Rather, he is standing outside of it and being gently invited in by his father. What is keeping him outside, since, after all, he is doing everything correctly? Bitterness and anger. A bitter, unforgiving heart can be just as much a blockage to entering God's house as is any moral transgression. We can be scrupulously faithful and still find ourselves standing outside of God's house and outside the circle of community and celebration because of a bitter heart. Christian discipleship is as much about having a mellow and forgiving heart—like the father—as it is about believing and doing the right things.

Over the years, I have learned how important these ideas are for me. I knew that I didn't want to end up an angry and bitter man. I needed to find my warm heart.

3) From Resentment to Gratitude

When you live in a monastery for over twenty-five years, it is easy to cultivate resentments. Living together in such close quarters creates an atmosphere where resentments can eat away at you. However, I have learned over the years, that living with, and dwelling on resentments can cause a lot of anger and bitterness. They can lead to becoming a negative person and depression. Eventually, they can rob you of joy and gratitude.

One resentment that was especially difficult for me to overcome over the years is what the Catholic Church and my religious order put me through in order to get my dispensation. This was extremely painful for me and seemed so unnecessary. There was nothing positive about it. In fact, it made me feel shame and guilt at a very deep level. According to the church, not only was I doing a bad thing in wanting to leave, but it also made me feel like I was a terrible person. There was no understanding, no empathy, no compassion for my struggle in coming to this decision— only that I was a bad person if I left.

In addition, there was no gratitude for my years of service, no thank you for my efforts to live monastic life, and no recognition of the many ways I had tried to help people through my years in the monastery.

So, because of this process, I had some resentments through the years. In fact, one of the major focal points that I worked on when I continued in therapy after I left were these feelings of resentment. Eventually, I saw where they were hurting me and dragging me down. Gradually, I learned to let them go.

Rather than dwell on the resentments that I felt while living in the monastery, I began to think about the positive things that I knew were a part of my life during those years. I remembered my many years teaching theology, especially my courses in the area of spirituality and psychology, the retreats and days of recollection that I conducted, the many people I helped to find peace through my spiritual direction, counseling, and especially through the sacrament of reconciliation. But maybe even more importantly, I began to think about the many holy men that I had the opportunity to live with. Some of these friars had truly been inspirational to me and I am forever grateful to them.

Dwelling on these much more positive aspects of my years in the monastery, began a process in me of becoming more grateful for what I had learned and experienced during these twenty-five years. The resentments were still there, but the idea of gratitude gradually became more predominant for me. I was trying to move from resentment to gratitude. Even if I couldn't completely forget about these resentments, this growing sense of gratitude helped me to cope with them in a healthier, more positive way.

As I began to remember these positive things I had done while living in the monastery, I slowly began to incorporate this idea of gratitude into my own prayer life. One of the things that helped me immensely was that one day, long after I left the monastery, I began to read again the story of the ten lepers in chapter seventeen of Luke's Gospel. Although, I had read this story many times before, it struck me in a very powerful way when I was thinking about this idea of gratitude. St Luke writes:

> As he entered one of the villages, ten lepers came to meet him. They stood some way off and called to him, 'Jesus! Master! Take pity on us.' When he saw them he said, 'Go and show yourselves to the priests.' Now as they were going away they were cleansed. Finding himself cured, one of them turned back praising God at the top of his voice and threw himself at the feet of Jesus and thanked him. The man was a Samaritan. This made Jesus say 'were not all ten made clean? The other nine, where are they? It seems that no one has come back to give praise to God, except

this foreigner.' And he said to the man 'stand up and go on your way. Your faith has saved you' (Luke 17:11–19).

In some ways, it seems hard to believe that all the lepers who had been cured would not have come back to thank the Lord. In the time of Jesus, leprosy was such a dreaded disease with so many social implications. To not come back and say thanks is almost unthinkable. And you can almost here the disappointment in the words of Jesus, "were not all ten made clean? The other nine, where are they?"

When we reflect on this story, it is easy for us to believe that if this happened to us, we would certainly come back to say thanks. It is also easy for us to wonder why the other nine never came back. Yet, in our own lives, there can certainly be gaps in our gratitude. We can easily be people who remember to say thanks once in a while to the Lord or other people for one thing or another, but how can we grow in a life of gratitude so that it permeates our entire being? How can we cultivate a grateful heart?

The well known English writer, G.K. Chesterton, once wrote: "Nothing taken for granted; everything received with gratitude; everything passed on with grace."[27] So, how can we receive everything with gratitude and pass it on with grace? Often, finding meaning and cultivating a grateful heart is not about doing things differently. It's about seeing familiar things in new ways. For me, it was about seeing and understanding my years in the monastery in a new way. This has allowed me to move from my resentments to possess more of a grateful heart.

In more recent years, I have come to understand that gratitude is ultimately the basis of all virtue. Soren Kierkegaard said that to be a saint is to will the one thing, "namely, God and the life of service to which our faith in God calls us."[28] In addition, to be a saint, one must also be fueled by gratitude. Some spiritual writers believe that gratitude is the basis of all holiness. The holiest person you know is the most grateful person you know. This is also true for love. The most loving person you know is also the most grateful person you know because even love finds its basis in gratitude. If our love and service of others does not begin in gratitude, we will end up as one writer said, carrying people's burdens and crosses and sending them the bill!

27. Kea, *Amazed by Grace,* 164.
28. www.goodreads.com/Purity_of_Heart/SorenKierkegaard.

The real task of life then is to recognize that everything is a gift and that we need to keep saying thanks over and over again for all the things in life that we so much take for granted.

4) From Anger to Forgiveness

Close to the end of Morrie Schwartz's life, author Mitch Albom in *Tuesdays with Morrie*, asked him about the idea of forgiveness. Morrie seemed eager to share his thoughts on this topic. "Forgive yourself before you die. Then forgive others. There is no point in keeping vengeance or stubbornness. These things I so regret in my life. Pride. Vanity. Why do we do the things we do?"

Mitch wondered if Morrie had any need to say "I'm sorry" to anyone before he died. "Do you see that sculpture?" he asked, pointing to the figure on a shelf against the wall of his office. Cast in bronze, it was the face of a man in his early forties, wearing a necktie, a tuft of hair falling across his forehead. "That's me," Morrie said. "A friend of mine sculpted that maybe thirty years ago. His name was Norman. We used to spend so much time together. We went swimming. We took rides to New York. He had me over to his house in Cambridge, and he sculpted that bust of me down in his basement. It took several weeks to do, but he really wanted to get it right."

Mitch studied the face. Since Morrie was in the final stages of his life suffering from ALS, he thought how strange it was to see a three-dimensional Morrie, so healthy, so young. Even in bronze, Morrie seemed to have a whimsical look about him.

"Well, here's the sad part of the story," Morrie said. "Norman and his wife moved away to Chicago. A little while later, my wife, Charlotte, had to have a pretty serious operation. Norman and his wife never got in touch with us. I know they knew about it. Charlotte and I were very hurt because they never called to see how she was. So we dropped the relationship. Over the years, I met Norman a few times and he always tried to reconcile, but I didn't accept it. I wasn't satisfied with his explanation. I was prideful. I shrugged him off. A few years ago he died of cancer. I feel so sad. I never got to see him. I never got to forgive. It pains me now so much."[29]

Morrie went on to say that "it's not just other people we need to forgive. We also need to forgive ourselves." "Ourselves," Mitch said. "Yes.

29. Albom, *Tuesdays with Morrie*, 164–66.

For all the things we didn't do. All the things we should have done. You can't get stuck on the regrets of what should have happened. That doesn't help you when you get to where I am. I always wished I had done more with my work. I wished I had written more books. I used to beat myself up over it. Now I see that never did any good. Make peace. You need to make peace with yourself and everyone around you. Forgive yourself. Forgive others. Don't wait, Mitch. Not everyone gets the time I'm getting. Not everyone is as lucky. I mourn my dwindling time, but I cherish the chance it gives me to make things right."[30]

In her book, *The Way of Grace,* Miranda Macpherson said that "forgiveness begins when you want true peace more than you want to be right, to be in control, or to hold the moral high ground."[31] As I have grown older, I have learned how important forgiveness truly is. But I have also learned that it is never easy. Whether we are trying to forgive ourselves or someone else, it is always difficult. This is because it always involves so many dimensions of our humanness. It is difficult because all of us have been hurt in life and these hurts often cause emotional turmoil which takes time to work through. This is why forgiveness usually involves a process. We have to work our way through many emotions in order to come to a point where we can truly forgive. Everett Worthington put it bluntly in his book *Forgiving and Reconciling* when he said, "the way of forgiveness is hard. Forgiveness isn't for wimps."[32]

After living for twenty-five years in the monastery, there were many people, situations, and experiences that I had which called for forgiveness on my part. But, over the years, I have learned how important this dimension of life is. Trying to forgive has helped my own heart to heal. It has helped me find freedom and not hold on to grudges.

Carl Jung said that the major psychological and spiritual task for the second half of our lives is to forgive. We need to forgive those who have hurt us, forgive ourselves for our own failings, forgive life for not being fully fair, and forgive God for seemingly being so indifferent to our wounds. We need to do that before we die because ultimately there is only one moral imperative: not to die an angry, bitter person, but to die with a warm heart.

---

30. Albom, *Tuesdays with Morrie,* 164–66.
31. Macpherson, *The Way of Grace.*
32. Worthington, *Forgiving and Reconciling,* 15.

5) From Talking to Listening. Becoming a Wounded Healer

All of us have been wounded in life. No one comes to adulthood with his or her heart fully intact. In ways small or traumatic, we have all been treated unjustly, violated, hurt, ignored, not properly honored, and unfairly cast aside.

Spiritual writer Henri Nouwen also makes this point that we are all wounded people and this allows us then to become "wounded healers." But in order to become a wounded healer, we have to first face our own woundedness and struggle for healing. What we learn from our own personal struggles helps us to discover ways of trying to help other people heal from their wounds.

Although I had tried to heal from these wounds before I left the monastery in 1982, I realized I needed to continue to work on these issues if I wanted to find peace. The wounds that I experienced in the monastery, were, for the most part, similar to what we all experience. After all, people are people whether they are in a monastery or not, and each of us can be wounded by our interactions with others. However, the unique life style and daily living of monastery life, offers its own set of interesting challenges.

For me, the wound of depression for years found me struggling to understand emotionally what was going on inside of me. I struggled to find reasons for my depression so I could make changes and search for healing. Working with my spiritual director, a psychologist, and a psychiatrist over the years certainly helped to some extent. The medicine I began to take also helped me to some degree. Yet, owning the reality that I might be in the wrong life style was terribly difficult to admit. Trying to live a life style that was so difficult for me and finally coming to the realization that "I just couldn't do it anymore," created a deep wound within me that I have struggled with for years.

A second area of woundedness that came from living in a monastery for a long time was connected with living community life on a daily basis. When disagreements of all kinds would emerge, I simply couldn't avoid people. I had to continue living with them each day. This was especially true for me in the example that I wrote about earlier in the book in which the superior and I were tasked with investigating if any kind of gay activity was going on in our house of theology. This investigation stirred up a hornet's nest with community members being angry at me and the superior of the house. The students would shun me and avoid me as much as they could and resented the fact that we had done this. Then, this wound was compounded by the fact that our provincial did not do anything about this situation after we presented him with our findings. The superior and I felt betrayed by him and we were left "holding the bag" so to speak, trying to pretend that all of this never happened. It all felt like such a charade.

A third wound that was very difficult for me to deal with in relation to community life was finding someone who could truly listen to me about staying in or leaving the monastery. I don't think anyone was ill intentioned. It's just that they had their own personal bias which was natural for them I think. For example, my spiritual director was inclined to encourage someone to remain in religious life unless there was a very good reason for them to leave. Perhaps it was me. Maybe I didn't explain my conflict well enough. Maybe it was because my spiritual director was not a counselor. In any case, finding someone to listen with a "third ear" as one writer said, or "behind my words," was difficult and this prolonged my struggle and woundedness in this regard for years. Because of this experience, being a good listener has always been important to me.

Furthermore, I have also discovered over the years that perhaps one of the most important dimensions of understanding woundedness, healing, and being a good psychotherapist is the power of listening. Reflecting on my own years in the monastery, I believe finding someone who was a good listener among my spiritual directors, psychologists, and psychiatrist, was the one element that was missing in my effort to sort out for myself whether I should stay in the monastery or not.

The power of listening was brought home to me in a day long continuing education course that I attended many years ago conducted by Carl Rogers, a pioneering humanistic psychotherapist. It made a profound impact on me. Rogers approach to therapy, called unconditional positive regard, was very popular at the time.

Rogers was a deeply intuitive man, and as he spoke to us about how he worked with his patients, he often paused to put into words what he did instinctively and naturally. After explaining his approach to his clients, Rogers offered us a demonstration. One of the participants from the audience volunteered to act as his client and they rearranged their chairs to sit opposite one another. As Rogers turned toward him and was about to begin the demonstration session, he stopped and looked thoughtfully at the audience. Then he turned to speak. "Before every session, I take a moment to remember my humanity," he said. "There is no experience that this man has that I cannot share with him, no fear that I cannot understand, no suffering that I cannot care about, because I too am human. No matter how deep his wound, he does not need to be ashamed in front of me. I too am vulnerable. And because of this, *I am enough.* Whatever his story, he no longer needs to be alone with it. This is what will allow his healing to begin."

The session that followed was profound. Rogers conducted it without saying a single word, conveying to his client simply by the quality of his attention and a total acceptance of him exactly as he was. The participant began to talk and the session rapidly became a great deal more than the demonstration of a technique. In the safe presence of Rogers' total acceptance, he began to shed his masks, hesitantly at first and then more and more easily. As each mask fell, Rogers welcomed the one behind it unconditionally, until finally we glimpsed the struggle and the beauty of this person's life. It was truly amazing to see how this kind of profound listening, total acceptance and being received in such a complete way could allow a person to become vulnerable and begin the journey toward healing. I have never forgotten this presentation.

What Rogers was pointing out is, of course, a very wise and basic principle of a healing relationship. Whatever the expertise we have acquired, the greatest gift we bring to anyone who is suffering is our humanness.

I have learned over the years, that listening is the oldest and perhaps the most powerful tool of healing. It is often through the quality of our listening and not the wisdom of our words that we are able to effect the most profound changes in the people around us. When we truly listen, we offer an opportunity for healing. Our listening creates a safe place—a sanctuary—within a person to explore those parts of ourselves that have been hurt or wounded by our life experiences. It is because of our listening and acceptance that others find healing.

The Dalai Lama said, "when you talk you are only repeating what you already know. But if you listen, you may learn something new."[33] I suspect that the most basic and powerful way to connect with another person is to listen. Just listen. That is what Carl Rogers understood in a very profound way. Perhaps the most important thing we ever give each other is our attention. And especially if it is given from the heart. When people are talking, there is no need to do anything but receive them. Just take them in. Listen to what they are saying. Care about it. Most of the

33. www.brainyquotes.com_authors_dalai-lama.

time, caring about it is even more important than understanding it. Many of us don't value ourselves or our love enough to believe in the power of simply listening, and saying "I'm so sorry," when someone is in pain, and sincerely meaning it.

Most people are much better talkers than they are listeners. One of my clients once told me that when she tried to tell her story, people often interrupted to tell her that they once had something just like that happen to them. Subtly, her pain became a story about themselves. Eventually, she stopped talking to most people. She said it was just too lonely. We connect through listening. When we interrupt what someone is saying to let them know that we understand, we move the focus of attention to ourselves. When we listen, they know we care. Many people who are hurting talk about the relief of having someone just listen.

In my own counseling practice, I have even learned to respond to someone crying by just listening. In my earlier years as a therapist, I used to reach for the tissues, until I realized that passing a person a tissue may be just another way to shut them down, to take them out of their experience of sadness and grief. Now, I just listen. When they have cried all they need to cry, they find me there with them.

Listening creates a holy silence. When you listen generously to people, they can hear the truth in themselves, often for the first time. And in the silence of listening, you bring healing to the other person. A loving silence often has far more power to heal and connect than the most well intentioned words.

Perhaps the most important thing we bring to another person is the silence within ourselves. The great Irish poet, William Butler Yeats said, "we can make our minds so like still water that beings gather around us that they may see . . . their own images, and so live for a moment with a clearer, perhaps fiercer life because of our quiet."[34] This kind of quiet or silence that Yeats speaks about is not the sort of silence that is filled with unspoken criticism or punishing withdrawal. Rather, it is a place of refuge, of rest, of quiet acceptance of someone as they are. We are all hungry for this kind of silence. It is difficult to find. However, when we experience this kind of silence, we can remember something beyond the moment, a strength on which to build our life. Silence is a place of great power and healing. I wish I had found this kind of silence during my time in the monastery.

34. Yeats, *The Celtic Twilight*, 136.

L. Monsters in the Church

For over seventy-seven years, I have been a member of the Catholic Church. In some ways, I have had a unique vantage point from which to step back and try to understand what the church has meant to me over these years. As I reflect on what I have learned about the church, I have discovered that there are three distinct phases to my understanding of the Catholic Church.

1) 1942–1962

As a young boy, I grew up in the Roman Catholic Church as it existed prior to the changes ushered in by the Second Vatican Council in the 1960s. I spent my childhood in the church which in many ways, was the center of life. During these years, it seemed like everyone went to church and the church's rhythms pretty much dictated things. The Mass was celebrated in Latin and virtually all Roman Catholics identified strongly with a number of common devotional and ascetical practices. These ranged from not eating meat on Fridays, to not going to dances during Lent, to praying the rosary. As a child, we were made to memorize a common Baltimore catechism. Rectories, convents, and seminaries teemed with life and, by and large, the church enjoyed considerable respect within the larger culture.

For Roman Catholics in the Western world, this was like a certain golden time. There was a universal ethos within the body of Roman Catholicism that we may perhaps never again approximate. As children in this environment, we were taught that the pope, bishops, and priests were next to God and we did whatever they said. Clearly, they were admired and possessed a great deal of power over the faithful.

It was in this environment that I went to the seminary in 1957 as a sophomore in high school. As seminarians, all of us quickly got caught up in the clerical culture which began to indoctrinate us into the belief that we, as seminarians, were special and that attaining the goal of the priesthood was the highest calling that anyone could have.

2) 1962–1982

After spending five years in the minor seminary, I entered religious life and began my journey of living in the monastery. For the next twenty-years, I had the unique perspective of seeing and understanding the church "from the inside."

In 1963, the Second Vatican Council began which would have a major impact on the life of the church. In the United States, the Mass would now be celebrated in English and the priest would now celebrate Mass facing the people rather than with his back to them. The church was to be understood as the "people of God," and priests were called to be servants of the people.

I was ordained to the priesthood in 1968 and remained in the active ministry until 1982. As a priest, I got to experience what we had been indoctrinated with, i.e. that among the people, we were somehow special. Outside the monastery, I was treated with admiration and respect. But inside the monastery, the view was very different. Here, I saw the human side of the church. Although I lived with some very holy priests, I also lived with others who were angry, depressed, and isolated. There were alcoholics, power struggles, resentments, in-fighting, and relationship issues. First hand, I began to see the human side of the church and the priests who were thought to somehow be "holier" than others. Clearly, from my vantage point, we, as priests, had no inside tract to God.

3) 1982–present

I left the monastery and the active ministry in 1982. Since that time, my wife and I have continued to be active members of the church. We find comfort and strength here. But we also find sadness and anger, especially with regard to the sexual abuse crisis in the church. It is difficult to believe that there can be so much evil perpetrated by men who are supposed to lead us to God.

Some years ago, a colleague shared with me a story about his very troubled family life. One year he said that around Halloween he and his wife went to visit a haunted house. As they went to enter one of the rooms, suddenly a teenager dressed in a scary costume, jumped out and tried to frighten them. They both jumped back a bit and then he said he laughed out loud. He went on to tell me that he actually enjoyed haunted houses in all their varieties. In fact, despite the scary things, he said that a haunted house is one of the few places where he actually felt safe.

The reason was simple. For all their efforts to frighten him, a haunted house was actually entertainment. It was designed to give the appearance of danger. But if it ever crossed the line into actually hurting people, it would quickly be shut down. He went on to say that a haunted house has rules, and he trusted that the rules would be followed. So, he walked into the haunted house with the assurance that the teenager who jumped out to scare him really wouldn't hurt him and, as weird as it might sound, he was able to relax.

He continued to share with me that he never had this same feeling of assurance about the house he grew up in. It was a place that looked safe from the outside, but a whole lot of scary moments took place on the inside. In his house, he said that you never really knew when you were going to come face-to-face with a monster. There were no rules that kept him safe. Walking in, there was always a chance somebody would get hurt.

Houses like the one he grew up in are ruled by demons, and they are haunted by secrets. Violence, substance and sexual abuse loomed out at him from the shadows. He said that the worst part of it was that because his house looked safe and normal from the outside, everyone expected him to keep up the appearance that everything was fine.

As we talked, I couldn't help but draw parallels between what my colleague told me about growing up in his house and what is happening in the Catholic Church today. For decades, the church has tried to polish and protect the reputations of its priests and bishops, when, in reality, we have harbored and protected monsters—real monsters. Keep everything looking good on the outside, while stories of horror have occurred on the inside. Move these priests around to protect them while they inflicted untold damage on thousands of children.

Then, my colleague said that as his kids get older, he wished that he could tell them that he felt safer taking them to his parish than he does to a haunted house, but he didn't. And, until we become more honest and truly face our monsters in the church, he said that he will stick with the haunted house. At least there, he would have confidence that his children would come out on the other side, unharmed.

Since 2002, the sexual abuse scandal in the Catholic Church has been for me, and for millions of other Catholics, devastating. So many of us feel betrayed, scandalized, demoralized, and angry beyond words. It has made thousands of Catholics drop out of the life of the church. It has eroded Catholic credibility so completely that the church's mission of evangelization, catechesis, preaching, outreach to the poor, recruitment of vocations, and education has been crippled. And most terribly, the children, our most vulnerable members of the church, have been forced to live through a nightmare from which it seems impossible to wake.

The hurt and alienation felt by many catholics goes so far and deep that it is scarcely possible to gauge. Every particular act of sexual abuse by a priest brings about an extraordinary ripple effect through families, parishes, and communities. A single child might have been abused, but the anger, fear, and shame radiate out to mothers and fathers, brothers and sisters, aunts and uncles, friends and classmates. Now, think of the thousands of cases of sexual abuse by the clergy and the sickening influence that has gone out from each one of them. The rot and stench has reached virtually every cell in the church.

In the summer of 2018, the attorney general of Pennsylvania issued a report of the cases of sexual abuse of minors by the clergy in that state over roughly the past seventy years. The results, just for this one state, were astounding! The number of abusive priests was depressing enough, roughly 300 priests and 1,000 victims. However, the details of the cases sickened the members of the church and indeed, the entire country. Just one example exemplifies how some of these monsters operated. A group of priests in the Pittsburgh diocese actually acted as a predatory ring, identifying potential candidates for abuse and passing information about each of them back and forth. They would take Polaroid photos of the children, in one case requesting a young man to take off his clothes and stand on the bed in the attitude of the crucified Jesus. To children that they found particularly attractive, they would give gold crosses to wear around their necks, so as to signal their availability to other pedophile priests. Now, how evil and sick is that? One priest even raped a girl in the hospital, just after she had her tonsils removed. Another raped a girl, got her pregnant, and then arranged for the young woman to have an abortion. Another Pittsburgh priest would give homeless boys drugs, money and alcohol in exchange for sex.

While these crimes were being committed, the priests in question were typically removed from a parish or institution where the complaint originated and then reassigned somewhere else in the diocese, free to abuse again. As is now well established, this pattern of abuse, reassignment, and cover-up was repeated again and again across the catholic world, fueling the massive anger and frustration of the faithful.

In that same terrible summer of 2018, it was also revealed that then Cardinal Theodore McCarrick, retired Archbishop of Washington, DC, had been a serial abuser throughout his entire clerical career. The case that broke open the story concerned a young altar server whom McCarrick, then a priest of the Archdiocese of New York, sexually abused in the sacristy of St. Patrick's Cathedral just before midnight Mass, as the boy was vesting for the liturgy. But as more and more victims came forward, it became clear that the Cardinal, in his various assignments as Bishop and Archbishop, preyed especially on seminarians, those young men over whom he had almost complete control.

Just as bishop after bishop around the country quietly reshuffled abusive clergy from parish to parish, so it seems that numerous bishops, archbishops and cardinals both in this country and in the Vatican, knew all about McCarrick's outrageous behavior and did nothing. Maybe even worse, they continued to advance him up the ecclesiastical ladder, from auxiliary bishop to bishop of a diocese, to archbishop, and finally to cardinal. This increase in power, prestige, and control emboldened him to become even more abusive. Even after he resigned from his post in Washington, DC, immediately upon turning seventy-five, apparently at the urging of Pope Benedict, McCarrick continued to be a roving ambassador for the church in the American hierarchy, again while everyone knew about his disturbing and abusive behavior. The average American catholic certainly could be forgiven for thinking that there was a conspiracy of silence and a very deep corruption going on in the institutional life of the church. What is particularly galling about this whole McCarrick situation was that catholics had heard, since 2002, that protocols and reforms were in place that would prevent this kind of abuse. They seemingly made little difference.

As if this is not enough evil, lest we think this sexual abuse problem is confined to the United States, consider briefly for a moment two other examples. First, Ireland. The Ryan Commission published its 2,600 page report in 2009. Despite government inspections and supervision, catholic clergy had for decades violently tormented and abused thousands of children. The report found that children held in orphanages and reformatory schools were treated no better than slaves—in some cases, sex slaves. Rape and molestation of boys was all pervasive. Other reports were issued about other institutions, including parish churches and schools, and homes for unwed mothers. The notorious "Magdalene Laundries," were places where girls and women were condemned to lives of coercive servitude. The ignominy of these institutions was laid out in plays and documentary films, and in *Philomena*, the movie starring Julie Dench, was based on a true story. These homes for women scandal climaxed in 2017, when a government report revealed that from 1925–1961, at the Bons Secours Mother and Baby Home, in Tuam, County Galway, babies who died—nearly 8,000 of them—were routinely dumped in mass graves or sewage pits. Not only priests had behaved despicably. So had the nuns!

Another example is what happened in Germany. Here, an investigation revealed in 2018, that from 1946–2014, 1,670 clergy had assaulted 3,677 children! Where will it all end?

It has been extremely difficult for me to wrap my head around these evils that individuals in the Catholic Church have perpetrated. Someone might say that over the centuries the church has been embroiled in other scandals and survived. And, while this is certainly true, it doesn't feel very comforting at the moment. Other people might point out that this same type of sexual abuse is also prevalent in other church denominations and certainly in families and societies in general. And while this also might be true, for me and for so many catholics, this scandal constitutes the darkest moment in the history of the Catholic Church in the United States.

After I left the monastery in 1982, I became a psychotherapist and had my own counseling center for over twenty-four years. During that time, I have worked with children and adults who were sexually abused and I know first hand from my experience how this kind of abuse has negatively impacted their lives. Almost everyone I ever worked with suffered from anxiety and depression. Self-esteem issues plagued them for years. Their ability to trust had been severely damaged, causing all kinds of relationship problems. Sexual identity issues were always problematic. In order to numb the pain, they often tried to cope with what happened to them by using alcohol and/or drugs. Holding down a job was often a major problem for these victims, as well as behavioral problems which sometimes led to time in prison. In a word, many of my clients were devastated.

During my twenty-five years in the monastery, I lived with guys who were gay and involved in gay activity, but over the years since I left, I have discovered that several other priests and brothers were also pedophiles and sexually abused children. I knew these guys, lived with them, and prayed with them. One of my own classmates is in jail for sexually abusing children. Sometimes, we can literally live with people, and not really know them. It takes time for secrets and secret life styles to emerge.

Because all of this has made me so angry, I have studied this problem in the church in order to try and understand what caused this scandal where thousands of children have been abused. One of the reasons that most authors agree with, and one that I have certainly lived with in the monastery, is called "clericalism." Unfortunately, Vatican II was unable to deal with this issue of clericalism but Pope Francis has pointed out how dangerous it can be.

The origins of this idea of clericalism has existed in the Catholic Church for hundreds of years. It is at the heart of the sexual abuse crisis and needs to change so that the Catholic Church can truly be a servant church. Essentially, clericalism is a disordered attitude toward the clergy, an excessive deference and an assumption of their moral superiority. As Pope Francis said, clericalism occurs when clerics feel they are superior and when they are far from the people. It's also when lay people fall into thinking that their contributions to the life of the church are only second rate or that in all things, surely "Father knows best." It is a contradiction to the life of Christ, an obstacle to the Holy Spirit present in and among his people. Those who get caught up in clericalism, seek to keep the attention on themselves, seeking to be the center of everything, always the most important person in the room, an inappropriate self-centeredness extending even to the celebration of Mass. And they exercise their authority in such a way as to maintain continuing dependence in those they rule. Usually, it is obsessed with status. I believe that clericalism is both the underlying cause and the continuing reason of the present catholic catastrophe.

Historically, the conceptual underpinnings of clericalism can be laid out simply: women were subservient to men, lay people were subservient to priests, who were defined as having been made "ontologically" superior by the sacrament of Holy Orders. When I was ordained in 1968, I was taught that I would receive an "indelible mark" on my soul in Holy Orders, allowing me to act in the person of Christ. I was to become an "alter Christus, another Christ." This theological notion that the priest undergoes an "ontological change" at ordination, so that he is different from ordinary human beings, is a dangerous component of this "culture of clericalism." The idea that the priest is a sacred person contributed to exaggerated levels of unregulated power, trust, and control, which perpetrators of child sexual abuse were able to exploit. In many ways, it is the culmination of what I experienced in the minor seminary and in the monastery. "Seminary culture" early on, began indoctrinating seminarians with the belief that somehow we were special, different, on a higher plane than other people. This belief was intensified when I entered the monastery. Now, our "monastery culture" said that we were even more special because we were professing our vows and giving up so much in order to serve God. This idea once again made us feel important and admired. The final step in this culture of clericalism was the teaching that this ontological change happens to the priest at ordination. With this belief, a priest feels more special than ever.

However, when I was ordained, it did not mean that I was automatically wiser or possessed any better judgment or was morally superior to anyone else. Those of us who were ordained, remained human beings, prone to all sorts of errors and sins—just like every other human being. The apostles themselves made all kinds of mistakes, from misunderstanding the words of Jesus to betraying Him, and we shouldn't think that their successors are immune from these defects.

Over the centuries, these ideas about the priesthood and the culture of clericalism have dramatically affected the laity and the way in which the laity relate to priests. Clericalism treats priests as beatified ministers, merely because of the formal role that they occupy in the church. With this understanding, priests are thought to be holier than the rest of us, capable of greater moral perfection, insight, wisdom, and fortitude. They are the only real, complete examples of religious life, while lay people mostly occupy a second best, helper status. Pope Francis recently repeated his warnings against this "culture of clericalism," in which holiness is seen as largely reserved to ordained religious leaders.

When priests and bishops are taught all through their formation years, that they are special, somehow better and holier than others, and lay people actually believe this, it greatly impacts the life of the church. When the laity are told repeatedly that the priest is special and uniquely holy because of this ontological change, they are not inclined to believe that the clergy are capable of sin. Moreover, with their state in life, lay people fall into the trap of believing that there is a kind of caste system in the church. Priests and certainly bishops are holy and special. They are number one. Those in religious life are number two. They also have a special calling which makes them holier than the laity, and lay people are down at the bottom of the ladder at number three. In this view of the church, the lay state of life is like a concession to human weakness, a less perfect commitment to following Christ.

Most historians agree that this "culture of clericalism" is at the heart of the sexual abuse crisis. There are also other reasons, but this is a major one. This way of looking at priests gives them tremendous power. It encourages adults and children to trust them without question. This belief that a priest is automatically holy, next to God, allows a priest to gain favor with people very easily. This kind of power and trust that the priest possesses, unfortunately gives them the opportunity to abuse children. How many times have we not heard that a priest seemingly becomes a very good friend to a family where he is trusted and ends up abusing a child. This kind of blind faith in a priest often sets the stage for abuse. If we are ever going to change this behavior and stop this abuse, then we need to change this culture of clericalism. We need to see all vocations in the church as equal. Each one of us is called to holiness. And, most importantly, we are all called to be *servants,* building up the Body of Christ.

M. Why I Stay in the Catholic Church?

In the sixth chapter of John's Gospel, there is a scene that is vitally important. Finding the Lord's words concerning the Eucharist simply too much to take, the majority of Jesus' followers abandoned him. "Because of this, many of his disciples turned back and no longer went about with him." Turning to his inner circle, the tiny band of his most ardent apostles, Jesus said, simply and plaintively, "do you also wish to go away?" The entire future of the Christian movement was hanging in the balance as Jesus awaited an answer. Finally, Peter spoke: "Lord, to whom shall we go? You have the words of eternal life" (John. 6:66–68).

This sexual abuse scandal has shaken me to the core. It is so difficult to understand the horrific nature of these crimes, committed by the very people who are supposed to be leaders in the church. But this wickedness has also forced me to take a hard look at why I stay in the Catholic Church. Let me briefly share four reasons.

1) The Catholic Church has been my community of faith for 78 years. It is where I have learned about Jesus. It was he that I wanted to serve when I went to the seminary sixty-three years ago. He was the reason I spent over twenty-five years in the monastery trying to grow closer to him and wanting to serve him and his people. I have grown up in this community of faith and it has had a major impact on my life in terms of the way I think about life and how I have tried to live my life. And, despite the evil and wickedness of some of its members, I still believe that I find Jesus in the midst of this community.

2) I also remain in the Catholic Church because of the holiness that I have experienced there. Living in the monastery for over twenty-five years, I have had the opportunity to live with some very holy men who have greatly inspired me. True, I have also lived with some who manifested all kinds of problems. But, over the years, I have tried to remember the lives of these holy men who taught me a great deal about life.

In addition, since I left the monastery over thirty-eight years ago, I have also met so many wonderful people in this faith community. Often, these are the people most of us would never hear about. In their own quiet way, they live out the reality of their faith each day in a life of service to others. These are the saints that I meet in the Catholic Church, my community of faith, who encourage me to live out my faith as best I can.

3) The third reason I remain in the Catholic Church is because of the virtues of the catholic faith that have been obvious to me my whole life. The world is better for those virtues, and I cherish the countless men and women who bring the faith alive. The Catholic Church is a worldwide community of well over one billion people. North and south, east and west, rich and poor, intellectual and illiterate, it is the only institution that crosses all such borders on anything like this scale. As James Joyce wrote in *Finnegans Wake*, Catholic means "here comes everybody."[35] Around the world, there are more than 200,000 catholic schools and nearly 40,000 catholic hospitals and health care facilities, mostly in developing countries. The Catholic Church is the largest non-governmental organization on the planet, through which selfless women and men care for the poor, teach the young, heal the sick, and work to preserve minimal standards for the common good. The Church needs these people to continue the work of Jesus and I want to be a part of this.

4) The fourth reason I remain a member of the Catholic Church is because it is here—in this church—that I am able to receive the sacraments, especially the Eucharist. In the church, we receive the seven sacraments that bring the life of Christ to us as we make our journey through the various stages of our lives. Baptism, Confirmation, and Eucharist, initiate us into the Christian life. Marriage, and Holy Orders give that life purpose and direction. The Sacrament of Reconciliation and Anointing of the Sick restore the life when it has been lost. As necessary as food and drink are to the body, so are the sacraments for the health of the soul. The great medieval theologian St. Thomas Aquinas said that although all of the sacraments

35. James Joyce: Here Comes Everybody by Cleo Hanaway at http://writersinspire. org/content/james-joyce-here-comes-everybody.

contain the power of Jesus, only the Eucharist contains Jesus himself. When we consume the Eucharist, we are taking the whole Christ—body, blood, soul, and divinity—into ourselves, thereby becoming conformed to him in the most intimate way. It is here in the Eucharist that we find the grace and strength to live our Christian lives on a daily basis.

St. Augustine clarified that the validity of the Eucharist is in no way compromised by the immorality of the priest involved in its consecration. For me, therefore, the Eucharist is the single most important reason for staying in the Catholic Church. You can't find it anywhere else and no wickedness on the part of priests or bishops can detract from it.

The horror of the abuse cases, the sheer number of victims, the longevity of the crisis, its scope, and the fact that it has proved so hard to change these institutional patterns and habits that cause it—all this has been for me and for so many of the faithful, a profoundly shocking and disorienting experience. It has eroded the trust we used to give to our church leaders and structures. In addition, it has shamed us in the eyes of the world. It will only be when the church addresses this "culture of clericalism" and adopts a model of humility and service that the church will survive this scandal and thrive.

Conclusion

ERNEST HEMINGWAY ONCE WROTE that "the world breaks everyone and afterward many are strong in the broken places." From 1957–1981, most of my world had been living in a monastery, and so this was the world that broke me down. But after I left in 1981, I became a psychotherapist where I tried to "become strong in my broken places," by helping others make important decisions in their own lives. Like me, many to these individuals found such decisions difficult to make because of feelings of guilt, shame, and depression.

Anne Morrow Lindberg, in her book, *War Within and Without,* said that "one writes not to be read but to breathe . . . one writes to think, to pray, to analyze. One writes to clear one's mind, to dissipate one's fears, to face one's doubts, to look at one's mistakes—in order to retrieve them. One writes to capture and crystallize one's joy, but also to disperse one's gloom. Like prayer—you go to it in sorrow more than joy, for help, a road back to grace." My hope is that in writing my story, I have accomplished some of these things for myself, and that what I have written will help others find some peace in their lives.

Bibliography

Albom, Mitch. *Tuesdays with Morrie: An Old Man, A Young Man, and Life's Greatest Lesson.* New York: Doubleday, 1997.

Berry, Wendell. *Standing By Words.* Berkeley: Counterpoint, 1983.

Cummings, E. E. *A Selection of Poems.* New York: Harcourt, 1965.

de Chardin, Teilhard. *The Divine Milieu.* New York: Harper & Row, 1960.

de Mello, Anthony. *The Heart of the Enlightened.* New York: Doubleday, 1989.

de Sales, Francis. *Introduction to a Devout Life.* New York: Doubleday, 1989.

Eliot, T. S. *Murder in the Cathedral.* New York: Harcourt Brace, 1935.

———. *The Complete Poems and Plays, 1909–1950.* New York: Harcourt Brace, 1971.

Greene, Robert. *Mastery.* New York: Penguin, 2012.

Heschel, Abraham. *I Asked for Wonder.* New York: Crossroads, 1983.

Jones, Alan. *Journey into Christ.* San Francisco: Harper & Row, 1971.

Jorgensen, Johannes. *St. Francis of Assisi.* New York: Image, 1955.

Jung, Carl. *The Structure and Dynamics of the Psyche. Collected Works of C. G. Jung 8.* Translated by R. F. C. Hull. New Jersey: Princeton University Press, 1960.

Kea, Elizabeth. *Amazed by Grace.* Nashville: Thomas Nelson, 2003.

Keating, Thomas. *The Heart of the World.* New York: Crossroads, 2008.

Keefe, Patrick. *Say Nothing.* New York: Doubleday, 2019.

Kelly, Thomas. *A Testament of Devotion.* New York: Harper & Brothers, 1941.

Kierkegaard, Soren. *Purity of Heart.* Translated by Douglas Steere. New York: Harper & Row, 1938.

Lewis, C. S. *The Four Loves.* New York: Harcourt, 1960.

Lindberg, Anne Morrow. *War Within and Without: Diaries and Letters of Anne Morrow Lindberg, 1939–1944.* New York: Harcourt Brace Jovanich, 1980.

Macpherson, Miranda. *The Way of Grace.* New York: MacMillan, 2018.

May, Rollo. *The Courage to Create.* New York: Bantam, 1975.

Merton, Thomas. *Conjectures of a Guilt Bystander.* New York: Image, 1968.

———. *New Seeds of Contemplation.* New York: New Directions, 1961.

———. *The New Man.* New York: Farrar, Straus & Giroux, 1961.

———. *The Intimate Merton.* New York: Harper Collins, 1999.

———. *Thoughts in Solitude.* New York: Image, 1968.

Miller, Arthur. *After the Fall.* New York: Viking, 1964.

O'Connor, Elizabeth. *Our Many Selves.* New York: Harper & Row, 1971.

Painter, Christine. *The Soul's Ripening.* New York: Sorin Books, 2018.

Pearson, Carol. *The Hero Within.* San Francisco: Harper & Row, 1986.

Rilke, Rainer Maria. *Letters to a Young Poet.* New York: Norton, 1934.

Satir, Virginia. *The Family Networker.* 13, (January–February), 28–32.

Shea, John. *Stories of God: An Unauthorized Biography.* Chicago: Thomas Moore, 1978.

Wiesel, Elie. *Night.* Translated by Stella Rodway. New York: Avon, 1960.

Williams, Daniel. *The Spirit and Forms of Love.* San Francisco: Harper & Row, 1968.

Worthington, Everett. *Forgiving and Reconciling.* Downers Grove, IL: Intervarsity, 2003.

Yeats, William. *The Celtic Twilight: Faerie and Folklore.* London: A. H. Bullen, 1902.

Zohar and Marshall. *Connecting with Our Spiritual Intelligence.* New York: Bloomsbury, 2000.